THE AMERICAN ANIMAL HOSPITAL ASSOCIATION
ENCYCLOPEDIA OF DOG HEALTH AND CARE

Also by the American Animal Hospital Association

The American Animal Hospital Association
Encyclopedia of Cat Health and Care

THE AMERICAN ANIMAL HOSPITAL ASSOCIATION

ENCYCLOPEDIA OF DOG HEALTH AND CARE

with Sally Bordwell

Special Consultant,
Alan Dubowy, DVM

Produced by The Philip Lief Group, Inc.

Quill

WILLIAM MORROW   New York

Library of Congress Cataloging-in-Publication Data
Bordwell, Sally, 1947–
    The American Animal Hospital Association encyclopedia of dog
health and care / with Sally Bordwell ; special consultant, Alan
Dubowy.
        p.   cm.
    Originally published: 1st ed. New York : Hearst Books, c1994.
    Includes index.
    ISBN 0-688-14771-2 (alk. paper)
    1. Dogs—Health—Encyclopedias. 2. Dogs—Diseases—Encyclopedias.
3. Dogs—Encyclopedias.   I. Dubowy, Alan.   II. American Animal
Hospital Association.   III. Title.
    [SF427.B625   1996]
    636.7'089—dc20
                                                    96-21453
                                                    CIP

Printed in the United States of America

First Quill Edition

          5   6   7   8   9   10

CONTENTS

PART III. THE ENCYCLOPEDIA OF DOG HEALTH

ABOUT THE AMERICAN ANIMAL HOSPITAL ASSOCIATION (AAHA)

FOUNDED IN 1933, the American Animal Hospital Association is an international association of more than 12,000 veterinarians who treat companion animals, such as cat and dogs. Located in Lakewood, Colorado, the association sets widely observed standards for veterinary hospitals and pet health care, inspects and accredits these hospitals, and assists veterinary professionals in meeting AAHA standards. AAHA hospital members are known throughout the world for providing the highest quality care for pets. There are currently more than 2,500 AAHA member hospitals in the United States and Canada.

One of our organization's aims has always been to promote responsible pet ownership. Every companion animal deserves to have its most basic requirements, including food, warmth, and shelter, fulfilled. Every companion animal also deserves attention and affection, and to be cared for when ill. With this reference and its companion, *The AAHA Encyclopedia of Cat Health and Care,* we have aimed at disseminating sensible, practical information to pet owners in order to help build strong, loving, and mutually beneficial relationships between people and their pets.

For more information about the American Animal Hospital Association, write to P.O. Box 150899, Denver, Colorado 80215–0899.

INTRODUCTION

DOGS ARE FIERCELY LOYAL animals who will desert other dogs to be with us, and will fight other dogs to protect us. In return, we must show our furry companions the respect such friendship deserves. The best way to show your dog respect is give it the most informed, consistent care you can.

Many of the books available on dog care use a dizzying array of impenetrable scientific terms when describing ailments, bodily functions, and conditions. Others focus on a single aspect of dog care, such as reproduction or dog shows.

THREE BOOKS IN ONE

The American Animal Hospital Association Encyclopedia of Dog Health and Care is a unique and valuable addition to any dog owner's library. This refer-ence book is actually three books in one: a guide to breeds and tempera-ments, a guide to caring for your dog, and an encyclopedia of dog health. Whether you are involved in the raising of puppies or are interested in knowing more about canine health, the special problems of elderly pets, or what to do in a canine emergency, you will find all this information and much more at your fingertips in easy-to-understand language. All the information in this book is up to date, authoritative, and culled from leading veterinarians and other expert sources.

A GUIDE TO BREEDS AND TEMPERAMENTS

In Part One, "A Guide to Breeds and Temperaments," you'll learn everything you need to know about more than 130 breeds of dog, from akitas to fox terriers to whippets. An at-a-glance breed chart provides you with essential information about appearance, behavior, exercise requirements, and more.

You will also learn about the history of dogs, dating back to the first interaction between human and wolf. You will discover how certain contemporary traits and habits can be traced to your dog's primitive ancestors. You will also find tools for deciphering your dog's attempts to communicate with you and the world it lives in, as well as pointers for coping with problem behavior.

CARING FOR YOUR DOG

Part Two presents six chapters that will show you how to become your dog's caretaker. You'll glean essential information about the responsibilities and obligations of dog ownership, from providing adequate space for your pet to community concerns. This section also contains information on how to choose the right dog, where to get a dog, and how to prepare for its arrival in your household.

Chapter Four is a complete primer of basic dog care. It covers virtually every aspect of dog ownership, from the feeding of dogs to such special situations as the best way to handle a dog on moving day. Other subjects discussed in this chapter include grooming, exercise, and dogs' nutritional requirements.

Later chapters detail how to raise puppies, make certain that your dog or puppy is properly vaccinated, general procedures to follow when your dog is ill, including feeding, monitoring a dog's temperature, and maximizing its comfort (including a list of supplies that should be on hand in every dog's home).

Anyone who owns a dog will ultimately have to deal with two stages of their dog's life that may not be the happiest of times: old age and death. Chapter Seven provides important information about the special needs of elderly dogs, while Chapter Eight will help you consider the difficult issue of euthanasia and cope with that saddest of moments—the death of a longtime pet.

THE ENCYCLOPEDIA OF DOG HEALTH

This section begins with an at-a-glance guide to signs and symptoms and will quickly refer you to the disorders usually associated with a given symptom. For example: If you notice that your dog seems to be scratching constantly at its ears, consult the symptom guide under the heading "Scratching." The heading will then refer you to the pages in this encyclopedia that deal with the subject of ear scratching and subsequent irritation.

Chapters Nine through Twenty-one present a comprehensive list of illnesses and disorders most likely to beset your dog, from infectious diseases to cancer. In clear writing free of medical jargon, each disorder is discussed in terms of underlying causes, symptoms, and what treatments are available. These chapters are designed to be used as a general reference guide so that you can better understand and cope with any illnesses that may affect your dog's normal good health. This section, however, is *not* a substitute for getting veterinary help when your dog is ill.

Because male and female dogs often have special medical problems that are gender-related, Chapters Nineteen and Twenty focus on each gender's unique problems, disorders such as urological infection in males or false pregnancy in females. The care, growth, and development of puppies (including raising them by hand) is discussed in Chapter Twenty-one.

Chapter Twenty-two is divided into three sections designed to provide you the information you need if an emergency befalls your dog. "Emergency Procedures" outlines techniques for approaching an injured dog, checking for breathing and pulse, and performing mouth-to-nose resuscitation. "Common Emergencies" advises on procedures for threatening situations, from burns to fractures to unconsciousness. Finally, "Poison Control" shows you how to respond if your dog has ingested a toxic substance. Such information can help you make the right choices in that critical period before your dog can receive veterinary help.

AN ESSENTIAL HEALTH AND CARE REFERENCE

More than 57 percent of American families own some kind of pet. According to the latest figures available, there are more than fifty-two million dogs in the United States; 36 percent of all households in this country contain at least one dog. The best way for these dogs to receive all the loving care they deserve is for their human caretakers to be fully informed about all aspects of dog life. We hope this book helps the dog in your household to live longer, and enhances your enjoyment of this special family member.

PART I

A GUIDE
TO BREEDS
AND
TEMPERAMENTS

1

BREEDS OF DOGS

THE CANINE KINGDOM is amazingly diverse. It is populated by dogs of every size, color, look, temperament, and talent. Dogs have been bred to be helpers, playmates, and creatures of beauty.

BREED GROUPS

Up to 400 breeds are recognized worldwide, with several other mixed-breed or mongrel dogs equally impressing us with their uniqueness and character. To begin learning about the different types of dogs, we can turn to the seven general groupings of the 137 breeds recognized by the American Kennel Club.

WORKING DOGS

Akita
Alaskan Malamute

Bernese Mountain Dog
Boxer
Bullmastiff
Doberman Pinscher
Giant Schnauzer
Great Dane
Great Pyrenees
Komondor
Kuvasz
Mastiff
Newfoundland
Portuguese Water Dog
Rottweiler
Saint Bernard
Samoyed
Siberian Husky
Standard Schnauzer

These dogs have worked for their popularity, pulling carts and sleds, guarding homes, businesses, and property, serving in the military, or rescuing

3

victims from dangerous waters and mountainsides. Today, many working dogs are only family companions. So instinctual is their knowledge of their former existence, however, that many could still be excellent workers at their prescribed tasks. Keep this in mind when considering a working dog as a pet, as these dogs take pride in learning and being useful and often require a savvy owner who can focus their behavior. Without such an owner, their independent personalities can take over, making them very difficult to handle.

HERDING DOGS

Australian Cattle Dog
Bearded Collie
Belgian Malinois
Belgian Sheepdog
Belgian Tervuren
Border Collie
Bouvier des Flandres
Briard
Collie (Rough and Smooth-Coated)
German Shepherd Dog
Old English Sheepdog
Puli
Shetland Sheepdog
Shiloh Shepherd Dog
Welsh Corgi (Cardigan)
Welsh Corgi (Pembroke)

Like the working dog, the herding dog has been raised to help people get the job done. The herding dog's specific duty is to watch over and organize herds of sheep and cattle. Although the use of the herding dog has somewhat

diminished, sheep and cattle owners in such countries as Scotland, Australia, and Turkey still rely on herding dogs. In other countries, many are simply domestic pets and are prized for their loyalty, intelligence, and awareness.

SPORTING DOGS

Brittany
Pointer
Pointer, German Shorthaired
Pointer, German Wirehaired
Retriever, Chesapeake Bay
Retriever, Curly-Coated
Retriever, Flat-Coated
Retriever, Golden
Retriever, Labrador
Setter, English
Setter, Gordon
Setter, Irish
Spaniel, American Water
Spaniel, Clumber
Spaniel, Cocker
Spaniel, English Cocker
Spaniel, English Springer
Spaniel, Field
Spaniel, Irish Water
Spaniel, Sussex
Spaniel, Welsh Springer
Vizsla
Weimaraner
Wirehaired Pointing Griffon

The sporting group consists of three basic types of dogs: the pointers, the retrievers, and the spaniels. All were raised to be intelligent, loyal, athletic companions and helpers to the hunter. For this reason, a typical dog from the sporting group tends to be easy to train, friendly, patient, and usually good with children. They thrive especially well when they have access to an open environment in which they can run, swim, and fetch.

HOUNDS

Afghan Hound
Basenji
Basset Hound
Beagle
Black-and-Tan Coonhound
Bloodhound
Borzoi
Dachshund
Foxhound, American
Foxhound, English
Greyhound
Harrier
Ibizan Hound
Irish Wolfhound
Norwegian Elkhound
Otter Hound
Pharaoh Hound
Rhodesian Ridgeback
Saluki
Scottish Deerhound
Whippet

Despite the varied appearance of the dogs in this group, all were bred for their sharp sight or hearing in order to hunt, chase down, and catch small game. Many breeds in the hound group have adapted well to the more passive domestic lives they now typically enjoy. Don't expect, however, to keep the hound out of the hound dog. These

smart, curious, athletic canines need to run, explore, and challenge themselves, and they need an owner who will not only be able to let them express some of their natural behaviors but will also be able to control them when they dart off after an inviting scent.

TERRIERS

Airedale Terrier
American Staffordshire Terrier
Australian Terrier
Bedlington Terrier
Border Terrier
Bull Terrier
Cairn Terrier
Dandie Dinmont Terrier
Irish Terrier
Kerry Blue Terrier
Lakeland Terrier
Miniature Schnauzer Terrier
Norfolk Terrier
Norwich Terrier
Rat Terrier
Scottish Terrier
Sealyham Terrier
Skye Terrier
Smooth Fox Terrier
Soft-Coated Wheaten Terrier
Staffordshire Bull Terrier
Standard Manchester Terrier
Toy Fox Terrier
Welsh Terrier
West Highland White Terrier

The word "terrier" is a derivation of the Latin *terra firma*, meaning "earth." It is no surprise, then, that these bright, playful, active, cheerful, and loyal dogs are called terriers, as they were bred to hunt and bolt rats, foxes, otters, and other small vermin from their earth dwellings and dens. Terriers were always popular pets who after a day of work curled up with their human companion. Today, however, the domestic terrier typically expresses its terrier instincts only in the backyard, where the curious dog will often dig holes and bark, without knowing why, at anything that is small and moves. Terriers are sometimes smaller than other dogs, but they are always hardy and active. The terrier owner must be prepared to keep up with the energetic terrier and its need for play.

Toys

Affenpinscher
Brussels Griffon
Chihuahua
English Toy Spaniel
Italian Greyhound
Japanese Chin
Maltese
Miniature Pinscher
Papillon
Pekingese
Pomeranian
Pug
Shih Tzu
Silky Terrier
Toy Manchester Terrier
Toy Poodle
Yorkshire Terrier

Dogs in the toy group were bred and raised purely as companions. Their sense of dignity, sometimes bordering on stubbornness, as well as their love for attention and pampering, is probably a reflection of their prestigious past, living with emperors, nobility, royalty, and the wealthy elite who, in some cases, considered these dogs sacred. Their small size, low need for exercise, affectionate disposition, and love of comfort make them wonderful domestic pets for today's dog owners, especially those living in apartments or those who are elderly and need a less athletic companion. Don't be fooled by this canine's timid appearance, however. Toys often have no sense of their size and status in the canine kingdom. They are very courageous and will try to take on anything. In the absence of a clear sense of when to stop pampering this type of dog, many can become a little too spoiled quite easily.

Non-Sporting

American Bulldog
Bichon Frise
Boston Terrier
Chow Chow
Dalmatian
English Bulldog
French Bulldog
Keeshond
Lhasa Apso
Miniature Poodle
Schipperke
Standard Poodle
Tibetan Spaniel
Tibetan Terrier

The non-sporting group describes dogs who are now simply domestic companions, and therefore cannot be classified in any of the other groupings. Don't underestimate the potential of these breeds, however. Their present role as a pet often hides an interesting history. Some were bred to be workers; others, like the Chow Chow, may have been bred to be eaten!

BREED CHART

If you are planning on getting a new dog, this chart can provide you with essential information on the size, history, grooming needs, suitability for children, exercise requirements, typical temperament, and the ailments that commonly afflict the breed you are considering. If you are getting a pedigreed dog, simply look up the dog's breed name on the chart. If you are getting a mixed-breed dog, you can still get an idea of what to expect by looking up all the breeds you suspect have contributed to your dog's makeup.

Of course, no chart can summarize exactly what to expect from a dog. Each dog differs, and how you handle it as an owner can play a significant role in whether or not it will be a good companion.

BREED/ AVG WT	ORIGIN/HISTORY	COAT/GROOMING
Afghan Hound (50–70 lbs)	The lineage of this ancient breed can be traced to the Afghanistan desert and mountains, where the dog's keen sight and agile athleticism were relied upon to track down gazelles, hares, and leopards over often rugged terrain. The Afghan was being bred in Britain and America by the beginning of the twentieth century.	Long, silky, luxurious mane that requires daily brushing and occasional trimming.
Airedale Terrier (45–52 lbs)	This dog originated in the English river valley of Aire, where it was bred to hunt small vermin. The Airedale later went on to become a police and military messenger dog. Today, it is a good watchdog and companion.	Thick, wiry, short coat that gets bushy around the eyes and muzzle. Brush this dog about twice a week and take it to the groomer for shaping every three to four months.
Basenji (21–25 lbs)	This dog was originally a vermin hunter from central Africa. It came to England in the nineteenth century, but was not successfully bred until some fifty years later. Today, it is a companion dog.	Smooth, short coat that requires a quick brushing once a week.
Basset Hound (30–55 lbs)	This hound derives its name from the French word *bas,* meaning "low." The name describes its body, which remains low to the ground at all times. It might also describe its baying, which alerts hunters that this keen scent hound is on the trail of a badger, rabbit, or fox.	Dense, short coat requires only a quick weekly brushing.
Beagle (25–35 lbs)	This dog's origins may date back to Greece or France, but its true history belongs to England, where this hound trailed rabbits either singly or in packs. Today, it is a very popular companion.	Short, thick coat that needs a quick brushing once a week.
Bedlington Terrier (17–23 lbs)	The Bedlington Terrier takes the name of its English town of origin. It was bred to assist miners and became a hunter of rats and small vermin. Today, it is typically a domestic pet favored for its distinctive silhouette.	Short, thick, curly coat that should be groomed twice a week. Coat shaping is needed every two to three months.

GOOD WITH YOUNG CHILDREN?	EXERCISE REQUIRE-MENTS	COMMENTS	COMMON AILMENTS
No	Abundant	This quiet, dignified, affectionate indoor dog can become boister-ous, energetic, and independent to the point of unruliness when outdoors. Its owner, therefore, should be experienced with dogs, patient, and sensitive. Also be aware that the Afghan is often aggressive toward cats, rabbits, and other small animals.	Hip dysplasia Allergic dermatitis Cataracts Ear infection
No	Moderate, with long walks.	The dignified and courageous Airedale can be a good companion and guard dog, provided its owner is experienced and can focus this dog's independent, aggressive dis-position.	Hip dysplasia Gastritis Eczema
Yes	Moderate	The Basenji is generally cheerful, energetic, and eager to play and explore. It is also very alert. Since it cannot bark, when it hears an odd noise, it will express concern by wrinkling up the fur on its forehead.	Hernias Gastritis Anemia
Yes	Moderate	This dog's unique droopy and kind eyes give away its true dispo-sition. The Basset Hound is a calm, good-natured, sophisticated, loyal dog that makes an excellent companion.	Herniated disc Ear infection Entropion Ectropion Glaucoma Conjunctivitis
Yes	Moderate	This gentle, smart, happy, curious, and energetic dog adapts well to both country life and—provided it is walked frequently—city life.	Ectropion Cherry eye Cataracts Heart disease Epilepsy Allergic dermatitis
No	Moderate	This dog can be affectionate and loyal, but only if properly trained. Otherwise, it tends to be stub-born and can be aggressive toward other dogs and pets. It also loves to chase after cats, rab-bits, and other small animals as well as dogs.	PRA Cataracts Kidney disease

BREED/ AVG WT	ORIGIN/HISTORY	COAT/GROOMING
Bichon Frise (7–12 lbs)	The Bichon Frise is thought to have originated on the Canary island of Tenerife. Its true popularity, however, arose when Spanish sailors began using the dog as barter, introducing it to many European cities. The dog first established itself as a companion to the Italian and French nobilities. Later it became a companion to circus performers.	Curly and puffy coat that needs a good daily brushing and a clipping every two months.
Borzoi (55–105 lbs)	Seventeenth-century Russian aristocrats bred the Borzoi for its swift gait and keen sight, which made it a good hunter of wolves, hares, and other prey. The Borzoi often hunted in packs, leading their human companions who were on horseback. This dog enjoyed later popularity among royalty and fashionable sets, due to its beautiful and sophisticated lines.	Long, curly, or wavy coat that is full on the chest, stomach, legs, and tail. Needs a good brushing a couple of times a week.
Boston Terrier (15–25 lbs)	This dog originated in America in the nineteenth century and is thought to be a mix of an English Bulldog and English Terrier.	Smooth, glossy, thick coat that only needs a quick brushing once a week.
Boxer (55–70 lbs)	The Boxer originated in Germany, where it was raised to fight other dogs, bulls, and bears in cruel spectator sports that are now banned. The Boxer later served as a police dog. Today, it makes an excellent companion.	Short, thick coat that only needs a quick weekly brushing.
Bulldog (45–55 lbs)	The Bulldog grew in popularity in England, where it was bred to fight bulls in a cruel spectator sport. Many of today's Bulldog's characteristics are different from those of its early ancestors.	Short, shiny coat that needs a quick weekly brushing.
Bull Terrier (40–55 lbs)	The Bulldog, Dalmatian, and local terrier types were interbred to produce the Bull Terrier. Once used in England for dogfighting, it is now a domestic pet.	Short, thick coat that only needs a quick weekly brushing.

GOOD WITH YOUNG CHILDREN?	EXERCISE REQUIRE- MENTS	COMMENTS	COMMON AILMENTS
Yes	Light	The Bichon Frise is an active, playful, sturdy, curious canine. He can sometimes be bashful.	Runny eyes Cataracts Ear infections Skin disorders
No	Abundant	The Borzoi is generally a docile, aloof dog who probably would not be happy around prodding children. It loves to stroll and run. But be careful: The Borzoi can run very quickly and should always be kept far away from traffic if let loose.	Allergic dermatitis Leg fractures Gastritis
Yes	Light	A playful, Intelligent, and gentle dog who is sensitive to a person's ups and downs. The Boston Terrier can be somewhat independent at times.	Cataracts Cherry eye Respiratory problems Heatstroke Patellar dislocation Difficult whelping
Yes	Moderate	The Boxer is an intelligent, courageous, straightforward dog that, with proper training on the part of every family member, can be a loving, playful, obedient, and protective pet.	Cancer Tooth and gum disease Respiratory problems Heatstroke Heart disease Hip dysplasia
Yes	Moderate	Despite its stocky, fighting appearance, the Bulldog is prized as a companion for its gentle, friendly, calm, and reliable disposition.	Obesity Respiratory problems Heatstroke Heart disease Cherry eye Entropion Whelping problems
Yes	Moderate	This former gladiator of the canine kingdom is now bred to be a sweet, charming, playful, gentle companion whose distinctive muzzle, expressive face, and squat body can be amusing to watch. This dog is also good with children, but can be aggressive toward other dogs and cats.	Deafness Allergic dermatitis Obesity Heart problems Umbilical hernia

BREED/ AVG WT	ORIGIN/HISTORY	COAT/GROOMING
Cairn Terrier (13–16 lbs)	This dog is originally from the Highlands and islands of Scotland, where it was bred to become a fearless hunter of foxes and rats. Its name derives from the rocky dens, or cairns, where its hunted prey took refuge. Today it is a popular domestic dog.	Shaggy coat that needs grooming twice a week.
Chihuahua, Smooth or Long Coat (2–6 lbs)	Although some trace this dog's origins to China, Egypt, or Spain, it is most commonly believed that it originated in Mexico, where it took its name from the city of Chihuahua. The dog enjoyed popularity with the Aztecs; due to the number of Aztec sculptures that resemble this little dog, it is thought that the Chihuahua was a symbol of good luck. Today it is a popular breed in many countries.	Smooth-coat Chihuahas have a short coat that needs a quick brushing every other week. Long-coat Chihuahuas have fine, wavy hair that needs a quick weekly brushing.
Chow Chow (44–70 lbs)	This dog, with its distinctive purple tongue, originated in China, where it was raised to guard herds and hunt small prey. Whether or not this dog was also used as food or simply served as trade barter (also called "Chow Chow" by Chinese sailors) is a detail that remains unknown. Today, the dog is a companion and household protector.	Thick, bushy coat that requires daily grooming.
Cocker Spaniel (26–34 lbs)	Fourteenth-century Spain may have been the birthplace of this established Spaniel breed. Its popularity, however, grew in England, where it would assist the hunter in "cocking" or flushing game. Today the Cocker Spaniel is a very popular companion.	Long, silky mane that needs to be brushed twice a week.
Collie, Rough and Smooth (40–75 lbs)	Originally a sheepherder from the Scottish Lowlands, this breed became popular when it was the favorite of Queen Victoria, and, later, the star of the *Lassie* films and TV series.	The Rough Collie has a thick, long, bushy coat that needs a daily grooming; the Smooth Collie has a thick, short coat that needs brushing once a week.

GOOD WITH YOUNG CHILDREN?	EXERCISE REQUIRE-MENTS	COMMENTS	COMMON AILMENTS
No	Moderate	This courageous, curious, adaptable, energetic, and cheerful dog makes a wonderful companion. It is very loyal, becoming jealous when your attention is divided. It may enjoy digging and barking.	Ingrown nails, unless regularly clipped Allergic dermatitis
No	Light	The Chihuahua is a loyal dog; sometimes this loyalty, however, borders on jealousy. This dog is very intelligent. It also needs a lot of attention and activity. It does have a tendency to yap.	Fractures Tooth and gum disease Heart disease Hydrocephalus Patellar dislocation
No	Moderate	The Chow Chow is an alert, smart, fastidious dog who is typically loyal, but only to its closest companion. It requires a firm trainer because it is fiercely independent, aggressive, and stubborn, characteristics that, if handled well, can make it an excellent guard dog.	Eczema Hip dysplasia Heatstroke Entropion
Yes	Abundant	This gentle, playful, easy-to-please dog makes an excellent companion. It can, however, be independent, and will behave best with an owner who can be firm when necessary.	Umbilical hernia Cleft palate Patellar dislocation Ear infections Eczema Obesity Entropion Ectropion Cataracts Cherry eye Glaucoma
Yes	Abundant	Collies can be high-strung and stubborn, but they are also loyal, affectionate, eager-to-please, intelligent dogs that will be obedient with some training.	Collie Eye Anomaly PRA

BREED/ AVG WT	ORIGIN/HISTORY	COAT/GROOMING
Dalmatian (45–59 lbs)	The origins of this dog are unknown, but the breed was established in the eastern European region of Dalmatia, where it was raised to be a versatile working dog. The Dalmatian has also served as a rat hunter, herd dog, sled dog, stable guard, and firehouse mascot. It became a companion dog only recently and rose in popularity after the 1961 release of the Walt Disney film *101 Dalmatians*.	Short, thick, glistening coat that needs a quick brushing once a week.
Doberman Pinscher (55–90 lbs)	This dog gets its name from its nineteenth-century breeder, Louis Doberman, who mated guard dogs with terriers to perfect what has served as a military, police, and guard dog as well as a wonderful domestic companion.	Short, thick, shiny coat that lies close to the body. Brush quickly once a week.
English Springer Spaniel (40–55 lbs)	This English land dog gets its name from "springing" hunted pheasants into the air. It is considered one of the very best sporting gundogs.	Silky and wavy coat that needs grooming a couple of times a week. A light trim may also be required once every two months.
German Shepherd (60–85 lbs)	This dog was bred and raised in Germany to herd sheep. Over the years, however, this canine has been used as a guard, police, military, rescue, search, and guide dog. The German Shepherd also makes an excellent, loyal companion.	Thick, short, smooth coat that frequently sheds and could use a brushing twice a week.
German Short-haired Pointer (45–70 lbs)	This dog originated in Germany, where it was bred as a hunter of fowl and small vermin. Today, the German Short-haired Pointer is still used as a hunting dog, but it is also a popular domestic companion.	Short, smooth, thick coat that needs only a quick weekly brushing.

GOOD WITH YOUNG CHILDREN?	EXERCISE REQUIRE-MENTS	COMMENTS	COMMON AILMENTS
Yes	Abundant	The Dalmatian can be overeager at times and needs an energetic owner who not only lets the dog have fun, but also can control it when it gets too excited. The Dalmatian is also courageous and makes an excellent guard dog.	Hip dysplasia Deafness Allergic dermatitis Eczema Bladder stones
No	Abundant	The intelligent, bold, strong Doberman makes an ideal watch-dog. It can also be gentle, loyal, and great fun. Due to its aggressive, independent disposition, however, a Doberman should be enjoyed only by an owner who can train the dog and be sensitive to its personality. It can also be a good family dog, provided all family members take part in its obedience training.	Gastritis Immune deficiency disorder Hemophilia Heart disease Osteochonditis dessicans
Yes	Abundant	The English Springer Spaniel tends to be vivacious and playful, and loves an equally athletic and energetic companion. It needs plenty of attention and can grow destructive if ignored or left indoors over long periods of time.	Eye disorders Hip dysplasia Skin disease Ear infection
Yes	Abundant	Inexperienced handlers can make monsters of this dog. Good, firm, and fair obedience training can, however, bring out the dog's acute intelligence, loyalty, and affectionate disposition.	Hip dysplasia Gastritis Eczema Diabetes
No	Abundant	This is an intelligent and proud dog that typically makes a good companion. However, it is excitable and needs a lot of exercise. When ignored or cooped up, it will bark and may take to chewing off-limits objects.	Hip dysplasia Eczema around the paws

BREED/ AVG WT	ORIGIN/HISTORY	COAT/GROOMING
Golden Retriever (55–75 lbs)	The English and Scottish originally bred this dog to retrieve waterfowl. Today, this dog is a popular domestic companion and guard dog.	Moderately long, wavy, thick coat that needs brushing a couple of times a week.
Great Dane (more than 100 lbs)	The Great Dane established itself in medieval Germany as a boar hunter and guard dog. Today, the Great Dane has a more dignified character and is enjoyed as a domestic companion.	Short, thick, smooth coat that lies close to the skin. Brush quickly once a week.
Greyhound (60–90 lbs)	This breed is thought by some to be the oldest in existence. Its lineage may be traced back to ancient Egypt, where it is depicted on wall engravings. It was most likely then (as it is now) prized for its keen sight and tremendously fast gait, allowing it to chase down small prey across open fields and to race after mechanical rabbits in the popular spectator sport of Greyhound racing.	Short, thick, smooth coat that only needs a quick brushing.
Irish Setter (60–70 lbs)	This dog was bred and raised in Ireland for locating and retrieving fowl. It received its name because it freezes or "sets" when it smells its prey. Irish Setters are popular companion dogs today.	Long, wavy, red coat that is more abundant on the chest, stomach, legs, and tail. Brush a few times a week and occasionally trim long hair.
Italian Greyhound (7–13 lbs)	The ancient Egyptians and Romans enjoyed this elegant breed, decorating the walls of their tombs with its image. Its fame grew, however, in the Renaissance courts of Italy and Spain, where many noble ladies prized the dog's companionship and beauty, and many artisans depicted it in tapestries and paintings.	Short and soft coat that only needs a quick brushing every other week.
Japanese Chin (4–7 lbs)	The Japanese Chin originated in China, but grew in popularity in Japan, where it was a pampered companion to members of the imperial court. Its popularity spread in the West during the nineteenth century.	Fine, silky, long hair that needs daily grooming.

GOOD WITH YOUNG CHILDREN?	EXERCISE REQUIRE-MENTS	COMMENTS	COMMON AILMENTS
Yes	Abundant	Golden Retrievers are one of the most beloved breeds. Intelligent, playful, eager to please, affectionate, loyal, and gentle, this is the ideal dog for a family or a person who loves the outdoors.	Hip dysplasia PRA Cataracts Entropion Heart problems
Yes	Abundant, and room to stretch its legs.	This giant, almost horselike breed requires an owner who can provide it with the space it needs. Some Great Danes tend to be aggressive and dominating, but most are gentle, calm, affectionate, and loyal dogs who respond to obedience training with encouragement.	Entropion Hip dysplasia Bone cancer Cervical spondylopathy Tumors
No	Abundant, requiring a safe place to run.	This gentle, sensitive, affectionate dog can make a wonderful companion. It is intelligent, but it often needs a sensitive and patient trainer as it is easily distracted and sometimes frightened by discipline. The Greyhound can bother cats and small rabbits.	Weight fluctuations Allergic dermatitis
Yes	Abundant, needing wide-open spaces to play.	This energetic, highly excitable dog can be a handful without ongoing, patient training and lots of exercise. If handled well, the Irish Setter will be loyal and affectionate.	Hip dysplasia Ear infection PRA Entropion Heart disease Epilepsy
No	Light, with a good run from time to time.	Calm disposition and not so needy of constant attention. The Italian Greyhound can become nervous around too much excitement or other emotional situations. Don't let its occasional timid behavior convince you, however, that this is a fragile dog. It is a strong, hardy breed.	Fractures Progressive Retinal Atrophy (PRA) Epilepsy
No	Light	The Japanese Chin is playful, alert, and bright, but somewhat resistant to obedience training. It loves comfort and pampering.	Respiratory difficulties Heatstroke Lacerations of the eye

BREED/ AVG WT	ORIGIN/HISTORY	COAT/GROOMING
Labrador Retriever (55–65 lbs)	This dog originally came from Newfoundland, Canada. It was the British, however, who raised it to be the excellent retriever of fowl that it is today.	Dense, straight coat that sheds regularly. Brush once or twice a week.
Lhasa Apso (13–15 lbs)	The breeding of this ancient dog was for many centuries monopolized by Tibetans, who thought it sacred, symbolizing the lion who protected the Buddhist lord. Lhasa Apsos began to be bred outside Tibet only in the early 1900s, when both a male and a female dog were given as gifts to a British official.	Long, abundant mane that requires daily grooming and an occasional trim.
Maltese (4–9 lbs)	This dog may have originated in Egypt, but its popularity evolved on the Mediterranean island of Malta, where the dog lived with elite and wealthy families. Today's Maltese closely resembles its early ancestor.	Straight, silky long coat that needs a daily grooming and an occasional trim.
Mastiff (170–200 lbs)	This ancient breed was once a Roman war dog and gladiator. The breed traveled to England in the sixth century, where it was bred to control wolves and to fight bulls, bears, and lions in cruel spectator games. The breed almost became extinct during the 1940s. Today it once again is popular, serving as a watchdog and companion.	Short, dense coat that is close to the skin. Brush quickly once a week.
Miniature Pinscher (8–10 lbs)	Originally, the Miniature Pinscher was a German dog that predated the larger Doberman Pinscher by many centuries. Its popularity outside Germany grew in the early 1900s.	Short, smooth coat that needs a quick brushing once a week.
Miniature Schnauzer (13–15 lbs)	The origins of this dog date back to the Middle Ages, when German herders raised the dog to rid their fields of rats. Its name derives from its characteristic mustache or muzzle, which in German is called a *schnauze*.	Wiry, thick coat that is bushy around the nose, eyes, and legs. Grooming twice a week is recommended. Coat shaping every three months is also needed.

GOOD WITH YOUNG CHILDREN?	EXERCISE REQUIRE- MENTS	COMMENTS	COMMON AILMENTS
Yes	Abundant	This is a gentle, intelligent, affectionate, patient, and loyal dog that is a perfect pet for a family or energetic owner who loves the outdoors.	Hip dysplasia Cataracts PRA Entropion Obesity Hemophilia
No	Moderate	A good Lhasa Apso will be trusting, playful, and alert. A spoiled Lhasa Apso, however, can become needy, manipulating, and overly dependent. If you are persistent without being too aggressive, the Lhasa Apso will be a wonderful companion.	Runny eyes Eye lacerations Kidney problems
No	Light	The Maltese is playful, energetic, gentle, and craves attention. It is also hardy and strong.	Runny eyes Eye infections Tooth and gum disease Hypoglycemia
Yes	Moderate, with long walks.	The Mastiff can be aggressive, stubborn, and overly independent if not trained properly. A well-trained Mastiff, however, is gentle, good-natured, and loyal.	Hip dysplasia
No	Light	Unlike many other toy dogs, the Miniature Pinscher is not a lapdog. It has an independent, loyal, intelligent, bold, and courageous personality that makes it act like many of its larger canine counterparts. If you want a large dog but don't have the space or time to exercise one, the Miniature Pinscher might be an ideal alternative.	Kidney stones
No	Moderate, accompanied by long walks.	A sharp, playful, loyal, flexible dog who loves to be pampered, but will rarely become spoiled.	Cataracts Liver disease Heart disease Diabetes

BREED/ AVG WT	ORIGIN/HISTORY	COAT/GROOMING
Norfolk Terrier (11–12 lbs)	The English farm was this dog's first home, where he spent his working hours catching pesky rats. This breed grew popular in America after 1914.	Wiry, short coat that needs a quick weekly brushing.
Norwich Terrier (11–12 lbs)	Like its close companion the Norfolk Terrier, the Norwich Terrier was originally an English rat-catching dog. Some countries don't distinguish between the lower-eared Norfolk and the perky-eared Norwich Terrier. America, however, has recognized both breeds.	Wiry, short coat that needs a weekly brushing.
Old English Sheepdog (60–90 lbs)	This dog was first bred in the west country of England to help farmers driver their sheep and cattle to market. Today, the Old English Sheepdog is a domestic companion.	A bushy, abundant, dense coat that needs to be brushed every other day and occasionally trimmed.
Papillon (8–10 lbs)	The origins of this dog are uncertain, but it is known that it became a popular breed in the Renaissance courts of Spain, Italy, and especially France, where its name, which means "butterfly," was bestowed on the dog thanks to its winglike ears.	Silky, long-haired coat that is especially fine on the ears, chest, legs.
Pekingese (8–13 lbs)	This dog's origins date back to ancient China, where it was bred and raised purely for its sacred presence in the imperial palace. The 1860 British capture of Peking almost wiped out the breed. Fortunately, a few specimens were saved and transported to Britain, where the breed grew in popularity.	Long, straight, thick coat that requires daily grooming.
Pembroke Welsh Corgi (17–25 lbs)	This cattle herder was originally from Pembrokeshire, Wales. Its popularity remained steady throughout history, but soared when Queen Elizabeth II posed for a portrait surrounded by her Corgis.	Short, thick coat that needs a weekly brushing.

GOOD WITH YOUNG CHILDREN?	EXERCISE REQUIRE-MENTS	COMMENTS	COMMON AILMENTS
No	Moderate, with plenty of walks.	This spitfire of a dog loves to chase, dig, play, and interact with everything and everyone. It is very affectionate and loyal. It is also very vocal and can be noisy at times.	Allergic dermatitis
No	Moderate, with plenty of walks.	The Norwich Terrier is similar in disposition to the Norfolk Terrier.	Allergic dermatitis
Yes	Abundant	This dog is sometimes called the "nanny" dog because of its instinctive tendency to watch children as if they were part of its flock. Extremely lovable, playful, easygoing, and loyal, the Old English Sheepdog is an excellent domestic pet, and especially good with families.	Hip dysplasia Cataracts Autoimmune deficiency disorder Skin disease
No	Light	The Papillon is energetic and playful to the point of being high-strung. It loves attention and affection, and is very protective of its owner. It appears timid, but responds well when treated like a hardy and strong dog.	Fractures
No	Light	The Pekingese is proud to the point of obstinacy. It often rejects obedience training, but doesn't tend to be a mischief-maker. Frequently barks.	Entropion (inward-rolled eyelid) Eye lacerations Respiratory problems Herniated disc Patellar dislocation Umbilical hernia Difficult whelping
No	Moderate	The Corgi is a very intelligent, obedient, adaptable, hardy, friendly, and playful companion. It is an excellent pet for somebody who travels frequently, or wants a "big dog" personality but can't have a big dog. The Corgi is fine for the city (provided it gets exercise) or country.	PRA Glaucoma Herniated disc Hip dysplasia

BREED/ AVG WT	ORIGIN/HISTORY	COAT/GROOMING
Pug (14–18 lbs)	The exact history of this breed is unknown, although most agree it enjoyed early popularity among the Buddhist monks of China and was brought to Holland by sea merchants in the 1500s. The Pug's popularity grew among the European nobility; it was an especially prized companion of royal children and famous ladies. It still enjoys popularity today.	Velvety, thin, short coat that only needs a quick weekly brushing.
Rottweiler (85–115 lbs)	This dog's lineage can be traced back to Rottweil, Germany, where it was raised to drive cattle to market and to guard its owner's profits from highway bandits. Over time, this canine's courageous disposition made it useful not only as a guard dog, but also as a police, military, and security dog.	Short, thick, shiny coat that needs only a quick weekly brushing.
Saint Bernard (120–170 lbs)	Seventeenth-century monks from a hospice monastery near St. Bernard's Pass in the Swiss Alps raised these dogs to guide travelers over the dangerous mountains. Its keen hearing allowed it to warn of oncoming avalanches, and, over time, it also developed a talent for rescuing the unfortunate traveler who could not escape in time. Today the Saint Bernard is a companion dog.	The more common long-haired variety seen today has thick, moderately long wavy hair that needs to be brushed every other day.
Samoyed (35–55 lbs)	The Samoyed tribe of the northeast Siberian tundra raised this dog to herd their reindeer and pull their carts. Fur traders introduced the Samoyed to England in the 1900s, where it became a popular companion. In addition to its domestic life, the Samoyed is still used as a sled dog in some colder regions.	Thick, bushy, abundant coat that needs brushing every other day.
Scottish Terrier (18–23 lbs)	The Scottish Terrier originally populated the rocky Scottish Highlands, where it chased down fox and other small vermin. It is now a popular domestic dog.	Long, thick coat that gets bushy around the eyes and muzzle. A quick combing twice a week will keep the coat well groomed.
Shetland Sheepdog (14–18 lbs)	This sheepherder hails from the Shetland Islands off the coast of Scotland, where such other miniature animals including Shetland ponies originated. Their small size results from the limited diet Shetlanders feed their animals, not from breeding. Today, the Shetland Sheepdog makes an excellent companion.	Thick, long, bushy coat that requires a daily grooming and an occasional trim.

GOOD WITH YOUNG CHILDREN?	EXERCISE REQUIRE- MENTS	COMMENTS	COMMON AILMENTS
No	Light	This is a sturdy, playful, clever, and affectionate dog. Many enjoy being loyal to one person and covet being the center of atten- tion. They get cold easily, so be sure they wear a coat on chilly days.	Prolapse of the eye Eye lacerations Runny eyes Respiratory problems Gastritis
No	Abundant	If everyone in the family learns to handle this dog firmly, it will make an excellent household compan- ion. Otherwise, this stern, intelli- gent, and alert dog may be prone to behavioral problems.	Hip dysplasia Obesity Entropion Osteochonditis dessicans
Yes	Abundant, with space to roam.	The Saint Bernard is an easygoing, patient, cheerful, loyal companion who makes an excellent family pet.	Hip dysplasia Osteochonditis dessicans Entropion Ectropion
Yes	Moderate	This independent, intelligent, viva- cious dog may misbehave if it is not handled by an energetic, firm owner who can bring out this dog's affectionate, loyal, playful, and cheerful personality.	Hip dysplasia PRA Glaucoma Skin disorders
No	Moderate	The Scottish Terrier is a sophisti- cated, friendly dog. It tends to get very independent with old age, although it will remain loyal and affectionate to the one person it considers its companion.	Allergic dermatitis Deafness
No	Moderate, with at least one daily walk.	The Shetland Sheepdog has a gentle temperament, intelligence, eagerness to please, and loyalty to its owner that make it a won- derful companion. It likes to exer- cise, and provided it is allowed to run, it can enjoy both city and country living.	PRA Collie Eye Anomaly Heart disease Epilepsy Deafness

BREED/ AVG WT	ORIGIN/HISTORY	COAT/GROOMING
Shih Tzu (9–17 lbs)	This ancient mix between the Lhasa Apso of Tibet and the Pekingese of China established itself as a sacred court dog in the Chinese Tang and Ming dynasties. Not until the early twentieth century, when a few specimens were brought over to England and bred, did they achieve an international popularity.	Thick, long, silky mane that requires daily brushing to keep it from getting tangled and unkempt. An occasional trim is also needed.
Standard Dachshund, Wirehaired, Smooth, or Long-haired (11–25 lbs)	Today's Dachshund is a descendant of a slightly larger German dog used to hunt badgers. Its popularity as a domestic dog spread in nineteenth century Britain after Queen Victoria had some as her companions.	The Wire-haired Standard Dachshund has a thick, bushy coat that needs a quick weekly brushing. The Smooth Standard Dachshund has a short, dense coat that also needs a quick weekly brushing. The Long-haired Dachshund has a long, silky coat that needs to be brushed twice a week.
Toy Poodle (7–12 lbs)	Many assert that this breed of dog originated in Germany, where it was used to retrieve hunted fowl out of the water. The Toy Poodle, however, probably originated in France, where it was bred down to become a circus dog. Today, the Toy Poodle is a very popular companion.	Curly, silky hair that needs a grooming every other day, and clipping and shaping every month and a half.
Weimaraner (45–70 lbs)	This dog was originally raised in the German state of Weimar to help the aristocracy hunt bear, mountain lions, and, later, to retrieve fowl. Today the Weimaraner is a family companion and favorite portrait sitter of photographer William Wegman.	Short, shiny, thick coat that needs only a weekly brushing.
West Highland White Terrier (15–22 lbs)	This terrier is said to have originated in Argyle, Scotland, where it was bred as a hunter of fox, otter, and other small vermin. Today, this dog enjoys popularity as a domestic companion.	Dense, thick, straight coat that should be brushed twice a week and trimmed every three months.

GOOD WITH YOUNG CHILDREN?	EXERCISE REQUIRE-MENTS	COMMENTS	COMMON AILMENTS
No	Light	The Shih Tzu is a proud dog who craves affection, play, a comfort-able environment, and a good owner to which it can loyally devote itself. Spoil a Shih Tzu too much, however, and its stubborn personality can take over.	Obesity Respiratory problems Tooth and gum disease Ear infections
No	Moderate	Lively and loves to be the center of attention. His cleverness and stubbornness, however, demand good and persistent training.	Herniated disc Diabetes Heart disease PRA
No	Moderate	The Toy Poodle is perky and play-ful to the point of sometimes seeming high-strung. It is intelli-gent and trainable, but can become stubborn if spoiled. Some Toy Poodles yap at almost any-thing.	Glaucoma Runny eye Cataracts Dry eye Ear infection Allergic dermatitis Heart disease Heart murmur Epilepsy Hydrocephalus Patellar dislocation
No	Abundant	The Weimaraner requires an experienced owner who can con-trol this dog's stubborn, indepen-dent, domineering, boisterous dis-position. If well-trained, the Weimaraner will be a loyal, digni-fied, friendly, charming companion.	Hip dysplasia Allergic dermatitis Tumors
No	Moderate	The "Westie," as some call it, is a sturdy, flexible, spirited dog who is affectionate and loyal to its owner.	Allergic dermatitis Liver disease Hernias

BREED/ AVG WT	ORIGIN/HISTORY	COAT/GROOMING
Whippet (18–30 lbs)	This relatively modern breed originated in northern England, where greyhound racing fans who could not afford to feed and maintain the large Greyhound bred the dog with local terriers to produce the smaller whippet.	Short, dense, smooth coat that only needs a quick weekly brushing.
Yorkshire Terrier (5–7 lbs)	This dog first appeared in the nineteenth-century English town of Yorkshire when a Maltese mix was bred with local terriers. Today it enjoys great popularity.	Long, silky hair that needs daily grooming.

GOOD WITH YOUNG CHILDREN?	EXERCISE REQUIRE-MENTS	COMMENTS	COMMON AILMENTS
Yes	Moderate, but needs to run from time to time.	The Whippet is gentle, affection-ate, and bright. It enjoys long walks and a good run. Keep it monitored, however; if the dog should run off, it will probably be too fast to catch.	Gastritis
No	Light	Lively, intelligent, courageous, and affectionate, this dog makes an excellent companion. It can, how-ever, bark a lot and become stub-born if pampered.	Runny eye Tooth and gum disease Patellar dislocation

2

CANINE BEHAVIOR: UNDERSTANDING DOGS

THE MODERN DOMESTIC DOG belongs to the *Canidae* family, along with wild beasts like jackals, coyotes, foxes, and wolves. When you compare a domestic dog to a fox or wolf, you may be surprised at the resemblance. Each member of this family has a comparatively long head that ends in an elongated jaw. *Canidae* members also boast plenty of teeth.

Many scientists now believe that the domestic dog descends directly from the Asiatic wolf. The first interaction between humans and wolves probably occurred about 40,000 years ago. Interestingly, while some speculate that humans first approached wolves benevolently, offering them meat left over from successful hunts, other scientists think that wolves were actually the prey of prehistoric humans. According to this theory, some wolves were a versatile source of food and clothing. Some wolves may even have been raised from pups, just as we now raise cattle.

People realized quickly that certain dogs could earn their keep, and set them to work as protectors. As evidenced by paintings in ancient Egyptian tombs, we now know that other dogs were trained to become invaluable participants in the hunt. These original hunters evolved into today's Afghans and greyhounds.

Domestication of dogs served many other purposes. Household dogs were placed on treadmill-like contraptions attached to roasting spits. By running on the treadmill, the dogs were able to make the spit rotate above an open fire. By exploiting the strong backs of certain breeds, rural inventors learned how to create contraptions that would enable dogs to churn butter or work a well.

It was quickly learned that dogs made good herders; they possessed an ability to manage livestock very effectively, both in the pasture and on the way to and from the market. Romans found that this managerial aptitude could also be called upon to control people; dogs were used to keep slaves in line. In Rome, dogs quickly became status symbols—the wealthy used dogs to guard their homes. Romans, Greeks, and Persians learned how to breed huge, vicious dogs that made excellent warriors.

Some dogs were never bred for heavy labor. The toy breeds, which could be found in Europe and parts of Asia at least 2,000 years ago, were the precious pets of the wealthy. Many were bred to look like tiny versions of their larger, hardworking relatives.

The household dog certainly differs from its ancestors in both form and function. Evolutionary changes have occurred in response to demands made on the dog by its environment. One factor has been consistent throughout the dog's history: human life has always been vastly enriched by our canine friends.

HOW DOGS COMMUNICATE

Speech is the chief means of communication for humans. When we need to convey information, we reach into our vast supply of words and piece together a sentence that will convey our intended meaning. For us, in everyday interaction, other forms of communication like "body language" are usually secondary. Only by actively studying a person's gestures and movements during speech do we ever raise body language to the level of conscious communication. For the most part, it remains below the surface, underscoring or enriching meaning.

Dogs, in contrast, rely chiefly upon body language to communicate. The physical gestures a dog uses to "speak" to others of his species also constitute the language your dog uses to communicate with you. For example, a dog will have the same response to your scolding tone as he will to the reprimanding gestures of a dominant (i.e., larger or older) dog. The admonished dog will very obviously avert eye contact, signaling deference.

A dog spells out deference with many different parts of his body. His ears

A dog in total submission presents his groin as a sign of friendship, similar to the way we shake hands.

THE FIXED STARE

Dogs learn early that a fixed stare signals a challenge. You can stare a dog into submission on occasion. However, it's not a good idea to employ this technique with dogs you don't know. A dog who is unfamiliar with you may become very frightened and defensive, believing your stare is a signal of imminent aggression.

become flush against his head. His tail, positioned snugly between the hind legs, may wag in short, low strokes. He may drop to the ground, crawl, and then roll over onto his back. Total submission is usually indicated by this posture, with one hind leg in the air to reveal his groin. Presenting the groin is a peaceable gesture, one that an amiable dog may make toward a person or another dog. Some researchers compare this gesture to the human handshake.

If you look at them closely under a variety of different conditions, you will discover that dogs are capable of many facial expressions. A dog can question, challenge, or greet with his face. A dog may say hello or defer to you with a smile—the canine version of a smile, that is. The lips will stretch across the teeth and the mouth will open slightly. Sometimes, the tongue may even stick out a bit.

Another common facial expression conveys the desire to play. It looks like the greeting or submission smile, only it's more exaggerated. Along with this face, the dog may crouch, raise one foot, and lean to one side, his head sometimes approaching the ground. The dog may suddenly leap forward from the crouch and bite the air playfully, or leap backward and run off, asking you or another dog to give chase.

On the opposite end of the behavioral spectrum, a dog can use his body to intimidate and instill fear. One trick a dog relies upon is the ability to create the illusion of enlargement. A dog sensing challenge or danger will stretch his head, neck, and tail to full extension. He will wag his tail in tight, stiff motions. This can be dangerously

A dog asking to play may raise one paw and lean to the side.

A dog makes his appearance seem more imposing when he knows he needs to be aggressive.

sion may indicate potential violence, with the lips drawn back and teeth bared. Dogs about to bite in fear sometimes seem like they are conveying submission with their faces, so always be sure to look at all the elements of a dog's body language—and the sounds he emits as well. A fearful dog that may become aggressive will growl low and ominously.

Dogs are capable of many different sounds. The various tones and intensities of a sound, in combination with body language, can effectively communicate feelings and intentions. A dog will adjust the sound of a bark, for instance, to accurately reflect his excitement or agitation.

To read a sound accurately, you must consider the context in which it is made. If a dog is hovering over a dinner bowl in your kitchen, he may growl to make sure he is left alone to enjoy his meal. He may make the same sound outside; in a field where other animals are approaching, the growl can signal a challenge.

Growls themselves have many shades

confusing for those who automatically interpret tail-wagging as a gesture of friendliness.

As his perception of danger intensifies, the dog may change his head position, lowering it and extending the neck in the direction of the opponent. The dog will seem to grow "taller" as he stretches all four legs to their maximum length. The dog may raise one leg, release urine, and scratch the ground with his paws. His scratching and urine marks the turf as his own, and demands that others stay away.

Sometimes, a fearful dog will show signs of aggression and submission at the same time. His ears may be cocked back in a submissive position, but his hair will stand straight up, his muscles will tense, and his hind legs will be prepared for motion. His facial expres-

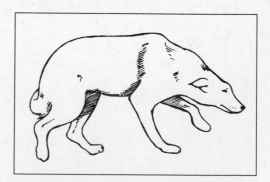

The fearful dog prepares itself for rapid movement, and also shows signs of submission.

of meaning. A frightened dog may emit a low, constant growl at first. As his posture changes to prepare himself for aggression, the pitch of his growl may rise. A playful growl, on the other hand, wavers repeatedly in pitch.

As you can see, while dogs don't have words, they are certainly equipped to speak to the world, using a complex combination of sound and gesture. By closely observing the subtle shifts in what we see and hear, we can forge better communication with our canine companions.

PROBLEM BEHAVIOR

Dogs are just as susceptible to emotional problems as we. Often, the seeds of canine neuroses are found in the way a dog is treated. Overcoddling, as well as abusive disciplinary measures, can create a neurotic dog. Long stretches without attention or companionship, as well as a lack of exercise and training, or overfeeding, can all lead to various forms of dysfunction.

Neuroses express themselves in different ways, all of which are unpleasant for both dog and human. Restlessness and excessive whining, barking, or whimpering are very common. Neurotic dogs sometimes seem as if they are on an emotional roller coaster; since they turn on people very easily, resentment between pet and caretaker builds quickly.

Let us take a look at other common neurotic behavior, and at some ways to handle it.

ANXIETY

Dogs are in some ways reflections of ourselves. They often copy our actions and patterns, which may include some of our less flattering attributes.

The symptoms of anxiety are restlessness and loud panting. The dog may lose control of his bowels or bladder. The key to coping with anxiety is to help your dog overcome his fear, either by removing the source or by reconditioning his behavior. If your dog is particularly prone to severe anxiety attacks, your veterinarian may want to prescribe a dog tranquilizer to help him through bad episodes.

HYSTERIA

Sometimes, a certain set of stimuli will turn normally nervous behavior into hysteria. Hysterical reactions are usually evidenced by severe trembling, panting, and possibly hyperventilation. Occasionally, this severe reaction will lead a dog to become destructive, tearing apart papers, fabric, and even furniture. Discuss hysterical reactions with your veterinarian. An important step in dealing with this behavior is to isolate the causative factor. For some dogs, thunderstorms trigger hysterical responses. Your veterinarian may suggest you give your dog a tranquilizer prior to confronting the triggering stimulus, i.e., before a thunderstorm or other feared event occurs.

PHOBIAS

A phobia is a persistent, long-term fear of someone or something. In dogs, if the fear is allowed to build unchecked, hysterical behavior may occur in the presence of a triggering stimulus.

Many dogs quickly develop a phobic response to going to the veterinarian. Some dogs become so frightened of the doctor's office that they display a phobic response to anything associated with such a trip, including getting into a car, even if it is only for a pleasant Sunday drive. Typical signs of phobia include trembling, panting, running in circles, and attempts to hide. To prevent this, take your dog in the car frequently for fun, reinforcing the idea that every drive will not end in a veterinary examination.

SEXUAL NEUROSES

Sometimes, dogs don't pay any attention to their own breeding timetables and try to mount other dogs of the same or different sex out of season.

Sometimes, a male dog's frustrations become pent up. Roaming allows him to let off steam, but this is often not an option, especially for city and suburban dogs. In response to this frustration, they mount a person's leg, or even a small child. The best solution to persistent sexually neurotic behavior is to neuter the male (see Neutering, p. 199).

TEMPER TANTRUMS

Dogs often lack the self-restraint needed to control their anger and frustration. Even adult dogs can be prone to aggressive displays of temper. When left alone too much, a dog may throw a tantrum by chewing and destroying property, perhaps knocking over a garbage pail in the kitchen and spreading its contents across the room. Scolding your dog when you get home will be of little help; he will not associate your reprimand with his prior behavior. Instead, try giving your dog a bone or toy the next time you leave him alone. Another solution is to leave the radio or television on. This will occupy your dog, easing his frustrations.

PART II

CARING FOR YOUR DOG

3

BEFORE YOU OWN A DOG

DOGS ARE INDEED our best friends—just look at the way they treat us. They lick our hand affectionately. They are unconditionally loyal. And in return they deserve nothing less than meticulous care for all their needs.

A dog requires more than water and food. Owning a dog means spending time with it. You must make sure that she is regularly groomed and kept healthy. You'll need to schedule veterinary checkups regularly and have your dog thoroughly vaccinated. All the accoutrements of pet ownership will come into play, including food, leashes, toys, bowls, carriers, sleeping material, and more.

Dogs become members of the communities in which they live. Neighbors will show respect to the well-behaved, friendly dog—in short, the dog who respects the humans who live in her neighborhood. However, she will only learn how to behave well if you train her to be sociable.

Once you become aware of the various responsibilities dog ownership entails, you can set about the task of deciding whether or not you feel you can give a dog a good home. If the answer is yes, the next step is narrowing down the myriad types of available dogs to the one that is most suited to your circumstances.

When you adopt a dog, you claim responsibility for her health and happiness. In return, you expect love and companionship. It's important to consider whether you can realistically meet the dog's needs in terms of time, training, exercise, and grooming. Perhaps most important: Is the dog's temperament compatible with your needs, and vice versa?

CHOOSING THE RIGHT DOG

In order to help you choose a dog that fits your life-style, here are some questions to consider.

* HOW MUCH TIME ARE YOU ABLE TO SPEND?

It's easy to fall in love with puppies at the pound, especially as they beckon you with their mournful eyes. If you are considering a pet, however, you'll need to detach yourself from the emotional pull long enough to consider how you might react when the puppy has munched on your moccasin, or awakened you before sunrise. Puppies demand your time and patience and plenty of one-on-one contact. It's important to nurture a puppy, otherwise she may grow up dysfunctionally, causing you and your household unnecessary grief.

If your household is empty for long stretches of the day, it's probably wisest to consider an adult dog. Older dogs are much more likely to know the ropes of household life, and are probably trained. Your local animal shelter is almost certain to have grown dogs that would fit into your schedule perfectly.

* DO YOU LIVE IN THE CITY?

Believe it or not, a studio apartment and a Great Dane are not necessarily a bad match. While space restrictions may make a small or medium-sized dog the more logical choice for a city dweller, your chief concern should be the amount and quality of time you have to spend with your dog. If you have the time and the inclination to take that Great Dane on long walks in the park, then the two of you could be a good match.

If you like to exercise and want a jogging companion, you probably want a larger dog with a sturdy build, not a small dog with short legs who won't have the endurance or speed to keep up with you.

One of the prime requirements for a city dog is an easygoing, gentle disposition. Look for a dog that can easily adjust to people, noise, and the general hustle and bustle of urban living.

Noise is one reason why some small dogs, such as Miniature Schnauzers or Toy Poodles, may not be the best choice for apartment living. Schnauzers and Yorkies often bark constantly, regardless of whether a visible stimulus is present. While a barking dog may keep prowlers out, an excessive barker may agitate others living in your building, resulting in complaints to your landlord or management company.

* ARE CHILDREN PART OF THE HOUSEHOLD?

Children and dogs are fast friends. In fact, a dog can play a vital role in a child's life. Every youngster at some time or another feels lonely or insecure. At these times the companionship and loyalty of a dog can make a child feel like he belongs. In turn, learning to care for a pet's needs inculcates a sense of responsibility that a child will carry into adult life.

Although the relationship between a child and a pet has the potential to be mutually beneficial, there are some things to think about before bringing a dog into a household with children.

The first is the age of the children. Wait for them to reach three or four, at the very least, for safety's sake. Most children under the age of three can't really differentiate between the concepts of living animals and stuffed toys. Small children may yank the dog's tail or poke her eye just to see what happens. On the other hand, a heavyset adult dog or rambunctious puppy can unintentionally knock a small child down.

When a child grows sturdy enough not to be knocked down, a big dog is often a great companion, because many big dogs are as gentle as they are large. Toy breeds grow easily irritated at rough handling, and prefer to be with adults. A Collie is often a good choice with children; the Collie's herding instinct makes her a great babysitter.

Mixed breeds (mongrels) make wonderful pets for children. They may not live up to the aesthetic standards of a purebred, but mixed breeds are known to adapt easily to new situations and also possess sweet temperaments. Besides, children don't discriminate between mongrels and purebreds—they just want a pet to love and play with.

Although it's tempting, never give a child a dog as a holiday or birthday present. Holidays and birthdays involve too much noise, excitement, and activity. The poor dog will be frightened or excessively excited, making introduction to the household difficult. If your child is old enough to have a dog, make a birthday or holiday present out of a collar, bowl, and a few pictures of dogs, along with a commitment to bringing a new pet into the household. Then, a week or two later, take your child with you when you pick out the dog.

When you arrive at the store, shelter, or breeder, observe the interaction between your child and potential pet. Dogs that cower upon your child's approach, or bark viciously, will probably not make good pets. You want a dog to be a lively companion for the child, but not too lively. A hyperactive dog may nip and knock down a child and play too aggressively.

While you will make the final choice, it's a great idea to incorporate your child into the decision-making process. This will give your child a sense of responsibility and will help forge the bond between child and pet from the start.

* IS THE DOG TO BE A COMPANION FOR AN ELDERLY PERSON?

The joy that appears on an elderly person's face after she embraces a friendly pet is a beautiful thing. Affectionate, lively dogs can help mitigate the loneliness often associated with aging; the love dogs give, coupled with the tactile sensation of touching soft fur, make dogs welcome companions. "Pet therapy" programs in which the SPCA or humane societies take pets to visit nursing homes and hospitals have been very successful, sparking up even the most feeble residents in a way that medication could never accomplish.

But if you are a senior or are choosing a dog to be the companion of an elderly person, you'll need to exercise common sense in your selection.

The elderly may have time to care for a puppy, but they may not be willing or able to walk the puppy in the rain, to housebreak her, or to discipline her when she chews up the rug.

Large dogs may be difficult for older people to manage. An older, medium-sized dog or a toy breed might be the ideal companion.

* HOW CONCERNED ARE YOU ABOUT THE APPEARANCE OF YOUR HOME?

If you are very particular about your home's appearance, length of fur, shedding, likelihood of responding to training, and the age and sex of a dog are all issues to explore when assessing a potential pet.

Puppies, like children, get themselves into messes. If you aren't crazy about constantly picking up after a puppy, an older dog who has gone through the puppy stage is a better choice.

If cleanliness is an important issue but you still want a puppy, keep in mind that females often respond to training better than males, and are less likely to destroy objects in a house.

If you want to adopt a dog that won't shed throughout your house, investigate terriers. Most terriers don't require much more than sporadic trips to the groomer.

* ARE ALLERGIES PREVALENT IN YOUR HOUSEHOLD?

Just because you are an allergenic person, you don't have to rule out adopting a dog. Most dogs may make you sneeze and leave your eyes watering, but there may be a breed or two that never trigger an allergic reaction.

An allergic person is likely to find a successful match in a wire-haired breed like a Schnauzer, poodle, or terrier. These breeds do not shed much. Also, they give off very small amounts of dander, the skin- or hair-produced particles that aggravate allergies.

* IS A CAT ALREADY PART OF THE HOUSEHOLD?

Kittens and puppies are usually a good match, but an adult cat that has spent a lot of time indoors and had little or no contact with other animals probably won't like a newcomer, especially a dog.

Try a test run. Ask a friend to have her dog accompany her to your house and see how your cat reacts. This will give you a good opportunity to see how your cat acts.

This may come as a surprise, but if

you already have more than one cat in the household, taking in a new dog usually isn't a problem. This is because the two or more cats have already set up a feline hierarchy among themselves, whereas a single cat may compete against the new dog for dominance.

* IS A DOG ALREADY PART OF THE HOUSEHOLD?

Two female dogs will usually get along with no problems, as will a male and female. (If you combine a male and a female, you will have to neuter and spay them for obvious reasons.) Two males tend to compete, even if neutered, and the combination may be difficult to handle.

When a second dog comes into the household, and especially if the dog is a young puppy, the new dog will almost always submit to the will of the first dog. These hierarchies are natural; dogs gravitate toward dominant-submissive relationships with each other. It is wise to allow them to work it out between themselves.

Just be sure when you bring in a new dog that you pay attention to the old dog, too, so you do not create any jealousy between the two dogs. (See Introducing Your Dog to Her New Home, p. 46.)

* CAN YOU AFFORD A DOG?

Shelters provide inexpensive opportunities for adoption. There are low-cost spay and neuter clinics as well as other medical facilities aimed at making pet care affordable for people who have lower incomes.

No matter what your income is, however, you must consider that your dog could become significantly ill or suffer a life-threatening accident. Ask yourself the following important question: How much of a financial burden would you be willing to take on in order to provide your dog with adequate medical care?

Obviously, a big dog will eat more than a smaller one, and more food equals more money. Keep in mind too that a beautiful long- or curly-haired dog will be expensive to groom if you're not equipped or disposed to maintaining her coat at home.

MALE OR FEMALE?

Females are more amenable to training and housebreaking. While males often long to roam, females are likely to focus their attention strongly upon their human companions.

If a male dog gets the instinctual urge to roam, he may be gone for several days. If he is prone to aggression, he may also return with battle injuries. Some aggressive males will fight for any reason, just to assert themselves.

A neutered male will make an excellent pet, similar in affection and temperament to a female, but still a good watchdog. Neutering will usually mitigate his tendency to roam, and make him less aggressive.

PUREBRED OR MIXED BREED?

Whether purebred or mixed, all dogs share certain wonderful qualities that make humans crave their companionship. However, the debate between proponents of both types of dog has been waged for years.

With a little research, you can look into purebreeds armed with clues about their temperaments and what they will look like as adults. In some mixed breeds, lineage is so obvious from a puppy's appearance that you can make some educated guesses regarding future personality. Don't forget that nature and nurture both affect a dog's temperament.

Some people shy away from purebreds, believing they are more prone to behavioral problems than mixed breeds. As a result of faulty breeding, some purebreds do display difficult qualities like nervousness and a tendency to become overexcited. However, this is more indicative of specific breeding problems than characteristic of purebred dogs in general. A dog whose pedigree is strong and who has been properly bred should be as trainable as a mixed breed.

Dog shows are a passion all over the world. In order to participate competitively, you must show a purebred. Dog shows offer great opportunities to indulge your love for dogs, either as a competitor or a spectator. Professional breeders look forward to shows as an opportunity to display their hard work—which in turn can increase their sales.

"Obedience" and "conformation" are the two arenas of competition that make up a dog show. Dogs in the obedience competition respond to commands; this displays their abilities to be trained and to perform. Conformation judging is more aesthetically oriented. The breed club sets up a set of physical ideals for a breed, and each entry is judged according to that standard, which usually shifts slightly over the years.

Whether or not you plan to show your dog, it is crucial that you choose a pet whose needs you will be capable of satisfying, and whose personality is most likely to be compatible with that of your household.

ON CHOOSING A PUREBRED

Like any sport, showing your dog takes hard work, determination, and time. Here's an important tip for the uninitiated: Always research your breed. Then purchase the dog that has the best combination of strong pedigree conformation to the current breed standards. (See Finding the Right Mate, p. 204.)

WHERE TO GET YOUR DOG

Now that you have made the decision to get a dog and perhaps know what type of dog you are interested in, you are ready to start your search.

In addition to newspaper ads, which are sometimes a good source, you can also buy a dog from a pet shop or breeder or adopt one from an animal shelter.

PET SHOP

There are many reputable pet shops. Unfortunately, some shops give the good ones a bad name by buying their puppies from "puppy mills"—mass-production animal farms where dogs are bred for resale with no particular regard for temperament, genetic problems, or any of the other finer points of breeding. A puppy-mill dog has never lived in a home or had human companionship.

Here are some things to look for should you choose a pet shop:

- Store is neat, clean, and orderly
- Store employees are helpful and knowledgeable
- Dealer gives you a lifetime guarantee against inherited disorders such as hip dysplasia (see Hip Dysplasia, p. 161). These disorders often appear later in life and cannot be prevented once they appear. Selective breeding—i.e., only breeding dogs who do not carry the gene for these disorders—can eliminate the possibility of such a disorder from appearing.

ANIMAL SHELTER

Animal shelters provide an excellent opportunity to adopt a dog. Most are very adept at creating strong matches between pet and human, and will help you make the right choice based upon your needs and life-style. Often, they are familiar with the life a dog lived prior to her arrival at the shelter, and are thus able to supply you with important clues regarding her health and temperament. Keep in mind that when you adopt a dog from an animal shelter, you are giving an unwanted animal a home and a chance for happiness.

BREEDER

If you're looking for a purebred dog and you want to make sure that genetic problems have been eliminated as much as possible, your best bet is a private breeder.

One way to find a reputable breeder is to contact a national breed club. These groups are composed of breeders, owners, and people who have a passion for specific dog breeds. If you are unsure how to get in touch with the club representing the breed you're considering, write to the American Kennel Club, 51 Madison Avenue, New York, New York 10010. Other strong sources include magazines devoted to dogs, as well as the classified sections of newspapers.

One of the best methods is to get a recommendation from your veterinarian. There's no need to settle for the first breeder you meet—visit several. Once you find a potential breeder, pay close attention to the physical condition of the kennel. A good breeder will keep a tidy, well-organized kennel. A good breeder will be very responsive to your questions. Find out about the breeder's recent participation in dog shows. Ask if and how she has attempted to improve the breed. Based upon your observations, is the breeder's passion for dogs evident? One way to tell is to see if the breeder asks *you* questions and is concerned with your ability to raise the dog properly.

If possible, pick a breeder located near your home; a local breeder is more accessible if there's a problem with the dog. A reputable breeder will stand by the quality of her or his puppies, but make sure that any guarantees concerning the dog are finalized before purchase.

ADOPTING A STRAY

Giving a stray dog a home is an act of charity that may prove to be an intensely rewarding experience for all involved. However, you need to consider several issues.

After you take the stray in, be on the lookout for notices posted in your area announcing that someone has lost a dog. As adorable as your stray may be, she could have wandered away from a family that loves her very much.

You don't know the dog's history, and thus may encounter some of the longterm ramifications of abuse. Personality disorders can be worked through, but such a task requires patience, care, and knowledge. If you can get the dog to trust you, however, you'll find you're on the right track toward healing.

Take your dog for a complete veterinary examination as soon as possible. The veterinarian will diagnose current illnesses and disorders, and may be able to shed some light on the quality of the dog's former care.

HOW TO JUDGE TEMPERAMENT

One of the best ways to determine compatibility between you and a potential pet is to examine the dog's temperament. Temperament is often the force that guides day-to-day behavior as well as a dog's responses to specific circumstances. In actuality, it is important to know yourself well in order to choose a dog properly suited to your own temperament.

Here are the basic varieties of canine temperament:

RESPONSIVE

A responsive dog is mirthful, extroverted, and loves to make people happy. Because of the latter trait, responsive dogs are relatively easy to train, and can be expected to fit com-

TESTING FOR TEMPERAMENT

TEST #1

As long as you can lift the dog comfortably, you can use this test to determine how instinctively trusting the dog is.

Cradle the dog in your arms firmly, as if you are holding a small baby. *If the dog growls or barks loudly, do not continue.* If the dog seems reasonably calm, slowly adjust her orientation so that her feet are pointing upward, her head down. Her reaction to this new position will indicate temperament as follows:

BEHAVIOR	TEMPERAMENT
Lies calmly, looks at you peacefully, and may even give you a gentle lick or two.	Responsive or sedate
Squirms, whimpers, attempts to escape.	Nervous
Lies still and stiff, trembles slightly, and may scream.	Shy

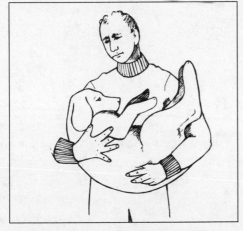

To test temperament, cradle the dog like a baby.

Slowly tilt the dog until his head is pointing downward, and then assess his response.

TEST #2

From several feet away, call the dog and clap your hands energetically.

BEHAVIOR	TEMPERAMENT
Approaches you rapidly and with great enthusiasm; may lick and jump on you.	Responsive/Nervous
Responds with some trepidation, may be frightened by sound of hand clap.	Shy
Stands still or slinks toward you.	Sedate
Emits a low growl and stands still.	Aggressive

fortably into your household. The Whippet and Bernese Mountain dog are both highly responsive, good-natured breeds.

NERVOUS

A nervous dog has more energy than she can handle. She may be skittish and easily excited. Nervous dogs are not always immediately responsive to training, but do eventually learn to behave properly. Additionally, they tend to be loyal and grateful. Due to overbreeding, many German Shepherd Dogs today are nervous, but with time and patience, they make excellent companions.

SHY

Timidity usually reflects fear. Shy dogs sometimes seem uncommunicative but respond well to gentle handling. Once a shy dog trusts you, her loyalty is unwavering. The Shetland Sheepdog is usually shy among strangers, but makes a highly affectionate pet.

SEDATE

Sedate dogs tend to take life easy. They don't make much noise, and like to lie about. As expected, they may be slightly resistant to training, but are a pleasure once trained. Because they don't require much exercise and tend to be very calm, sedate dogs make great pets for elderly people. Some pugs and Dachshunds fit this description.

AGGRESSIVE

Aggressive dogs are very forceful and sometimes prone to violence, especially when provoked. Therefore, all dogs that are naturally aggressive must be meticulously trained in order to curb potentially destructive behavior. Adult dogs demonstrating antisocial aggressive behavior should be brought to a professional trainer. The Rottweiler is highly aggressive toward outsiders, but once well trained, makes a terrific family pet.

INTRODUCING YOUR DOG TO HER NEW HOME

Try to arrange to bring a new dog into your home when there will be people (or at least a person) around to help her become comfortable. Even the most easygoing dog will need assistance and attention; the new surroundings represent a big change, and change can be stressful.

One way to ease the transition is to find out ahead of time what the dog had been eating prior to adoption. Prepare those foods for at least the first few weeks. Dogs sometimes react to traumatic situations by refusing to eat. If such behavior persists for more than two days, consult your veterinarian.

Introduce your new pet slowly to any

dogs already residing in your home. Take into account your established dog's feelings of territoriality. A good idea is to crouch down on the floor with your first dog, and then casually call the new dog to you. That way, you can lavish affection on both at the same time, rather than implying that you are rejecting your old dog for the new one. If the new dog causes strife or animosity among the resident pets, make sure all initial interactions are closely supervised until a comfortable hierarchy is established (see Is a Dog Already Part of the Household?, p. 41).

While the information you are about to read will be helpful for all dogs, turn to Chapter Twenty-one if you are bringing a puppy into your home. There you will find useful advice on puppy care, health, and training.

HOW TO CHOOSE A VETERINARIAN

Right after your puppy or dog enters your home, it is important for you to choose a veterinarian. Do not wait until the first sign of sickness. Rather, should your dog become ill, she deserves to see a doctor in whom you have already placed your trust. Choose a veterinarian by recommendation if at all possible. Ask your friends who have dogs whether or not they are satisfied with their veterinarians, and begin to explore the options based upon their advice. Other helpful ways of finding a reliable doctor include calling the American Animal Hospital Association—(800) 252–2242, or (303) 986–2800 in Col-

orado—or your local humane society for recommendations.

If you haven't already done so in the process of adopting your dog, take her to the veterinarian soon after she enters your home. This initial visit will allow you to assess the quality of the veterinarian and his or her staff, which should provide you with the information you need to make your choice. When you go for that first appointment, ask yourself the following questions:

1. Is the veterinarian's facility neat and orderly? If not, it may indicate a lack of organization and perhaps unhygienic conditions.

2. Can the veterinarian be easily reached outside regular office hours, on weekends, late at night, and on holidays? Does the veterinarian have an emergency service covering for him when he is not on call? If veterinary care is available on a limited basis only, go elsewhere.

3. Do you feel as if the veterinarian speaks freely and thoroughly with you? Does she explain everything clearly? Is she responsive to your questions?

4. Does the veterinarian perform a complete physical examination? A complete physical examination is the best way to resolve existing problems and prevent new ones from arising. This examination would include a survey of your dog's eyes, nose, ears, skin, coat, respiration, chest, lungs, heart, and sex organs. Vaccinations should be administered when necessary (see Chapter Five).

5. Does the veterinarian handle your

dog gently and with respect? Does he have a good rapport with animals?

BEDS

A puppy or dog will take great comfort in discovering there is a warm, soft sleeping space all ready for her in her new home. Once you choose the type of bed she will be sleeping in, be sure to place the bed in a place free of loud noise and distraction—a new dog needs to sleep in relative calm.

The most popular commercially made beds are made of wicker. One of the advantages of a wicker bed is that movement causes it to creak, a sound that seems to calm dogs. However, dirt and crumbs get easily lodged in wicker. Wicker also is an easy target for teething and destructive puppies. Not only is it prone to damage, it can break off and wind up inside your puppy's body. Therefore, avoid wicker beds for young dogs.

Another type of bed available in pet stores is constructed of hard plastic. This will both indulge and survive dogs that relieve their anxiety by chewing on their beds. Beanbag chairs can also work as long as the cover is very sturdy and can be easily removed and washed.

Of all beds, the one that makes the most sense is a collapsible crate or cagelike enclosure. A cage can be used for housebreaking purposes and often gives a new dog a sense of security. In essence, the new dog will "own" this structure, and consider it to be her very own space in the house. Standard crates suitable for dogs that never exceed thirty pounds are about two by four feet and stand three feet high. Larger enclosures are available to fit bigger breeds.

When the puppy first enters your home, place her in her cage and leave her alone there. After ten or fifteen minutes, return and release her. While the puppy is in the cage, do your best to resist her mournful howls, which should subside after a few minutes. Try to ease her fear by placing a light blanket over the cage to transform it into a cozy enclosure. Of course, the puppy's world should in no way be confined to the cage. Supervised ventures throughout the house are crucial to her becoming fully acclimated to her new environment.

Try to get a puppy used to eating inside the cage. Start by putting her dish in the room where the cage sits. Then, gradually move the dish closer to the cage until she is eventually eating inside. This should take about a week.

A puppy probably longs for the snug camaraderie of sleeping with her littermates. To reproduce the warmth a mother and litter provides, wrap a lukewarm hot water bottle in a towel and place it in the bed.

Puppies need gentle discipline to give them a sense of order. When it comes to bedtime, they need to learn early that sleep usually means temporarily leaving the fun and attention people provide. A puppy should be confined to her "room" when her natural sleeping time occurs. Stick to this schedule so that it becomes routine. A good way to ease the trauma of these nightly separations is to place a piece of your clothing in the puppy's bed. The scent that emanates from the garment will be calming.

For your dog's bedding, use a soft and warm blanket that will stand up to regular washing, regardless of the enclosure you decide to use.

HANDLING

Gentle handling is a very good way for a puppy to get used to humans. The best way to pick a puppy up is to lift her with one hand on her chest and the other supporting her bottom. This will not only give you a firm grip, but it also will make the puppy feel secure.

While the interaction between a child and a puppy can be very beneficial for both, children must be taught to respect a puppy's fragility. A child also must be taught that puppies are living beings, not dolls. Teach children

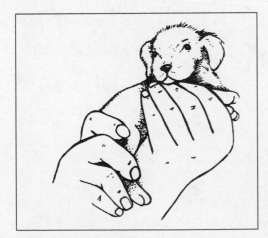

Gain a puppy's trust by supporting it from beneath.

to approach a puppy calmly and gently. Make sure they avoid brisk movements, roughhousing, or interrupting the dog's sleep or meals.

COLLARS AND LEASHES

Every dog needs a collar and a leash. Because this is such a basic necessity, you will find that there is a vast variety of both available in pet stores.

Small dogs, and larger dogs not in the process of being trained, do fine with nylon or leather collars that buckle closed. A half-inch-wide collar works well for most breeds, while larger dogs require a collar that is a little stronger—one to one and a half inches wide.

Once you put a collar around a puppy's neck, try to slip your middle three fingers through. If your fingers fit snugly with just a little give, the collar is probably well suited to your puppy's neck. It is important that the collar be tight enough to stay around the neck but loose enough to allow for easy, unrestricted breathing.

Once you begin to train a dog, use a buckle collar or a nylon choker (see below) for smaller breeds only. Larger breeds should wear a choke chain during training and walking, but you should change collars at other times. Choke chains tend to intermesh with other objects, and thus may cause an unsupervised dog injury.

Chokers tighten around a dog's neck when the leash is pulled, thus serving as an effective and safe training aid.

You will need to decide what type of choker you wish to use: nylon, chain, or angle-pronged. Nylon chokers work well on smaller breeds because they respond to lighter tugs during training. If you have a larger dog, try a chain choker first. If you find it isn't strong enough to withstand training, switch to an angle-pronged choker. This sort of choker, however, should only be used on very large breeds, and if the dog is at least nine months old and has a strong, muscular neck.

When you affix the choker, arrange the collar so that the weight of the chain loosens the loop after the collar has disciplined the dog. Above all, make sure all chokers fit loosely around the dog's neck. If you are unfamiliar with how a choker is worn, make sure to ask the pet store clerk for help.

When looking for a leash, your most crucial priority is strength. You want a leash that will stay firmly locked in place on your dog's collar, stay intact after countless pulls and yanks, and adequately restrain your dog. Leather and nylon leashes are the sturdiest; nylon is also easy to wash and comfortable to

use. However, both nylon and leather leashes often fall victim to a dog's desire to chew. Your dog probably won't chew a chain leash, but the metal may rust easily and can be uncomfortable to hold after a while.

Extending leashes have become very popular in recent years. These give you the flexibility to decide how much lead you would like to give your dog—often up to twenty feet. Dogs love the extra freedom, which you in effect control.

DOG TAGS

When you get a license for your dog (see Licensing Laws, p. 73), you will also receive a metal tag with her registration number on it. Attach this to your dog's collar and make sure she wears it at all times. You may also decide to purchase another tag and have your dog's name, as well as your name, address, and telephone number, engraved on it. Such tags are available through pet supply and hardware stores and will be of great benefit to your dog should she stray from home. If your dog wanders away and is found, these two markers will help concerned strangers or the dogcatcher quickly identify her and return her to you.

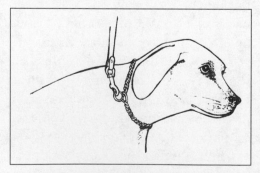

If your dog is large and has a strong neck, use a chain choke collar during training.

CARRIERS

The easiest and safest way of transporting a small dog is by way of a carrier similar to the type used for cats. A carrier will come in handy if you plan

---

BEWARE OF FOOTWEAR!

While it may be tempting to find boots to protect a dog against rain-soaked or snow-covered streets, most dogs have little interest in footwear. Also, protective coverings can be a detriment, as they could have the adverse effect of softening the pads, leaving them vulnerable to tearing and perforation.

---

to travel extensively with your dog, or if your dog ever becomes too weak or ill to walk by herself.

CLOTHING

A dog with a healthy, well-groomed coat has all the clothing she needs for life indoors. To protect your dog, however, several garments will come in handy.

Buy or knit a sweater to guard short-haired, small, fragile, or elderly dogs against winter weather. Sweaters are helpful because they cover a dog all around, while natural coats cannot fully protect a dog's underbelly. Investigate the various garments available in pet stores. They are sold in a variety of sizes; the store's clerk should be able to help you find the right fit.

Rainwear for dogs is mostly an aesthetic choice. Hats rarely stay on for long and may slip, making it difficult for your dog to see.

No matter what garments you put on your dog, make sure all removable objects, including buttons, gems, rhinestones, bows, or beads are far away from your dog's mouth. This will prevent choking.

BOWLS

Every dog needs two bowls: one for food and one for water.

Stainless steel bowls are practical because they are very easy to clean. However, dogs often paw at their bowls, or bump into them; for that matter, people knock into dog bowls rather easily as well. Because stainless steel is a fairly light material, you may want to consider another type.

Plastic bowls cost little but may become your dog's chewable toy. Food and dirt can easily accumulate inside the chew marks and scratches that accumulate on the plastic surface. Ceramic bowls are heavier and less likely to spill, but more prone to chipping.

Make sure the bowl isn't so deep that the dog can't get to the bottom-most layer of food or water. Also, food placed in shallow bowls tends to wind up on the floor very quickly.

Afghan Hound   *Airedale Terrier*

Akita   *American Staffordshire Bull Terrier*

Australian Cattle Dog   *Basenji*

Basset Hound   *Beagle*

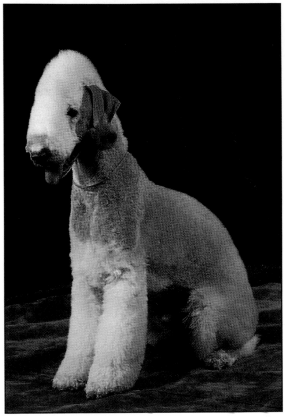

Bedlington Terrier   *Bernese Mountain Dog*

Bichon Frise   *Bloodhound*

Borzoi   *Boston Terrier*

Boxer   *Bull Terrier*

Cairn Terrier   *Chihuahua (Smooth)*

Chow Chow   *Collie (Rough)*

Dachshund (Standard)   *Dalmatian*

Dandie Dinmont Terrier   *Doberman Pinscher*

English Bulldog   *English Toy Spaniel*

German Shepherd Dog   *Great Dane*

Greyhound *Irish Wolfhound*

Italian Greyhound *Keeshond*

Lhasa Apso   *Maltese*

Mastiff   *Miniature Pinscher*

Newfoundland   *Old English Sheepdog*

Pekingese   *Pointer*

Pointer, German Shorthaired   *Pomeranian*

Poodle, Miniature   *Pug*

Retriever, Golden   *Retriever, Labrador*

Rottweiler   *Samoyed*

Scottish Terrier   *Setter, Irish*

Shetland Sheepdog   *Shih Tzu*

Siberian Husky *Skye Terrier*

Spaniel, English Springer *Spaniel, Cocker*

St. Bernard   *Standard Schnauzer*

Weimaraner   *Welsh Corgi, Pembroke*

West Highland White Terrier   *Whippet*

Wire Fox Terrier   *Yorkshire Terrier*

4

BASIC DOG CARE

Now that you have chosen your dog, introduced him to the household, decided on his veterinarian, and purchased some of his supplies, you will need to acquire some fundamental information about dog care.

Basic dog care includes knowing your dog's food and exercise needs, how to groom and board him, and, last but certainly not least, some of the best ways to have fun with him. First, let's take a look at the history of canine eating habits.

YOUR DOG'S EATING HABITS AND HOW THEY EVOLVED

When you feel like scolding your dog for taking pieces of food from his bowl and dragging them into the living room, take solace in the knowledge that he is only responding to an evolutionary instinct. By taking a look at how wolves, your dog's direct ancestors, satisfied their needs for food, you can better understand your dog's eating behavior.

Wolves traveled in packs and thus hunted together. A single wolf would grab its share of the kill and drag it off to a private space. It sequestered itself in order to ensure that it would be able to eat its entire meal privately, without the threat of interruption.

Dogs seem to swallow almost without chewing. Back in the wild, wolves needed to swallow their meals quickly, before packmates could gobble up more than their share. A dog's mouth is thus shaped to hold food for a very short period of time. His forty-two teeth are divided into several varieties: the long, pointed incisors or "dog teeth" snare the kill, then rend it; the back molars grind the most fibrous materials. The food quickly passes into the digestive system, where the stomach churns the food into usable form (see Chapter Sixteen, p. 175).

Dogs also seem to have a limitless capacity to stuff themselves. Their wolvine ancestors had to fill themselves whenever they found food. The prey they were able to catch often had to sustain them for a long time. Any leftovers would be buried to protect them from other animals, and then dug up when it was time for another meal. A domestic dog's tendency to bury bones in the backyard is a vestigial response to this instinct.

While wolves in the wild are flesh eaters, neither the ancient nor modern creatures are considered to be chiefly carnivorous. Domestic dogs need both plant and animal tissue to survive. In the wild, wolves and dogs would derive vegetable nutrition by eating the stomachs and other internal organs of their prey. The stomach contained partially digested vegetation, thus offering the predator a balanced diet.

YOUR DOG'S NUTRITIONAL REQUIREMENTS

Dogs get the energy they need from food, just as humans do. Every dog needs an adequate supply of proteins, carbohydrates, fats, vitamins, minerals, and water.

PROTEINS

Protein is essential for the growth of healthy tissues. Proteins also help repair damaged cells, and are important components in the production of antibodies, which ward off infection. The millions of chemical reactions that occur in a dog's body are regulated by hormones and enzymes, both of which depend upon a constant supply of fresh protein.

Dogs get much of their protein from meat and eggs. Cheese and milk are also good sources, but many dogs are sensitive to lactose products, which can produce digestive upset. Dogs also gain protein from vegetable sources, like the cereal that makes up dry dog food.

Protein should make up about 23 percent of a dog's diet. Female dogs nursing their litter, puppies, and dogs recovering from illness temporarily require more.

CARBOHYDRATES

Dogs, like people, rely on carbohydrates for energy. Glucose, the simple sugar that fuels the body, is a byproduct of carbohydrate metabolism. If a dog is not receiving an adequate supply of carbohydrates, he will turn to his protein reserve for fuel—protein intended for cell maintenance and growth.

Besides providing energy, carbohydrates are also a significant source of fiber. Fiber binds to water, adding bulk to fecal material. This bulk helps regulate bowel movements and prevents constipation. In obese dogs, adding extra fiber to the diet can help bring weight down. The bulking capacity of fiber works just as slimming tablets act in humans. While a normal dog's diet should consist of about 5 percent fiber, overweight dogs should take in two to three times that amount. Excellent sources of fiber include cereal, bread, wheat, brown rice, pasta, peas, green beans, and potatoes. Discuss with your veterinarian the possibility of combining fiber-rich table scraps with dog food (see Variety, p. 57).

Fiber is often recommended for ill dogs. If your dog is suffering from liver disease, for instance, fiber will help absorb the poisonous digestive wastes normally taken care of by the liver. Dogs who have difficulty absorbing glucose due to diabetes will also be helped by fiber's spongelike powers

A dog's diet should consist of no more than 65 percent carbohydrates.

FATS

Fats provide significantly more energy than proteins or carbohydrates. They carry fat-soluble vitamins A, D, E, and K through the body, and they add a luminous sheen to a dog's coat. Also, they assist in many different metabolic reactions.

Dogs who spend much of the time indoors often need a little extra fat in their food to enhance the quality of their normally dry skin and coat. Dogs whose life-styles demand great bursts of energy (workers and hunters) also benefit from increased fat.

While dogs enjoy fatty foods, fats should constitute no more than 5 percent of a dog's diet. This is because most fat is not absorbable by the gastrointestinal tract and is thereby wasted.

VITAMINS

Most dogs get the vitamins they need from their regular diet. If you are interested in exploring supplementation, speak to your veterinarian first. She or he will be able to help you understand what supplements will be helpful, and will also warn you about possible interactions and contraindications.

MINERALS

Minerals are crucial for many different physiological processes and for proper bone growth. For dogs, two of the most essential minerals are calcium and phosphorus, which play significant roles in the formation of a healthy skeletal system. While you will want to be sure your dog gets a sufficient supply of calcium and phosphorus, be careful not to overdo it. The proportion set up by a proper diet should not be altered. Heavy supplementation or a diet consisting chiefly of meat, for example, may create skeletal disorders, including rickets (see Rickets, p. 163). Do not give your dog any mineral supplements without consulting your veterinarian.

WATER

Water is essential to life; every living cell requires a constant supply of this crucial substance. About 50 percent of a densely built dog's mass is water; the percentage reaches 75 percent in leaner dogs.

Every dog requires a plentiful supply of fresh water each day. Some of this water comes from canned food, which usually contains liquids (canned food is sometimes 75 percent water). Provide your dog with water at all times, not just with meals. To calculate your dog's daily water needs, multiply his weight in pounds by .65. This product represents the number of fluid ounces of water your dog requires each day.

TYPES OF DOG FOOD

Because few people have the time or expertise to cook homemade dog food, producers of commercial food have striven to create products that are highly nutritional and palatable. Foods come in three forms: dry, canned, and semimoist.

DRY FOOD

Dry food contains approximately 10 percent water. In essence it is composed of cereal filled with vegetable protein. Bone and meat meal are also present. It is sometimes more expensive than other types of food, but its hard texture has the extra advantage of strengthening your dog's teeth.

CANNED FOOD

Dogs tend to favor canned food over all other commercial products. As often is the case, that which is most desired also costs the most; canned food is probably the most expensive of the three types of food.

Canned food is usually lacking in protein and loaded with water (again, as much as 75 percent). Because it is so soft, it does not help keep your dog's teeth clean like dry food. If the brand you use doesn't contain a cereal component, you will have to supplement your dog's diet with biscuit, either added directly into the meat (follow the instructions on the package) or as individual treats throughout the day.

SEMIMOIST FOOD

Many dogs who refuse canned and dry foods will eat semimoist food, which in most cases is nutritionally balanced. Like canned food, semimoist food requires that you give your dog a biscuit after eating to keep his teeth clean and strong.

Producers of semimoist food, which usually comes in individual packets, find it best to design the food so that it resembles real meat. In actuality, it is usually composed mainly of vegetable protein and meat byproducts. About a third of each semimoist serving consists of water.

While a dog will get more protein from semimoist than canned food, the additives in semimoist food can be somewhat detrimental. Semimoist food is likely to contain extra salt, as well as corn sweetener and syrup. For this reason, don't use semimoist foods if your dog suffers from diabetes.

TABLE SCRAPS (see VARIETY, below)

FEEDING YOUR ADULT DOG

Dogs who are getting the right amount of food are usually alert, enthusiastic, and healthy. They look neither emaciated nor obese, have a luster to their coat, and seem to be enjoying life.

Use the chart on page 58 as a general guideline, remembering that dogs vary in the amount of food they need. Besides differences in frame and build, other important factors to consider include exercise, metabolic rate, the amount of energy your dog needs to fulfill his life-style requirements, if it is female, whether it is pregnant or nursing, and whether it is ill.

VARIETY

Imagine how bored you would get if you were forced to eat hamburger day after day. Dogs face the same thing, and are extremely grateful for occasional variety.

It's fine to add any of the following delicious foods to your dog's bowl, as long as they never compose more than one third of your dog's diet:

nonfatty, bland stew or meat
vegetables
gravy
low-salt chicken broth
onions
liver
carefully filleted fish
cheese (unless your dog is lactose-sensitive)
eggs

SNACKS

Save treats and snacks as rewards. Otherwise, your dog will come to expect treats constantly, which could gradually add unnecessary weight to your dog's frame. Your dog will truly appreciate the snack if it associates it with your praise for a job well done.

BONES

Bones are perennial favorites among most dogs. However, we now know that many bones can cause a dog great harm. If a bone isn't tough enough to withstand your dog's persistent chewing, pieces of it could flake off and lodge inside his digestive tract.

Today, it is much safer to give your

SUGGESTED DAILY FOOD INTAKE

WEIGHT (POUNDS)	CALORIES NEEDED	DRY OZ.	SEMIMOIST OZ.	CANNED OZ.
5	250	4	4	4
10	450	8	8	8
15	600	12	8	10
20	700	16	12	12
25	800	20	14	14
30	900	24	16	16
40	1200	28	18	20
50	1400	32	20	24
60	1600	36	26	26
90	2100	48	32	32
120	3000	72	44	48

dog a rawhide or synthetic bone than the real thing. Rawhide is soft and digestible, but it will satisfy your dog and help keep his teeth clean and strong.

PICKY EATERS

Some dogs are very fussy about what they will eat. Commercial dog food companies now make foods specifically for finicky eaters, but even those products are often rejected.

Slowly introduce new foods, gradually escalating the amount with each meal.

FEEDING YOUR PUPPY

While it is important that any dog be fed a nutritionally sound diet, puppies require extra attention, especially during the first half-year of life, when development reaches its peak. Puppies need more protein and fat than adult dogs do.

The best puppy diet consists of about half canned and half dry food, created especially for puppies. They will get plenty of fat and calories from the canned variety, while the dry food will give them calcium, phosphorus, vitamins A and D, and protein.

If you decide to restrict a puppy's diet to dry food, add one teaspoon of polyunsaturated oil to the bowl each day. This will give it the fat it needs for a healthy coat. You should also feed a puppy two or three eggs each week (five or six eggs is suggested for larger puppies). Eggs are an excellent source of protein. Lightly scramble the eggs, and be sure to allow them to cool to avoid burning the puppy's mouth.

See Chapter Twenty-one for more information on weaning and other aspects of puppy care.

OBESITY

Obesity is a very common problem among domestic dogs. They have the same instinct to eat (and eat) as their ancestors, but food is much more readily available to the house dog than to the wild dogs of the past.

Obesity can be debilitating, if not life-threatening. Overweight dogs are more prone to musculoskeletal, circulatory, liver, and pancreatic disorders. They have trouble cooling off in hot weather and are prone to heatstroke (see Heatstroke, p. 256). Muscle strength decreases, making mobility and sometimes even breathing a chore.

Before you start your dog on a weight-reduction plan, have the veterinarian give him a complete checkup to rule out any serious problems that may be causing the obesity. Once your dog has been given a clean bill of health, you and your veterinarian must set a goal weight.

Suppose your dog weighs fifty pounds, but it would be more healthful for the scale to read "40" instead. First, figure out how many calories per day a forty-pound dog should consume (see table, p. 58); in this case, it's 1,200 calories. In order to slim down to the desired weight, your dog should first eat 60 percent of that figure, or 720 calories per day. If your dog seems to be very hungry all the time, add some low-calorie, high-bulk foods like cottage cheese. Weigh your dog consistently, at the same time every day if possible. As the goal weight approaches, gradually increase the amount you feed it until you reach the normal calorie figure for the desired weight (again, 1,200 calories).

Look around for a commercial dog food made for overweight dogs. These nutritious, high-fiber products are quite effective, but will result in an increase in bowel movements. This shouldn't be a problem unless no one will be home to allow your dog to relieve itself more frequently.

Approach a weight-reduction program with moderation. By all means, do not force your dog to drop significant amounts of weight too quickly. Rather, ease your dog into a gradual routine of decreased food and increased exercise (if possible).

EXERCISE

One of the joys of having a dog is being able to walk, run, and play with it. This can only be beneficial for animal and human alike. Exercise is crucial to warding off obesity and keeping all bodily systems working properly. Exercise can begin by the time a puppy reaches the age of three months.

JOGGING

Many breeds make suitable jogging companions. This form of exercise indulges their instinctive desire to run and provides an excellent opportunity to strengthen their respiratory and circulatory systems.

Jogging is an excellent recreational activity to share with your dog.

Ask your veterinarian if jogging will be in any way detrimental to your dog. Dogs with musculoskeletal problems like hip displasia should not be permitted to do much running at all, as the stress on their legs will aggravate their already weakened condition.

If you get the green light from the veterinarian, start by doing some light fetching routines first, as a warm-up. Then, start jogging gradually. An average-sized dog should soon be able to accompany you on five-to-seven-mile runs.

If your dog starts to show signs of fatigue, such as heavy panting, stop and rest. Try to get your dog water at this time. If your dog's gait becomes awkward, also stop. Don't overdo it

---

EXERCISE: SOME THINGS TO KEEP IN MIND

1. **Exercise in moderation. You should be the judge of when it is time to call it quits, as your dog may easily overextend itself. Make sure your dog's breathing does not become labored, or his gait awkward or irregular.**
2. **Choose activities that are appropriate for your dog's breed, size, metabolism, and temperament.**
3. **Behavior during exercise can often be an indicator of illness. If, for instance, your dog suddenly seems like it has had enough after only three minutes of your usual lengthy walk, consult your veterinarian. Such behavior may be indicative of a circulatory disorder.**
4. **Be very cautious of overheating, heat exhaustion, or heatstroke (see p. 256) in the summer. Extreme fatigue and panting are key signs.**
5. **By the time a dog reaches his tenth year, reduce (but do not eliminate altogether) his exercise.**

on hot days—a dog is always at risk for heat exhaustion in the summer. It's also a good idea to stay off hot pavement to prevent footpad injuries and discomfort.

When you finish your jog, carefully inspect each of your dog's feet. Look for pebbles, bits of ice, or broken glass in each of the toes. Make sure the footpads haven't been torn by the road. A tear will reveal flesh underneath the hard, dark skin. If you find a tear, flush it with soap and warm water, and then apply an antiseptic. Bandage the wound (see bandaging a paw, p. 86) until the skin has healed. Change the bandage every day.

SWIMMING

Dogs who enjoy the water should be encouraged to take supervised swims in safe water. Avoid steep banks or deep water. Beaches are usually perfect, because the bottom slopes gradually. However, keep your dog away from choppy surf. Don't allow him to become submerged in ocean water.

BICYCLING

If your dog can run on his leash alongside your bicycle, this makes a terrific form of exercise. However, avoid bicycling if your dog is likely to become easily distracted. Because you must keep him on his leash for safety purposes, a sudden lurch toward a per-son or animal at the side of the road could result in a dangerous accident.

CAMPING

Determine whether or not dogs are allowed at your point of destination. Protect your dog from any encounters with rabid animals by making sure his rabies vaccinations are up to date. Take along your dog's health certificate, as well as flea and tick preparations (see Fleas, p. 143, and Ticks, p. 150). Also, be sure to travel with your dog's complete first-aid kit (see First-Aid Kit box, p. 82).

Once you've set up camp, it's a very good idea to restrict your dog's movement by keeping his leash on. Supervise him at all times—do not allow him to wander off.

GROOMING

Grooming a dog is not just an aesthetic practice; it's important to keep a dog's coat healthy so that he has plenty of protection from the elements. When you groom, your goal is to get rid of dead hair as well as to cleanse the skin and the living hair. Grooming your dog at home can actually be an enjoyable experience—if you learn the basics and create a comfortable atmosphere. One of the most important things to remember is to groom prior to bathing. Bathing often complicates problem hair, worsening mats and tangles.

Stroke your dog from his head down

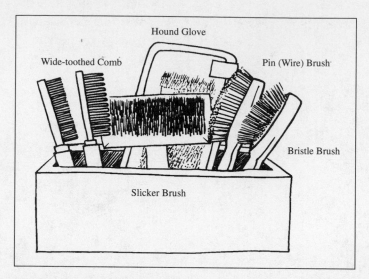

Set up a box filled with your dog's essential grooming tools.

along his back. Notice how the hair seems to be growing in lines that point toward the tail. These imaginary directionals called "hair streams" must be maintained during grooming. Always brush along the hair streams.

Once you are ready to groom, start with a wide-toothed comb in which the teeth are a twelfth of an inch apart. The space between the teeth helps to break up clumps of hair and eliminate mats. You may want to use a comb

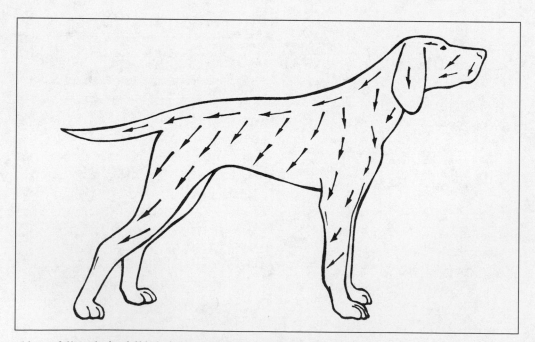

Always follow the invisible hair streams when grooming.

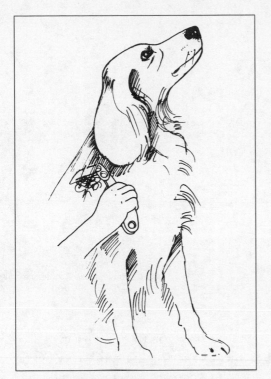

Use a mat and tangle splitter to remove kinks in your dog's coat.

whose teeth are close together if your dog has a particularly fine or problematic coat.

You can choose from plastic and metal combs. Metal combs are slightly more expensive, but are less likely to become your dog's chewable toy. Either way, look for combs whose teeth are rounded. These are safest, as they will not irritate (or even rip) the skin or hair.

Tangles can frustrate the grooming process. Your first approach should be to gently tease them out with a wide-toothed comb. Then, work through the hair with the wide-toothed comb, followed by the fine-toothed one.

A mat-and-tangle splitter is an essential grooming implement for dogs whose coat tends to form mats. Though it is similar to a razor blade, it

REMOVING STICKY SUBSTANCES

Sometimes, it seems as if a dog's coat is a magnet for sticky substances. Brushing a freshly painted wall or rolling in soft tar heated by the sun or even stepping in chewing gum all complicate the grooming process. Here are some handy tips for removing sticky substances:

1. Paint: Gently clip paint out of the coat. Never use turpentine or kerosene. These irritate a dog's skin. If ingested, they can cause serious internal injury.
2. Tar: If possible, clip. If there is extensive spread, work some petroleum jelly into the tar. Wipe with a rag, and then repeat until all the tar has been removed. Do not allow your dog to eat any of the tar.
3. Chewing Gum: Apply ice to the gum to eliminate stickiness. Gently clip the affected area. Again, do not allow your dog to eat the gum. It may become lodged in his throat.

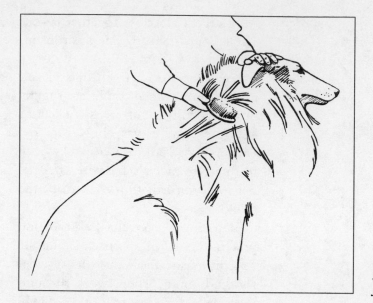

When brushing, use short strokes to twist the hair away from the skin.

has a safety component that will prevent injuries. Mats are often unresponsive to simple combing, so use a mat-and-tangle splitter to break down the hair before trimming.

After the coat is clear, apply the fine comb to the undercoat. Don't comb too forcefully; this may irritate your dog. By working the undercoat, you make sure that any extra lifeless hair will be brought to the surface. Also, remember to use the comb very gently behind the ears, along the tail, and under the chin.

After you have finished combing the dog, brush him. Brush in the direction of the hair streams. However, dogs whose breed standard requires some of the hair to project outward from the skin will need to be brushed against

TYPES OF BRUSHES

BRUSH	DESCRIPTION	FUNCTION
Bristle	Contains long bristles that penetrate the dense coat and extend to the skin.	For long-haired breeds
Hound Glove	Gives groomer good control via a slot in which to slip your hand; contains short wires, bristles, or rubber projections.	Brings out coat's sheen; eliminates dead undercoat; effective for short- to medium-length coats.

the stream. Using your brush, gently twist the hair away from the skin. Only do this in short strokes; you don't want to risk damaging the hair or the follicles.

TYPES OF COATS

Coats can be divided into five categories: long, nonshedding curly, smooth, silky, and wiry. Here are some specific tips on caring for each type of coat:

LONG COAT WITH UNDERCOAT

Breeds in this category include Collies, German Shepherd Dogs, Newfoundlands, and Old English Sheepdogs.

These dogs only need to be bathed twice a year. During shedding season, comb the undercoat thoroughly. Gently comb and brush the coat against the flow, over the shoulders and head. Then brush back into place. Keep an Old English Sheepdog neat and comfortable by restricting hair length to about one inch.

NONSHEDDING CURLY

Bedlington Terriers, Kerry Blue Terriers, and Poodles belong to this category.

These dogs don't experience a general drooping of their coats. However, their constant hair growth necessitates trimming and washing the coat once every two months. Start the clipping when a puppy reaches three to four months of age. On adult dogs, brush the short hair and comb the long hair thoroughly several times a week.

SILKY COAT

Breeds include Afghan Hound, Lhasa Apso, Maltese, Pekingese, Setters, and Spaniels.

Silky coats require diligent and consistent care. Regular brushing will eliminate mats and tangles. For most breeds, thoroughly comb and brush the entire coat, and bathe four times a year. This will rid the dog of the accumulation of dead hair and skin.

SMOOTH COAT

Breeds include Boxer, Corgi, some Dachshunds, Labradors, and Whippets.

Smooth coats can either be long or short. If the coat is long, comb and then brush with a bristle brush. Maintain shorter coats with a hound glove.

It's important to refrain from bathing a smooth-coated dog too frequently. Bathing washes out the special oils secreted by the skin to protect the coat against water.

WIRY COAT

Most terriers and Schnauzers have wiry coats.

To eliminate mats, comb at least once a week. Wiry-coated dogs require special plucking equipment, available in most pet stores. Use this equipment to extract dead hairs embedded in the coat. Pluck and bathe a wiry-coated dog three or four times a year, starting at four months old.

BATHING

Many dogs are averse to baths, especially if that first experience was particularly traumatic. When you give a puppy his first bath (at about four months old), make sure you do everything possible to keep it calm. Try to make baths something fun, rather than an unpleasant chore.

Keep the ear canals from filling up with water by inserting some soft, sterile cotton into the external ears. Even mild soaps can be irritating to a puppy's gentle skin, so rub a little petroleum jelly in tender spots, including over the eyes and on the scrotum.

While your dog is in another room and out of earshot, fill the tub or sink with about four or five inches of lukewarm water. Once you introduce your dog to the bath, speak in soothing, encouraging tones. Once it has been placed in the water, use one hand to stroke it while you rub a wet sponge along his coat with your free hand. A spray hose may be helpful, as long as you keep the pressure down so as not to frighten your dog.

Apply a dog shampoo, or a mild baby shampoo, in a thin line along the length of the coat. Rub the shampoo throughout the hair, and then rinse it out by pouring bowls of water over the body. Again, a hose will also do the trick, as long as the dog isn't terrified of the stream. It's important to eliminate all soap from the coat to prevent skin irritation.

Once the soap is all off, remove your dog from the bath and begin to dry it. A brisk rubdown with a soft, thick towel is both effective and invigorating. If you choose to use a blow-dryer, make sure the appliance is on warm; you want the air emitted from the dryer to be neither too hot (may cause discomfort or burns) nor too cold (may cause chilling and will probably fail to dry the hair thoroughly). Be sensitive to any signs of pain while you use the blow-dryer. Your dog should avoid the outdoors until you have determined that there is no dampness left in his coat.

You may want to try bathing your dog outside on a warm, breezeless summer day. A large metal tub makes a suitable spot for a bath, as does a kiddy pool. Or, if your dog allows it, you may want to simply use a garden hose—as long as the water is lukewarm and not too briskly applied.

Immediately after the whole experience is over, praise your dog repeatedly, offer him his favorite treat, show him plenty of affection, and play some quiet games with him. This will help make the next bath a little easier.

PROFESSIONAL GROOMERS

Some dog owners find grooming too difficult, or want a more handsome or glamorous look for certain occasions. If this is the case, look for a professional groomer who fits your price range. Your veterinarian, friends, breeder, or local humane society should be able to point you to a groomer in your neighborhood.

The professional groomer is likely to do more than merely clean and cut your dog's hair; he or she will clean the eyes and ears and also empty the anal glands, a hygienic practice that will prevent blockage. Nail trimming, often difficult for the layperson because of the dangerous proximity of nerves and blood vessels, is usually part of the package as well.

While some dogs become agitated when handled by a groomer, only the most unruly dog should be given a tranquilizer. *A veterinarian must be present when a groomer administers a tranquilizer.* Avoid any groomer who tries to tranquilize your dog without a veterinarian being present.

NAIL TRIMMING

A well-groomed dog has short, filed nails. Long nails are unsightly and pose a threat, since they can easily become snagged in carpeting or clothing. Also, they may become ingrown,

TIPS FOR SAFE TRIMMING

Nails contain circulating vessels, so it is important that you not sever any. If your dog's nails are white, look for where the pink area begins. The pink coloring is actually blood, so make the cut just beneath the pink border to ensure that your dog won't bleed. You can locate the vessels in a black-nailed dog by placing a small flashlight directly behind the nail.

Don't panic if trimming accidentally causes the nail to bleed. If this happens, apply direct pressure, followed by ten to fifteen minutes of a sterile towel soaked in cold water.

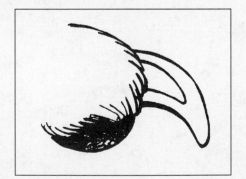

Beneath the hard layer of nail is a blood vessel. This must be avoided during trimming.

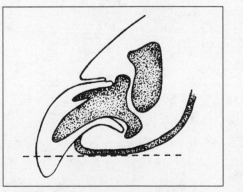

Cut where the nail curves downward.

causing pain and an awkward gait. The nail that needs the most care is the dew claw (which is similar to the human thumb). Because this is the nail farthest away from the ground, it is least likely to become worn down by walking, and thus must be trimmed.

Nail clippers specially tailored for dogs are available in pet stores. You can insert the nail through the hole at the end of the clippers, giving you good control over how much you will cut off. The pet store clerk should be able to help you find clippers that are suitable for your dog.

Nail trimming should start when a puppy reaches the age of three months. The force of the clipper, coupled with any hesitance on your part, is likely to scare a puppy, so introduce this practice gradually—perhaps one nail a day.

You probably won't have to do much nail trimming on a dog who takes regular walks on hard surfaces. The concrete will act as an abrasive and naturally file the nail to an acceptable length. If your dog rarely leaves the house or tends to walk on soft dirt, he is a candidate for trimming. The time to do so is as soon as you notice the nail starting to curve.

EAR CLEANING

Ears should be inspected regularly, not just when they emit a foul odor; by the time such a scent is detected, an infection has already set in. It's a good idea to clean your dog's ears once or twice a month. Dogs prone to infec-tion or irritation may require more fre-quent cleaning.

Use a Q-Tip soaked in diluted hydro-gen peroxide, alcohol, or mineral oil to clean around the bumpy folds of your dog's outer ear, as well as the opening of the ear canal. Keep in mind that ear-wax is not without function—a small amount of it is necessary to keep the vulnerable ear canal properly coated.

If your dog has long, floppy ears with plenty of hair, his ears might not be getting proper exposure to fresh air. Speak to your veterinarian about clip-ping this hair regularly and safely. You will want to provide good circulation while also preventing infection.

DENTAL CARE

Strong, healthy teeth are crucial to the digestive process. There are several steps you can take to help protect them:

1. Dogs love to chew, and chewing on safe objects will keep teeth clean and sharp. Offering him rawhide or syn-thetic bones a few times a week will be both pleasurable for him and beneficial.

2. Hard foods such as dog biscuits and kibble should be given daily. The rough texture will scrape waste parti-cles off the surface of the teeth.

3. Since dogs can't brush their own teeth, the job is up to you. Never use human toothpaste—the flavor is too strong for a dog, and can upset his stomach. Instead, scrub the teeth with a sterile cloth and water. Then, make a mild paste out of baking soda and water and apply the paste either to a rough piece of fabric or to a pet tooth-brush. Using firm but gentle pressure, brush each tooth. Then, rinse with a clean, wet piece of cloth. Commercial pet toothpaste is also available.

TRAVELING WITH YOUR DOG

If you are traveling with your dog overnight, always know ahead of time if the lodgings you plan to stay in allow dogs. Ask if there are any restrictions regarding a dog's size or quarters. Also ask if the hotel or inn charges extra for those with pets. If your stay will be lengthy, ask if the lodgings have any special accommodations for dogs, i.e. grooming or day care. Tourist attractions often provide such services, so make sure to ask.

Travel with some familiar objects from home, like his favorite toys, his bowls, and some of his bedding. This will help your dog adjust to the new environment. Try not to leave your dog alone in a hotel room unless he is comfortably confined to a cage. Otherwise, he may become destructive or bark loudly until you return.

Always ascertain the state of your dog's health before traveling, and find out from your veterinarian if your dog has any conditions or illnesses that might preclude certain types of travel. Make sure his vaccinations are current, and that he has a health certificate. Never travel without some form of identification (see Dog Tags, p. 50) firmly affixed to the dog's collar.

Here are some things to remember for specific types of travel:

AUTOMOBILE TRAVEL

Acclimate your dog to travel by car when he is a puppy. Always make sure your dog is secure in his seat and has no opportunity to suddenly climb or jump out of an open window. While a car is moving, a dog's entire body should be inside the car; he should not be able to interfere with the driver's mobility or concentration.

You should withhold food from your dog for about six hours prior to a long car ride. Feeding can occur after the last stop. While driving, give your dog a number of breaks for exercise, water, and relieving himself. Some dogs do become carsick; however, this is not an insurmountable problem. See the entry on Motion Sickness (p. 183) for tips on how to prevent digestive upset during car trips.

One of the most significant threats to a dog's safety is heat. Heatstroke (see p. 256) occurs when parked cars turn into furnaces in which temperatures often reach 125 degrees Fahrenheit in just minutes. Even if the windows are left partially opened, the car can still become very hot and endanger your dog's life. You may think it is safe to leave a dog in a parked car with the windows partially opened as long as the car is in a shady spot. However, shade is transient; what is shady one minute can become sunbaked the next. Therefore, avoid leaving your

---

ESSENTIALS OF SUMMERTIME TRAVEL

When driving with a dog in the summer, always keep the following items in the car:

- a jug of water
- a water bowl
- a thermos filled with ice chips
- wet towels

These will all help prevent dehydration, heat exhaustion, and general discomfort.

---

dog in a parked car, especially on a hot day. If you stop for a meal, take the dog with you—try to eat outdoors, where your dog will enjoy the fresh air.

PLANE TRAVEL

The key to successful air travel is planning. Find out precisely what requirements your specific airline adheres to for dogs, and then follow those guidelines precisely. The following must be done ahead of time:

- Find out what part of the plane your dog will be traveling in, and the type of pet carrier the airline requires you to use.
- Make reservations for both you and your pet.
- Ask about health certificates and proof of vaccinations required by the airline; it is better to initiate the inquiry than to discover right before boarding that you lack the necessary papers.

- Inform your veterinarian that your dog will be flying and ask if a tranquilizer is recommended.

Many airlines will allow small dogs enclosed in carriers to travel with passengers. If this is not possible, your dog will travel in the hold used to carry baggage. The dog will be safe there, but may be cold, so be sure to inquire about the temperature of the hold on your flight, and dress your dog accordingly. For summer travel, try to arrange for a nonstop night flight to avoid the risk of heatstroke incurred during a long rest in a baggage holding area.

Withhold food six hours before the flight, but feel free to give your dog water.

FOREIGN TRAVEL

Because you will be dealing with a different culture and a new set of laws and restrictions, you must research how traveling with your dog will affect your trip. First, call the local consulate for details regarding quarantine regulations. Also find out about what kind of health certificate and proof of vaccination is required by your country of destination. Explore the various restrictions posed by your airline.

LEAVING YOUR DOG BEHIND

Sometimes, it is impossible for a dog to travel with you. There is no need to feel guilty about this, because you can arrange for excellent care with a boarding or pet sitting facility.

BOARDING

Boarding facilities vary from simple places to sleep, eat, and play to elaborate resort-like setups. Either, if run efficiently and by people who truly care about animals, can provide your dog with a pleasant experience away from home.

Ask your veterinarian or friends to refer you to some facilities. Look into all the services provided. Will your dog have quality time with trained staff? Do you have to provide your own food, or will the facility feed your dog? Will the facility's food be palatable to your dog? What kind of exercise will your dog get? Will your dog have contact with other animals?

The best way to determine the quality of a boarding facility is to pop in unexpectedly. If you are welcomed by those in charge, there's a good chance they have little to hide. Examine the cleanliness of the kennels and the condition of the boarders. Be wary of facilities that are extremely noisy and chaotic; such an environment may be upsetting to your dog.

Be sure to reserve a space for your dog well in advance, especially during peak vacation time. Make certain your dog is in good health and thoroughly vaccinated. If the staff neglects to ask you for phone numbers where they can reach both you and your veterinarian, offer the numbers yourself.

Leave your dog with some items from home and a piece of your clothing. The scent will soothe him and make him feel more comfortable in his new surroundings.

PET SITTERS

Pet sitters allow you to leave your dog in your home, and thus offer an attractive alternative to boarding. It is best to ask your veterinarian or a friend for the name of a highly trustworthy sitter; after all, you will be allowing this person into your house.

The sitter will visit your dog at least twice a day, and charge for each visit. Each time, the sitter will allow your dog to relieve himself, make sure he is well fed and has plenty of water, and play with him, if the dog allows the sitter to do so. If your dog is trusting, he will accept affection from the sitter. At the very least, his basic needs will be satisfied.

A pet sitter is an excellent choice for well-trained adult dogs who have good bowel and bladder control. If your dog tends to be destructive when no one is around, or if he is a puppy or older animal, he may need more constant care.

SPECIAL SITUATIONS

Dogs have a far more difficult time adapting to new situations than people do. They assert little control over their environment, and come to rely upon the stability of familiar surroundings. Three abnormal occurrences that you and your dog might have to deal with are moving, the arrival of a new baby, and the fact that your dog has wandered off.

MOVING

A dog usually senses something strange is about to occur when he sees you start to accumulate empty boxes. By the time you begin to pack, he may become very anxious. Objects are moved from their ordinary places, robbing the dog of his touching-posts of normalcy.

You need to assure your dog that he will be moving with you and your home's contents, and that his new home will be safe and happy. Be understanding if the dog becomes slightly destructive or leaves little accidents in the house. Also, take your dog along for a visit or two prior to moving in. For safety's sake, leave the dog with a friend the day the movers come.

ARRIVAL OF A NEW BABY

Dogs see new babies as competitors and intruders. Although you will have your hands full, do your best to assuage any feelings of jealousy and reinforce your loyalty to your dog.

Supervise all interaction between dog and baby. Since dogs familiarize themselves with people and their surroundings through smell, allow your dog to sniff the baby. Be sure not to neglect the dog when company comes over, and give your dog a few extra toys. All of these tactics will help your dog during the adjustment period, and lay the groundwork for a healthy relationship between the dog and the new member of the household.

A LOST DOG

One of the most important items you can ever give your dog is a collar containing some form of identification (see Dog Tags, p. 50). If your dog wanders off and someone finds him, they need only read the tag to discover your name, address, and phone number. A license will further confirm that the dog is properly registered and belongs in your home.

YOUR DOG AND THE LAW

Because the pet population is so large, many states, cities, and municipalities have enacted legislation regulating how pets are cared for and are permitted to

---

SEARCHING FOR A LOST DOG

Here are some effective means of locating a lost dog:

PLACES TO CONTACT

- **The local police department**
- **The animal control officer**
- **Local shelters**
- **Local veterinarians**

PLACES TO POST NOTICES

- **The lost-and-found sections of local newspapers**
- **Supermarket bulletin boards**
- **The local post office, if it allows such notices to be posted**

---

interact with the rest of society. In most cases, such legislation is strictly enforced. Here are some important legal aspects of pet ownership:

LEASH LAWS

Laws that force you to keep your dog on a leash protect your dog from injury, and protect motorists from accidents caused by attempts to avoid hitting a stray dog. While you may be concerned with the loss of freedom a leash law imposes, take solace in the knowledge that a dog kept on a leash is less likely to stray from home or run out into the path of a moving vehicle.

LICENSING LAWS

When you purchase a license, you will have to pay a fee. The money is well spent, because licenses provide a ready-made registration system that will come in handy should your dog become lost. By registering your dog, you will also help the government accumulate accurate records reflecting the actual pet population, better enabling them to provide services necessary for efficient pet control.

"NO-PET" POLICIES

Many buildings refuse to allow pets and are run by landlords or management companies that are impervious to argument, even by the most earnest and conscientious pet owner.

However, in some instances you may be able to persuade a landlord into allowing your dog to live with you. One good suggestion is to have the landlord meet the dog. A well-behaved, clean, and personable dog can be a successful argument in itself. It may come down to paying a little extra for the privilege of keeping a dog, or putting up a small sum of money to protect the landlord from possible damage inflicted by your pet. Above all, it will be your responsibility to make sure your dog earns the right to remain in the apartment.

SCOOP LAWS

Thankfully, legislators fed up with sloppy sidewalks have enacted laws that force pet owners to pick up after their defecating animals. If you don't want to spend the money on a commercial contraption, always carry a plastic and a paper bag with you when you walk your dog. Use the plastic to grasp the waste, and then drop the plastic into the paper. Throw the paper bag into the nearest garbage can. Not only will you be complying with the law, but you will also be showing courtesy for your neighbors.

CITY LIVING

ELEVATORS

Elevators are common in the city, as well as in stores and commercial buildings. Ensure that you and your dog both make it into the elevator by allowing your dog to enter first, in front of you. Follow quickly behind.

Avoid packed elevators whenever possible, and try not to enter an elevator that already contains an animal. The combination of excitement and a confined space may make for unpleasant results.

ESCALATORS

Always avoid escalators. The collapsing steps can easily trap your dog's paws.

OFF-LEASH ACCIDENTS

It's never a good idea to allow your dog to roam freely. Allowing a dog to walk without a leash in a city is dangerous and illegal (see Leash Laws, p. 73).

ROOFTOPS

City dwellers who are usually deprived of open spaces might see a rooftop as a great stretch of freedom for a dog, making an ideal exercise "field." However, a dog's ability to judge both depth and distance is somewhat limited, which makes a roof a dangerous place for him. Try looking for a stretch of park instead—most cities contain some kind of grassy, recreational area or dog walk.

WINDOWS

If you have a dog, always maintain functioning window barriers. The last thing you want to happen is for your dog to accidentally fall out the window. In many cities, window barriers are mandatory for apartments containing children—take this as a cue to safeguard your apartment for your dog's sake as well.

WEATHER HAZARDS

HOT WEATHER

Dogs, especially long-haired breeds, the elderly, and the sickly, tend to overheat easily. Most dogs become sluggish when the mercury rises. Concrete heats up quickly and causes discomfort to a dog's feet. Leaving a dog in a parked car can lead to severe, life-threatening illnesses like heatstroke, which is characterized by loud, labored breathing, bright red mucus membranes, vomiting, and high fever (see Heatstroke, p. 256). Try to indulge in your dog's desire to rest during uncomfortably hot weather, and cut down on travel as much as possible.

COLD WEATHER

A dog's coat protects it from the cold. Dogs who are exposed to the cold consistently naturally grow thicker coats as the winter nears than those who stay indoors. It's important to know what type of coat your dog has (see Grooming, p. 61), in order to determine what type of attire cold weather demands (see Clothing, p. 51).

While it's fun to play with a dog in the snow, be certain to dry and warm your dog once you get him inside. Check his paws for ice particles and excess snow. Soak the paws in warm water to prevent frostbite (see Frostbite, p. 256).

Salt poured on the sidewalks goes a long way in preventing pedestrians from slipping on the ice, but the chemical nature of this substance can do damage to a dog's pads. Also, dogs who lick their burning paws may become poisoned by the salt. If you live in the city where this product is often used, try to avoid stretches of sidewalk covered by chemical salt. If possible, carry your dog to a salt-free space where he can walk and relieve himself.

HEALTH

PET HEALTH INSURANCE

Pet health insurance represents progress. Premiums are usually reasonable, and last for life. Many plans have some restrictions; for instance, annual checkups and neutering are often not covered, but insurance is a good guarantee that you will be able to afford care should an emergency or serious illness occur.

Ask your veterinarian for more information regarding insurance in your state.

VETERINARY CHECKUPS

Every dog should see the veterinarian for a complete physical at least twice a year. Not only will the veterinarian investigate all major systems, but he or she will also update your dog's vaccinations and be able to answer any questions you might have regarding health and care. Puppies, older dogs, and ill dogs need to see the veterinarian more frequently.

TRAINING

Training your dog is an important part of responsible pet ownership. While common puppy behavior problems and housebreaking are discussed in Chapter Twenty-One, here we'll discuss basic obedience training, which consists of teaching a dog to come when called, to sit and stay, to lie down, and to heel (walk at your side).

Obedience training can begin as early as three to four months if you train the dog yourself. Most trainers believe puppies aren't mentally or socially developed enough to benefit from group obedience class until they are six months old. Any sincerely interested dog owner can train his or her own dog, provided your dog hasn't already acquired a lot of bad habits. You and your dog may want to attend a couple of lessons at a good training club. You may also want to arm yourself with a good training book.

Wait until your dog is six months old before taking him to a group obedience class, which is a popular option for many dog owners. Obedience groups not only provide an excellent source of training, but also help socialize your pet with other dogs. When you first visit a class, make sure the instructors treat their pupils kindly— no punishment or yelling should be taking place or be permitted by those in charge. Your local parks department or school district may sponsor an obedience group. If you're having trouble finding one, ask your veterinarian.

Professional training is a good option for some larger breeds or for dogs that have acquired bad habits. If you are looking for a professional trainer, find one who favors working with your dog in your own home. No matter how appealing it may seem to send a problem dog away to be trained, the reality is that this often is a waste of time and money. The dog may behave perfectly with the trainer and then ignore you once it arrives home. A professional trainer will equip you with the knowledge and confidence you need to train your dog.

The best way to find a good professional trainer is through a veterinarian or breeder's recommendation. Arrange for an exploratory meeting with the potential trainer, you, and your dog. Then, make your decision.

Training takes time and patience—a capable trainer will stress this fact. Length of training depends not only on your dog's intelligence, temperament, and age, but also on how many bad habits he has acquired. Training requires you to take the lead, both as teacher and enforcer. After your dog has been trained you must not let him drift back into bad behavior patterns.

BASIC OBEDIENCE TRAINING

Before we get into individual basic commands, let's establish some essential guidelines for training.

1. The most effective training involves an exchange—your dog performs, and you reward him. When your dog gives his all to you, he has a right to expect praise from you. Praise, in the form of encouraging words and gestures, as well as concern and understanding, are the keys to successful training.

2. Training can—and should—be a pleasurable experience for both human and dog. Here's a tip: Keep training sessions to ten minutes for puppies, thirty minutes for adults. Limiting sessions will enable you to hold your dog's attention.

3. Make rules and stick to them. If you reprimand your dog for a specific behavior once, make sure the same reprimand is repeated every time the behavior recurs. This is the only way to keep your dog from getting confused between "right" and "wrong."

4. Some dogs only need a raised eyebrow to tell them to stop what they're doing; many respond immediately to a low-pitched reprimand; other, more strong-minded individuals might need occasional disciplining with a rolled-up newspaper. Never hit or shake your dog—this is abusive and unacceptable.

5. The way a command is conveyed is essential. In all but the "stay" command, the dog's name should precede the command word. This captures the dog's attention. Precise, short commands work best. Keep them to one or two words.

"COME!" AND "STAY!"

"Come!" is probably the easiest command to teach, because it indicates to the dog that you are calling it to give it affection. For that reason, never call your dog over to you and then punish him. It's best to do this training in a safe area (one where the dog cannot run off), such as an enclosed backyard. If you don't have access to this kind of space, attach a six-to-eight-foot leash to your dog's choke collar.

Raise your palm to your dog and say firmly, "Stay." If he rises, get him to sit (see "Sit"), raise your palm again, and repeat, "Stay!"

Walk away from your dog—ten to fifteen feet, or as far as your leash will allow you to travel. Turn and face your dog. Count to four, kneel, and count to four once more. Then, place your hands palm upward on your thighs. Say "Come!"; tug on the leash if your dog needs a little prompting. Praise your dog when he comes to you. Try to get your dog to "Stay" and "Come" three times before giving him a rest.

If you have taught your dog "Stay" and "Come" using a leash, it is important to eventually practice off-leash. This is an important element in training, preparing your dog to respond effectively to your call should he ever run out of your house or out of an enclosed yard.

"SIT!"

Put your dog to your left. Place your right hand on your dog's chest; place your left arm under his rump, flush against his rear legs. Say "Sit!" and apply pressure with your right hand and left arm—gently collapsing the dog's rear legs while raising the upper part of his body with your right hand. Hold the position and praise your dog. Repeat the process several times, with decreasing pressure from your hand and arms. Then, start to ask your dog to "Sit!" without your help.

"DOWN!"

Use a leash for teaching the "Down!" command. Have your dog sit. Raise your hand, palm toward the dog, and when you say "Down!" make a downward sweep with your hand and get the dog into a lying position. A small dog can be gently pushed down by the collar. A big dog may need a push at the shoulders or a gentle pull of the front feet. Once the dog is lying down, praise him. Keep practicing, making sure the dog associates "Down!" and the hand signal with the prone position.

"HEEL!"

"Heel!" will be helpful when walking your dog. Put his leash on, then wrap the leash around your hand so there is only a little space between you and your dog. Start to walk, with your dog on your left side. If he tries to scoot ahead of you, tug backward on the leash and say "Heel!" The goal is to walk with your dog at your side.

5

VACCINATIONS

PUPPIES ARE ABLE to defend themselves from disease during their first six to sixteen weeks of life because the mother usually successfully transmits antibodies, the body's agents for killing disease, through her blood while the puppies are in the womb and through her milk while the puppies are nursing. During this period, however, puppies become increasingly vulnerable to fatal diseases—including canine parvovirus, distemper, and rabies—unless they undergo a vaccination program administered by your veterinarian.

Vaccination programs evolved from the discovery that viral bacteria, or antigens, that have been chemically weakened and injected into the body could incite necessary antibody production while not exposing the puppy to their viral qualities. The so-called attenuated vaccine usually stays in your puppy's bloodstream for about a year.

As the production of antibodies subsides and the attenuated vaccine's protection wears off, your veterinarian will administer a booster shot consisting of a smaller amount of the attenuated vaccine. Booster shots trigger the puppy's amnestic response, or memory, of the original vaccine, allowing it to continue producing the antigens and protection necessary for her health.

Keeping up with your puppy's vaccination program can prevent many diseases from attacking her and can save you heartache down the road. Of course, you should always be sure to promote a vaccination's ability to help your dog by keeping her happy and healthy. An undernourished, fatigued, or sick dog's immune system may not

SAMPLE VACCINATION SCHEDULE

AGE OF DOG	VACCINE RECOMMENDED
5–8 weeks	Canine distemper-measles, CPI (parainfluenza)
8–16 weeks	DHLPP (distemper, hepatitis, leptospirosis, parainfluenza, parvovirus)
14–16 weeks	Rabies
12 months and annually thereafter	DHLPP
12 months	Rabies
At three-year intervals thereafter (check your local regulations)	Rabies

respond well to a vaccination or booster shot. Your vet may even suggest that a temporarily ill dog be revaccinated once she is back in excellent health.

The vaccination schedule that follows will give your dog adequate protection throughout her life, but some special circumstances may alter the schedule somewhat:

1. If a mother dies during delivery or early in nursing, her litter will be deprived of the all-important protective colostrum. Your veterinarin will vaccinate the puppies when they reach three weeks of age.

2. If you are planning to breed your female, she must have a DHLPP booster shot *before* she is bred. This will ensure that she and her puppies do not contract distemper, hepatitis, leptospirosis, parainfluenza, and parvovirus. Newborn puppies need all the protection they can get, so the mother's first milk should be as full of immunity as possible. If the immunity it provides is low, the puppies' survival is jeopardized. If a female is already pregnant, however, she should not be vaccinated unless your veterinarian recommends it.

3. If parainfluenza or leptospirosis are prevalent in your area, your veterinarian will recommend more frequent shots.

4. Some strains of live virus require booster shots every year, others every three years. Your schedule will vary depending upon what type of vaccine your dog receives.

6

WHEN YOUR DOG IS ILL

Sensible care and plenty of attention go a long way toward keeping a dog healthy and happy. However, every dog gets sick now or then, just like people do. Dogs are also prone to a host of accidents and injuries. As your dog's chief caretaker, it is incumbent upon you to familiarize yourself with the fundamental techniques and equipment necessary to care for an ill or injured animal. This chapter describes the basics, from taking a dog's temperature to stocking its first aid kit. The information you will find here can be applied to a wide variety of health problems your dog may encounter.

WHEN TO CALL A VETERINARIAN

As your dog's constant companion, you are probably very attuned to fluctuations in his behavior. If you observe that your dog seems more sluggish or less comfortable than normal, take a careful look at him.

Does your dog have a runny nose? A cough? Is his appetite normal? Does he have diarrhea? Is he drooling excessively? Is he whining? These are all examples of warning signs found in the "At-a-Glance Guide to Signs and Symptoms" at the beginning of Part Three of this book. Use the guide to find the specific condition indicated by your dog's symptoms. In Part Three you will discover the causes, notable symptoms, and points at which veterinary treatment is needed for a wide range of conditions and illnesses.

Remember that it is always better to call the veterinarian—even if it is a false alarm—than to wait and hope that a potentially serious problem will disappear without treatment.

81

YOUR DOG'S FIRST-AID KIT

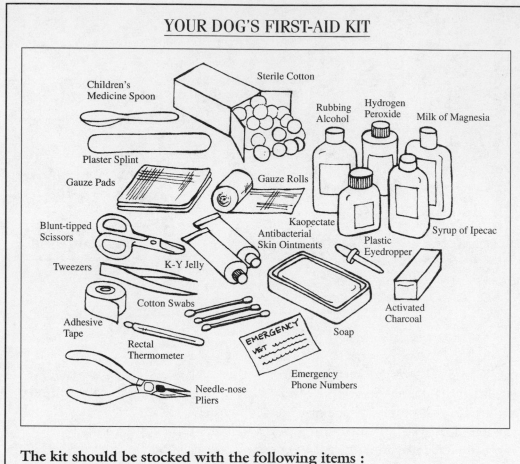

The kit should be stocked with the following items :

1. **Activated charcoal to absorb poisons.**
2. **Adhesive tape (a one-inch roll).**
3. **Antibacterial skin ointments to soothe minor rashes and burns.**

HOW TO TAKE YOUR DOG'S TEMPERATURE

If your dog seems sluggish, has a hot, dry nose, dull eyes, and/or feels warm, he may have a fever. The only reliable way to take your dog's temperature is with a rectal thermometer. Shake down the thermometer and grease it well with petroleum jelly.

Not many dogs will stand still while you insert a thermometer into their rectum, so it is best to get someone to help you. If no help is available, make your dog lie down on his side and hold him as best you can, all the while talking to him soothingly.

Lift his tail and gently push the thermometer in with a twisting motion. Insert the thermometer from one to

4. Blunt-tipped scissors.

5. Children's medicine spoon or syringe (with needle removed; ask a veterinarian to provide this) for administering liquids.

6. Emergency phone numbers: Keep your veterinarian's phone number handy, taped inside the lid of the kit. Some cities and towns have pet emergency ambulance services; keep that number in the kit as well.

7. Gauze pads (three by three inches).

8. Gauze roll (three-inch roll). Used for compresses, bandages, and tourniquets.

9. Hydrogen peroxide (the 3 percent solution is good for use as an antiseptic and to induce vomiting).

10. Kaopectate (for control of diarrhea; also good for coating the stomach to prevent the absorption of poison).

11. Milk of magnesia, liquid or tablets (these are used as laxatives; good for preventing absorption of poison).

12. Needle-nose pliers (to remove objects that are caught in your dog's throat).

13. Plaster splint.

14. Plastic eyedropper for administering liquid medication.

15. Rectal thermometer (either the type used by veterinarians or the hospital type).

16. A tube of K-Y jelly or petroleum jelly for taking temperature rectally.

17. Rubbing alcohol (effective for removing ticks).

18. Soap for cleaning wounds.

19. Sterile cotton (used for removing ticks, cleaning ears, and as a cushion under bandages).

20. Syrup of ipecac to induce vomiting in case of poisoning.

21. Tweezers for tick removal.

three inches, depending on the size of your dog. Hold the thermometer in place for at least two minutes. Remove it, wipe it clean, and determine the temperature by the height of the silver column of mercury on the thermometer scale. A

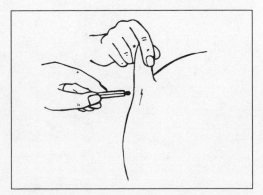

While taking your dog's temperature, have one person lift her tail while you gently insert the thermometer, using a twisting motion.

temperature of 100.5 degrees to 102 degrees is normal. A temperature above 102.5 or below 100.0 is cause for concern, and merits a call to your veterinarian. NOTE: Do not let go of the dog or of the thermometer. You do not want to risk having the thermometer break in the dog's rectum.

If the thermometer does break off, do not attempt to find and extract the broken end. Give the dog one to two teaspoonfuls of mineral oil and call your veterinarian.

HOW TO TAKE YOUR DOG'S PULSE

The most reliable way of taking your dog's pulse is to locate the femoral artery. Your dog can either be standing or can be lying on his back for this. Put your fingers inside your dog's groin, where the leg joins the trunk. Feel around until you detect a pulse. Another method is to press against the rib cage over the heart while your dog is standing. You should be able to detect a pulse just below the elbow joint.

Count how many beats there are in a fifteen-second period, and then multiply that number by four. The normal range is wide—anywhere from 70 to 130 beats per minute. Smaller breeds and puppies usually tend toward faster pulse rates, while larger breeds and healthy dogs who get plenty of exercise often have a slower pulse.

COLLECTING URINE SAMPLES

For male dogs, use a wide-mouthed jar. When your male dog lifts his leg to urinate during a walk, reach down gently and collect about a quarter cup of urine.

For a female dog, place a flat pan under her when she squats to urinate.

COLLECTING STOOL SAMPLES

Stool samples are used to determine the presence of intestinal parasites. A sample is often requested as part of your dog's routine examination. Try to collect as fresh a sample as possible and place it in a plastic bag. If you are taking it from outside, avoid soil; organisms on the ground could make their way into your dog's fecal material, resulting in an inaccurate reading.

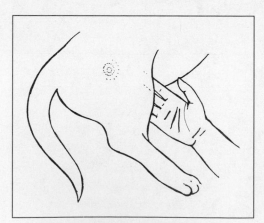

To take your dog's pulse, locate the femoral artery in the groin.

RESTRAINING A DOG

You can be a tremendous help to your veterinarian during exams and other procedures if you learn how to restrain your dog. The degree of restraint needed during an examination varies according to the dog and the procedure to be carried out. Usually your veterinarian will want your dog placed on a table.

To restrain a small dog: Grasp the scruff of the neck tightly, including the collar.
To restrain a medium-sized dog: Tuck the head under your upper arm, place the other arm around the body, and grasp one of the dog's forelegs.
To restrain a large dog: Place one arm under the neck and fix the head with your other hand by grasping the outer foreleg and leaning your body over the dog's shoulders. Someone else should hold the rear end.

BANDAGING A DOG

There are many similarities between the functions of bandages in humans and dogs. For both, bandages help control bleeding and expedite clotting. Skin torn apart is brought together by a bandage, which also keeps out harmful particles and infectious organisms. Bandages help prevent wounded dogs from interfering with the healing process. One crucial difference is that the common adhesive bandage that we use on our own cuts is far less effective on dogs because of their fur. Gauze strips, pads, and cloth are often necessary.

Here are some important guidelines to help you master bandaging:

1. To prevent infection or other complications, always clean out a wound before bandaging it.
2. Don't bandage too tightly, because this may impair circulation or breathing.
3. Change bandages every other day or when they get wet. Be on the lookout for infection whenever you change the bandage. If the wound is infected, you will see pus and may even detect a foul-smelling odor.
4. Don't allow a bandaged dog out of the house without close supervision.

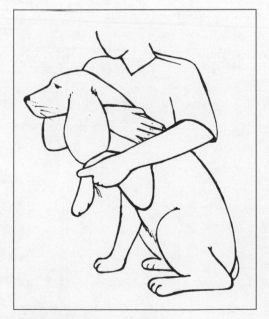

Restraining a large-sized dog.

Wrap a gauze roll around a wounded paw, covering the entire limb to prevent swelling.

PAW, LIMB, OR TAIL WOUND

Wrap a wounded paw, limb, or tail with a gauze roll, taping it in place without taping the limb itself. Then apply tape in overlapping strips over the entire gauze roll, from the toes up or from the tip of the tail down. Be sure to cover the afflicted limb in its entirety to prevent additional swelling.

CHEST OR ABDOMEN WOUND

A many-tailed bandage is required for this procedure. Make it yourself by tak-

ing a rectangular piece of clean cloth and cutting narrow strips extending from the two shorter edges one third of the way to the rectangle's center. The uncut part of the rectangle will cover the wounded chest or abdomen, while the strips will be used to affix the bandage.

First, clean the wound. Then, place a gauze pad over the wound. Fit the many-tailed bandage over the gauze pad, and tie along the dog's back.

EYE WOUND

Place a sterile bandage over the affected eye and hold it in place by taping around the head with one-inch adhesive tape. Remember not to pull the tape too tight, and make sure the ears are free.

EAR WOUND

An ear bandage should be applied in a manner that leaves the ear canals exposed to air, which will help avoid clogging and infection. This is especially important if your dog's ears hang close to his head.

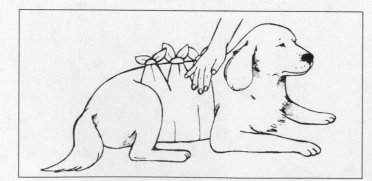

For chest or abdomen wounds, fashion a many-tailed bandage out of a broad strip of cloth.

First, fold the ears over the top of the head, bringing their tips together. Use adhesive tape to fix this position.

You can then slip a nylon stocking or sweater sleeve, with both ends cut out, over the muzzle and up over the ears. Be careful not to cover the eyes or the ear canal.

Tape the covering snugly to the dog's skin. If you decide to tape it to your dog's neck, be sure the fit is comfortable.

NURSING A SICK DOG AT HOME

For a dog, being sick or injured can be a very traumatic experience. It's hard for a dog to understand why he doesn't feel well, or why his mobility is limited. It is very important that a recuperating dog be made to feel as comfortable as possible, receive plenty of attention, and be permitted to relax in his familiar quarters as soon as possible. If home is to become a hospital, there are a number of nursing issues you will need to consider in order to create a healing environment.

Keep in mind that, while many may be tempted to scoop the ill dog up and lavish him with affection, serenity and rest are crucial to recovery. While remembering to show your dog he is being cared for, give him some time off from the rest of the world. Curtail visits from strangers, and warn any children in the household to approach the dog quietly and gently.

Recuperating pets need plenty of warmth, especially in bed. If your dog's bed is in a somewhat drafty place, think about using a supplementary heating source nearby. Even an infrared bulb will do. However, you don't want to give your dog too much heat, so touch his coat from time to time to make sure the temperature is appropriate. If your dog feels hot, lower the heat and move the heating source away from the bed. You might also consider putting some warm water in a hot water bottle and wrapping the bottle in a towel. This will definitely make the bed more cozy.

Exercise should be limited during recovery. If the weather is good, it's usually fine to take a patient outside briefly to relieve itself. However, do not take an ill dog out in inclement weather if at all possible. For this brief period, try to get your dog to relieve itself on newspaper inside. If this doesn't work, put a protective garment on your dog (see Clothing, p. 51) and let him out as briefly as possible. Once he is back inside, be sure to dry him off and warm him up. Return him to bed for rest.

FOOD

While it's fine to go along with an ill dog's rejection of food for a short period of time, you need to be certain the dog doesn't become dehydrated. Dehydration occurs frequently in puppies, older dogs, and dogs suffering from gastric upset, including vomiting and diarrhea. More fluids leave the body than are taken in, which is why

ELIZABETHAN COLLARS

Dogs with skin and eye irritations and dogs recovering from surgery often try to bite or scratch the affected areas. To prevent this, your veterinarian may recommend an Elizabethan collar, which resembles the fashion style popular in sixteenth-century Elizabethan England.

Pet-supply stores as well as veterinarians often keep vinyl Elizabethan collars in stock. However, they are fairly simple to make at home, using cardboard or plastic.

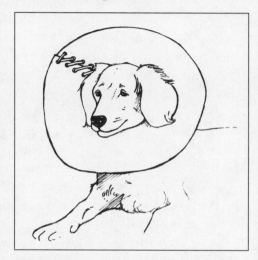

An Elizabethan collar constructed out of cardboard.

Take a circular piece of cardboard or plastic and cut a hole in the middle just wide enough to allow your dog to slip his head through. Punch two parallel arcs of eyelets through the lower half of the circle, each running along the circle's circumference. Run string through these eyelets, and fasten the string to your dog's leather collar. If you have made the Elizabethan collar to your dog's size, it should now be secure. Remove by simply untying the strings and slipping the collar over your dog's head.

An Elizabethan collar can also be made from a plastic bucket. Choose a bucket that, when measured against your dog's head, reaches to the end of his muzzle. A one-gallon size will fit small dogs; the two-gallon size is advisable for larger dogs.

Cut out the bottom of the bucket with an X-Acto knife. Pencil in marks for a line of holes two inches apart, two inches from the bottom of the bucket. Once properly measured, cut holes. Thread a long gauze bandage through the holes, leaving large loops of material on the outside of the bucket. Fit the bottom of the bucket over your dog's muzzle. Carefully insert your dog's leather collar through the loops hanging out of the bucket.

An Elizabethan collar constructed out of a plastic bucket.

The skin of a dehydrated dog's back loses its elasticity.

dog is dehydrated. Serious dehydration requires immediate veterinary intervention, as this condition can be lethal. Treatment is usually intravenous; a saline solution and glucose are pumped into the dog's body. Often, the veterinarian will also administer antidiarrheal or antivomiting medication to slow the outflow of liquids.

Prevent dehydration by force-feeding your dog—if he doesn't seem to be suffering from significant nausea (see below). Try giving him bits of food three to four times an hour. Even this much can ward off dehydration and its very serious effects.

it's important for an ill dog to drink plenty of water.

The hallmark of dehydration is a lack of elasticity in the skin on the dog's back. If you pull the skin and it doesn't spring back quickly, chances are your

FORCE-FEEDING

With solid material, only force-feed small bits. As confidently as possible,

---

BLAND DIET

When a dog's illness is digestive in nature, a normal diet is too harsh and irritating to the stomach and intestines to allow nature to heal the affected organs. For that reason, commercial dog foods should be removed from the diet, as should milk and fried foods.

You can feed your dog small portions of cooked rice, noodles, macaroni, or potatoes added to low-sodium chicken or beef broth, or flavored with boiled lean beef, chicken, or lamb. Boil the meat to remove the fat. Cooked cereals such as oatmeal, farina, pabulum, and baby cereals are all good choices.

If your dog's illness does not affect his digestive system, feed him small amounts of food at frequent intervals. Switch temporarily from his normal diet to his favorite nutritionally sound and easily digestible foods. Such foods include meat broths, cooked chicken, baby foods, cottage cheese (unless your dog suffers from colitis), and cooked eggs.

HOW TO OPEN YOUR DOG'S MOUTH

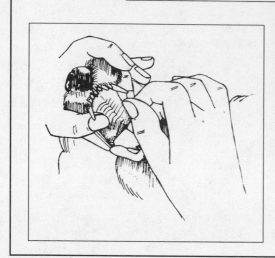

Open your dog's mouth by pressing in on the flews (the pendulous sides of his upper mouth) and at the same time rolling the lips over the teeth. This method will not only protect you from a bite, but it will also keep the dog's mouth open, because if he tries to close his mouth he will bite himself.

A safe technique for opening a dog's mouth.

open your dog's mouth (see box, How to Open Your Dog's Mouth), pull his head back so his snout is angled upward, and place the food as far back in his mouth as possible. For liquids, follow the instructions for giving liquid medications below.

HOW TO GIVE YOUR DOG MEDICATION

HOW TO GIVE YOUR DOG LIQUID MEDICINE

The easiest way to give your dog liquid medicine is to use an eyedropper—ideally one with liquid measures on it, available at any pet-supply store. You can use a tablespoon if an eyedropper isn't available, but it is harder to work with. Syringes (without needles) are also useful and are available at most pet stores as well.

For larger amounts of medication, use a turkey baster.

Do not use anything made of glass.

Once you've gotten the medicine into the device, hold your dog's snout in your free hand and point his nose into the air rather than down to the

Administer liquid medications using an eyedropper.

floor. Dogs have a gap just between their canine teeth. You can insert the device with the medicine in it through this gap while your dog's mouth is shut. To ease the swallowing process, gently stroke his throat. Check the sides of his mouth to make sure no medicine trickles out. If he doesn't like the taste of the medicine, he may struggle a bit, but he will swallow.

If you are giving your dog a prescription drug, do not try to compensate for any spilled medicine by giving an extra dose. **WARNING:** Make sure your dog swallows rather than inhales because you do not want the liquid to go to the lungs. If your dog starts to cough and can't seem to catch his breath, see Choking, p. 248.

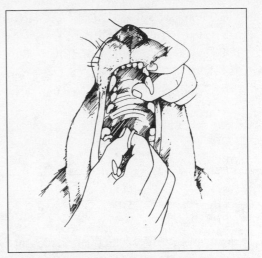

Use one hand to open the mouth and the other to place the pill at the tongue's base.

HOW TO GIVE YOUR DOG PILLS

Open your dog's mouth and tilt the head up slightly (see How to Open Your Dog's Mouth, p. 90). This usually causes the lower jaw to relax and drop a little. Use your other hand to pull the lower jaw open gently. Your fingers should be placed over the front incisor teeth.

With your thumb and index finger, place the pill in the center of the tongue near the back, where the tongue is first visible. Make sure the pill is in the center, otherwise it will not go down. Quickly remove your hand and the dog will close his mouth. Keep his head tilted upward while you stroke his throat to make him swallow.

Another way to make a dog swallow is to tap his nose with your finger, or blow gently on his nose. This will cause him to lick and swallow.

Another way is to crush the tablet and put it in food, but there can be problems with this method. Pharmaceutical companies often manufacture pills with coatings that regulate the speed at which they are digested. Crushing a coated tablet can alter the intended rate of digestion, thereby inhibiting the drug's healing properties. Also, many pills are coated with sugar and taste bitter inside. If you crush one of these tablets and put it in food, the dog probably will not eat it. Ask your veterinarian if this method will hinder absorption of your dog's medication.

Another method is to wrap the pill in a choice morsel. Pick a food with a strong odor that your dog loves, like cheese. Cheese works well because it can be easily molded to conceal the pill. Meat is also a good choice, but if you try to fold the pill in a piece of meat, your dog will probably find it and devour the meat but leave the pill. Try cutting a hole in the meat and placing the pill inside it.

HOW TO APPLY EAR MEDICINES

The vessels in which ear ointments are packaged have long nozzles for easy application. Hold the nozzle parallel to the dog's head. Be sure the dog is restrained so that you do not accidentally injure the ear canal's thin membrane in case the dog shows resistance. Then squeeze in a small amount of ointment.

If your dog has an ear infection, the medicine must reach the horizontal ear canal, so with your finger gently massage the cartilage at the base of the ears to disperse the medicine. Listen carefully—successful applications result in a squishing sound.

HOW TO APPLY EYE MEDICATION

If your dog is nervous, you may need help to keep his head still when applying eye medication. Always approach the eye from behind, to avoid scaring the dog.

EYE DROPS: Hold the bottle or dropper above the eye and press gently above the upper lid with your free hand. This will retract the lid. Squeeze

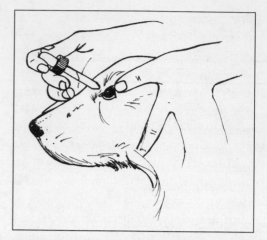

Preparing to administer eye drops. Prevent direct contact between the dropper and the eye itself.

in the drops, taking care that they actually drop into the eye. Be careful that the bottle does not touch the eye because that can contaminate the medicine. You'll want to ensure the drops stay in the eye. Gently press the corner next to the nose for about five seconds. This will inhibit drainage of the liquid into the tear ducts.

POWDER OR OINTMENT: Press just below the eye to turn down the lower lid. Then apply the medication on the inside of the lid. If the ointment is thick, you can make it flow more easily out of the tube by immersing the nozzle end of the tube in warm water in a shallow glass, by holding the tube under warm running water, or by warming it in your hands. If your dog has conjunctivitis, it is especially important to warm the ointment; cold ointments are less likely to reach conjunctival surfaces.

AFTER SURGERY

First and foremost, dogs recovering from surgery need rest. Make sure you follow all of your veterinarian's advice for postoperative care, and attend all scheduled follow-up appointments.

Consistently examine the area where surgery has been performed. Check for redness, swelling, or discharge; over the first few days, incisions normally cause all three. If pus begins to seep from the wound, or if the discharge has a foul odor, call the veterinarian. These are signs of infection. Also, call the veterinarian if you detect a moderate to large swelling in the incision area. Swelling may indicate an accumulation of fluid that needs to be drained, or a problem in the stitches themselves.

Watch for all other signs of complications, including prolonged nausea, vomiting, diarrhea, dehydration, fever, and severe pain.

7

CARING FOR
THE OLDER DOG

It is often thought that one year of a dog's life equals seven in a human life. In reality, however, by the time a dog is a year old she has surpassed a seven-year-old child's development. Once the dog reaches adulthood and middle age, her aging over one year equals the aging that takes place in a human over five years.

The aging process is even more difficult to pinpoint because different breeds age at different rates. Large dogs, for example, age quickly. Toy breeds, on the other hand, age slowly.

Therefore, the lifespan of a large dog such as a Saint Bernard is fairly short. A Saint Bernard may be considered elderly by the age of six. A Golden Retriever, meanwhile, starts to hit her golden years at the age of eight. The smaller Yorkshire terrier may not be considered a

AGE EQUIVALENTS		
Dog		Human
8 months	=	13 years
1 year	=	16 years
2 years	=	24 years
3 years	=	28 years
5 years	=	36 years
7 years	=	44 years
9 years	=	52 years
11 years	=	60 years
13 years	=	68 years
15 years	=	76 years

senior citizen until she has reached her thirteenth year.

THE AGING PROCESS

The first step in caring for an aging dog is to realize that your dog is getting old.

95

This is not always easy because many of the symptoms of age appear gradually and are often difficult to notice. For example, the hairs around your dog's muzzle will be turning white for several years. You may not notice this graying process until you glance at a photograph of your younger dog and realize that the characteristic gray mask forming around her eyes and nose is new. Likewise, you may suddenly notice one day that your dog's coat seems less shiny, clean, and groomed than it used to. This change may cause you to worry about your dog. It is, however, often a natural effect of aging, letting you know it is time to take special care of your elderly dog.

Other signs may also tell you that your dog is getting older:

FAILING HEARING. A dog who has always been alert and responsive may suddenly fail to come when you call her. Try whistling to a dog whose hearing is failing. It is usually the dog's ability to perceive the direction of the call that disappears. Her ability to hear high-pitched sounds often remains acute way into old age (see The Ear, p. 117).

FAILING EYESIGHT. Older dogs may bump into objects or appear generally disoriented. You may notice a bluish-gray tint in the eye caused by the hardening of the protein used to form the lens of the eye. Some signs of blindness may appear, but full blindness is rarely brought on by old age alone (see Blindness, p. 123).

FOUL BREATH, PLAQUE AND TARTAR BUILDUP, AND GINGIVITIS. All of these are common in old age, especially if you have not taken care to keep your dog's teeth clean throughout her life. Regular dental checkups may be necessary to ensure that any serious problems are quickly treated.

SKIN PROBLEMS. Even small scratches may take a long time to heal as the elasticity of the skin diminishes. Tiny wart-like bumps may appear on the dog's face and other parts of the dog's body. Hair may more readily shed as the follicles become less active. None of these changes is cause for alarm unless it seems to get in the dog's way. Scratching a bump, for example, may infect it, and it will then require attention.

TUMORS AND CYSTS. Usually these are benign cysts and fatty tumors. As older dogs are more susceptible to cancer, however, you should always have any lump or growth checked by the veterinarian.

HEART DISEASE. An older dog's heart often remains strong and healthy. As older dogs are prone to heart disease, however, do become aware of the symptoms of heart disease (see Heart Failure, p. 167). Early detection can prevent unnecessary pain and premature death.

SHAKY, UNSURE GAIT. Legs that are usually sturdy and agile may begin to shake with age. Your dog may have difficulty getting up after a long nap. The usual spring in her step is a little less pronounced. Due to a gradual weakening of the nerves and muscles in the legs, these changes are to be expected. If these changes seem unusually bothersome to your dog, or if your dog has had teeth infections, kidney illness, or other health problems that indicate arthritis, your dog's age may have made him susceptible to arthritic disease (see Arthritis, p. 160).

DIMINISHED APPETITE. You may notice that your dog is eating less and losing weight. This is often a normal result of the aging process; the dog's sense of smell and taste weakens, and she thus becomes less interested in food. A decrease in weight may also result from muscles becoming flabby once an older dog cuts back on her athletic activities.

INCREASED WATER INTAKE. An older dog may need up to two to three times more water than a younger dog. This is because her kidneys do not function as well and need the water to maintain their efficiency. Other signs of kidney disease (see Kidney Disease, p. 191) may also appear, since older dogs are vulnerable to this illness. Contact your veterinarian if you suspect your older dog may have a serious problem with this vital organ.

CONSTIPATION. In older dogs, constipation may be brought on by a loss of muscle tone in the bowel area, or, in older male dogs, by an enlargement of the prostate (see Prostatitis, p. 199).

Adding bran cereal, liver, or vegetables to the diet of an older dog who is constipated may provide the laxative effect needed to get rid of the problem.

INCONTINENCE. Older spayed female dogs may leak urine from the bladder without being aware of it. Urinary incontinence can usually be easily treated by your veterinarian, who will administer estrogen supplements to your female dog.

CHANGES IN BEHAVIOR. A dog who in her younger years loved to visit new places or who always became excited at changes will now suddenly become anxious and moody when anything upsets her daily routine. There is little you can do but be patient, and give your dog the care she needs in return for the years of companionship she has given you.

DIET

All dogs should be kept on a proper diet. Older dogs, however, have special dietary needs that must be met in order to keep up with the rapid changes taking place in the dog's maturing body. As you notice signs of aging, either in the last quarter of the dog's expected lifespan or when your veterinarian recommends it, you should begin modifying your dog's eating habits.

Gradually change the amount of food and the number of times that you feed your dog. Giving your dog smaller amounts of food at more fre-

THE OLDER DOG AND EXERCISE

A mature dog who continues to exercise is likely to remain more agile, toned, and healthy than an elderly dog who is mostly sedentary. You may need to inspire your dog to exercise. Encourage walks and other light forms of athletic activity. Do not push your dog, but allow her to exercise at her own pace. If you notice your dog becoming fatigued, breathing harder, or panting excessively, the activity is too taxing. If your dog is small, pick her up, bring her home, and let her rest. If you cannot pick up your dog, take a break from your walk. When your dog looks more rested, walk her back home at a leisurely pace, taking breaks along the way, if necessary.

quent intervals during the day can help to stimulate a poor appetite and ease digestion.

Invest in a dry food specially formulated for older dogs. Many pet-food companies market such products. Your veterinarian or local pet-supply store should carry some of the better brands.

As your dog's absorption of vitamins and minerals decreases with age, add vitamin and mineral supplements specially manufactured for canines to her food. Your veterinarian will be able to suggest the supplement best for your dog. This supplement may include zinc, vitamin B, and calcium.

Be certain that your dog is getting a diet of high-quality proteins. Small amounts of grilled lean hamburger, boiled egg, cottage cheese, or skim milk added to the dog's dry food can provide such a diet.

Do not overdo the amount of protein added to your dog's diet. A diet too rich in meat, for example, can overstrain an aging kidney or liver. Also be certain to cut out excessive amounts of sodium or phosphorus from your dog's diet.

Changes in exercise and in appetite may cause your dog to either gain or lose weight during old age. Be certain to monitor your dog's weight. If you notice any excessive weight fluctuations, be sure to put your dog on an appropriate diet recommended by your veterinarian.

If your dog has any other medical condition, discuss your dog's diet with your veterinarian to be sure it is providing the proper nutrition your dog needs.

8

SAYING GOOD-BYE

FOR MOST PEOPLE, losing a dog is like losing a member of the family. It is very difficult to imagine life without the creature that has given us such joy and love over the years. However, death is the inevitable end for all living beings. As a dog owner, you must be prepared to deal with the practical and emotional realities of losing your beloved pet, whether death is brought on by old age, accident, or sudden illness.

EUTHANASIA

Since you are your dog's primary caretaker, it may sometimes become your responsibility to answer the following question: Is my dog suffering from extreme and irreversible pain and suffering so much so that his life is devoid of pleasure? Make a rational assessment of your dog's condition, taking into account the quality of his life over a period of time. Consult your veterinarian, asking her or him to tell you the prognosis for relief or recovery. If, after much informed consideration, you can answer yes to the above question, it may be necessary to euthanize your dog. While your veterinarian may advise you, this difficult decision is ultimately up to you.

Your pet will not suffer during the procedure, which consists of a single, painless injection. Some veterinarians will administer the lethal dose in your own home, where you and your loved ones can surround your dog in its beloved environment.

Think about whether or not you would like to be present when the injection is administered. You may wish to be there for the dog's final

99

IF YOU THINK YOUR DOG HAS DIED

Perhaps your worst nightmare is coming home and seeing your dog lying on the floor, unconscious. If this happens, try your best to remain calm while you attempt to clearly establish whether or not your dog has died.

If you suspect your dog may be dead, the first step you must take is to check for a heartbeat (see Heart Massage, p. 240, and CPR, p. 239). Is he breathing? Hold a mirror in front of its snout and see if fog forms. Check the dog's eyes. When you press gently on the surface of the eye itself, does your touch elicit any response, i.e., a blink or twitch? Is the eye itself widely dilated, a characteristic sign of death?

If you discover he is not breathing, has no heartbeat, does not respond to your touch at all, and cannot be revived using emergency procedures, call your veterinarian for advice on how to proceed.

---

moments, or it may be too difficult a task. If you plan to be present, try to bring someone along who can help you through this trying event. If you can't bring yourself to be there, do not chide or accuse yourself of letting your dog down; it is very difficult to predict how one will respond to the death of a loved one. Concentrate on the warmth and sense of belonging you have given your dog throughout his life, and the gift of relief you are now bestowing upon your suffering pet.

BURIAL AND CREMATION

Once your dog has died, you will have to decide what to do with his remains. Ask your veterinarian about cremation and burial. Most veterinarians can arrange to have dogs cremated. If you

wish to retain your dog's ashes, be sure to warn the crematorium ahead of time.

Burying your dog in a pet cemetery allows you to visit your dog's final resting spot whenever you wish. Pet cemeteries offer plots, headstones, and monuments just as human cemeteries do. Aside from your veterinarian, you may also want to consult with your local humane society for respected pet cemeteries in your area.

LOSS AND GRIEVING

You may find that the sudden absence of your dog is too upsetting to bear alone. This is a perfectly natural response. If you feel you need some help getting through this traumatic period, seek professional counseling. Ask your veterinarian or the humane society for recommendations.

You should not keep a dog's death from your children, but you may need to exercise caution in explaining what has happened. Carefully explain euthanasia to older children. If you have very young children, you will probably want to shield them from the details. Instead, emphasize that, although your pet has had a long and happy life, he is now very sick and won't get better. Tell them that the veterinarian is going to help end the dog's suffering.

Be very respectful of a child's right to grieve, and keep watch over the various forms in which that grief may be expressed. Allow your child to be sad or angry, as long as the emotions do not become so overwhelming as to interfere with normal functioning after an initial period of mourning. Show that you too are saddened by the loss of your beloved pet, but concentrate on the positive, emphasizing that the terrific memories you all share of life with your dog will live on.

One positive step you can take during the grieving process is to make a donation in your pet's name to the local animal shelter, helping to give other animals the opportunity to find loving families.

PART III

THE ENCYCLOPEDIA OF DOG HEALTH

An At-a-Glance Guide to Signs and Symptoms

THIS IS YOUR QUICK reference guide to various symptoms. It helps you to identify the disorders with which they are associated and refers you immediately to the pages that discuss all problems that may be indicated by these symptoms.

For example, if you notice that your dog has suddenly begun to breathe noisily, consult this reference guide under Breathing problems. There you will see an entry for noisy breathing. Turn to the page indicated, and you will find information on that subject.

Remember that any given symptom has many possible causes. In addition, if a symptom is severe, it does not necessarily indicate that something serious is wrong with your dog. In fact, many minor disorders can provoke dramatic symptoms, while some far more serious ailments often have almost unidentifiable signs.

As with human beings, symptoms are the body's way of alerting you that something is wrong. Heed them, since early diagnosis and treatment of any ailment or disease increases the odds of a successful and speedy recovery.

It is especially vital that you pay close attention to your pet's health, because your pet cannot tell you that he is not feeling well. If you observe the slightest deviation from any of your dog's normal habits or any change in his appearance, contact your veterinarian immediately.

ABDOMEN
  painful   181, 183, 187, 191, 231,
      232, 244, 246, 260, 266, 268,
      269, 272
  rigid   231, 246, 260
  swollen   184, 191, 231, 234, 246
AGGRESSION   115, 227

9

INFECTIOUS DISEASES

INFECTIOUS DISEASES ARE caused by bacteria, viruses, protozoa, parasites, and fungi. They are most often spread from one dog to another by contact with infected urine and feces or by the inhalation of germ-laden droplets in the air.

CANINE PARVOVIRUS

CAUSES: Canine parvovirus attacks cells that reproduce often, such as those lining the gastrointestinal tract and heart, causing them to become debilitated and affecting the overall vital functions of the dog. Puppies under five months of age are highly vulnerable to this deadly disease, although all dogs can be infected.

Parvovirus was relatively unknown before its sudden worldwide spread during the late 1970s. Highly contagious, it can be transmitted by direct contact with an infected dog's saliva, feces, vomit, hair, or feet, or from contact with a contaminated cage or clothing. Humans cannot catch the disease but can carry the virus on their shoes and clothing.

SYMPTOMS: Most dogs affected by parvovirus suffer severe bowel distress, diarrhea, vomiting, lethargy, and high fever. Dehydration usually follows.

Parvovirus can kill puppies suddenly, since the virus affects the heart muscle. This is evidenced by loss of balance, labored breathing, and eventual collapse.

TREATMENT: See your veterinarian immediately if you suspect that your dog is infected with parvovirus. Treatment varies and depends on the symptoms and severity of the disease as well as the age of the dog. Hospitalization is usually necessary. Your veterinarian may also administer medication to stop vomiting and diarrhea, antibiotics to control secondary bacterial infections, and fluids to counteract dehydration.

PREVENTION: Parvovirus can be prevented. Be sure that your dog or puppy is properly vaccinated and that the immunization level is maintained by annual boosters.

NOTE: A properly vaccinated mother-to-be will pass along six weeks' immunity to her puppies.

DISTEMPER

CAUSES: Distemper is a viral disease that attacks the cells of the skin, respiratory tract, intestinal tract, and brain. It can cause a change in the dog's appearance, nervous disorders, and death. Young puppies are at highest risk of catching distemper, although all unvaccinated dogs are vulnerable to it.

Distemper is sometimes called the "canine plague" due to its contagious nature. Infected dogs and many other animals, including wolves, raccoons, foxes, and minks, can spread the virus, mainly in their breath. A dog's breath contains the virus particles in minute droplets, much as is the case with human measles. If the infection occurs through inhalation of the virus, it is spread throughout the body by the defensive cells that are trying to capture and kill it.

Humans are not susceptible to contracting distemper.

SYMPTOMS: A puppy may survive a very light infection showing only listlessness and a slight temperature. In acute cases, however, a wider variety of symptoms may appear.

In the early stages of the infection, dogs will suffer from fever, a loss of appetite, lethargy, dehydration, vomiting, and diarrhea. A white or green pus-like discharge may run from the eyes and nose, the skin may become spotted with red, pussy abcesses, and the dog's nose and footpads may become broken and dry.

In the advanced stages of infection, brain damage and nervous disorders may develop. Your dog may shake nervously, become restless and moody, and experience blindness and paralysis.

TREATMENT: If your dog shows any of the symptoms of distemper, *don't*

In the early stages of distemper, a dog's footpads may appear to be cracked.

delay. Call your veterinarian immediately. Treatment will be based on the stage of infection. Your dog may be administered canine distemper antiserum, anticonvulsants, antibiotics to prevent secondary bacterial infection, fluids to cure dehydration, medications to stop the diarrhea and vomiting, eye ointment, and vitamins.

If your dog survives this lethal disease, she can recover gradually from the symptoms with constant home care under the direction of your veterinarian.

PREVENTION: The key to preventing distemper is vaccination. The first distemper shot should be given shortly after weaning and before a puppy is brought into a new home where she will be exposed to other dogs.

Start vaccinating your puppy against this disease at six to eight weeks. This will consist of a series of shots that end when your puppy is about fourteen to sixteen weeks old.

During this time, keep your puppy out of any situation where she could come in contact with the disease.

Afterward, annual booster shots are necessary to adequately shield your dog from infection. Ignore anyone who tries to persuade you that early immunization will last a lifetime—that myth was repudiated long ago.

INFECTIOUS CANINE HEPATITIS

CAUSES: The word "hepatitis" means inflammation of the liver, but the disease also affects the kidneys and lining of the blood vessels. Infectious canine hepatitis is commonly confused with the human form of hepatitis, but it is not the same disease and so is not transmissible to humans. Infectious canine hepatitis is, however, a highly contagious viral disease among dogs. The principal sufferers are puppies, but dogs of any age can be affected.

A few days after a dog is exposed, the virus multiplies in the dog's tissues and is excreted in all her body secretions—saliva, urine, and feces. It is at this stage that the disease is most contagious. The virus is passed as dogs come into contact with contaminated food, water, or even air. Even dogs that have recovered can spread the virus through their urine for months after infection.

SYMPTOMS: In one form of hepatitis, the dog can suddenly become ill and die with no prior symptoms. This severe form mainly attacks young puppies.

In another severe form, the dog will have a fever that may reach 106 degrees Fahrenheit. She will have diarrhea (possibly bloody), may vomit blood, refuse to eat, and be extremely thirsty. Movement is painful, and often the dog walks with a hunched back, caused by her painfully swollen liver.

TREATMENT: Treatment will vary depending on the severity of the hepatitis. In acute cases, your dog may have to be hospitalized.

In most cases, your veterinarian will recommend antibiotics to prevent further bacterial complications, vitamin supplements, since the liver at this point cannot produce its own, and nondairy fluids, since the dog's throat is frequently inflamed.

During recovery, you will have to be sure the dog always has fresh water, protection from extreme heat and cold, and a diet consisting of several fat-free small meals per day.

PREVENTION: Infectious canine hepatitis can and should be prevented through vaccination. There are two types of vaccine available, modified live virus or killed virus. Modified live virus provides longer immunity to hepatitis. However, some dogs have developed "blue-eye"—a blue clouding of the eye's surface due to a fluid swelling of the cornea—from being immunized with modified live virus. To avoid the risk of this temporary side effect, the killed virus is commonly used.

Your veterinarian will begin a vaccination series when your dog is a puppy. A yearly booster is also needed.

KENNEL COUGH

CAUSES: Kennel cough is so named because it is spread by germ-laden droplets in the air when dogs are kept together in close quarters, such as kennels. Dogs outside kennels can catch the disease, but it is more prevalent in places where dogs are caged together, because the concentration of airborne virus particles is much greater in close quarters.

Kennel cough is an infection of the throat and bronchial tubes. The cough alone is akin to what is found in the human cold. The trick with kennel cough is to avoid complications and secondary infections, including bronchitis and pneumonia, which can be fatal.

SYMPTOMS: A coarse, convulsive cough is the characteristic sign. The cough becomes more severe with excitement or exercise. Otherwise, the dog seems normal and is bright and alert, with a healthy appetite.

WARNING SIGNS OF KENNEL COUGH

If your dog has kennel cough and shows any of the following symptoms, call your veterinarian immediately:

- fever
- continual harsh, dry cough
- lack of appetite
- nasal or eye discharge
- listlessness

TREATMENT: Isolate the dog so as not to infect other dogs. It is important that she rest in a humid atmosphere. Keep a home vaporizer running in one of her favorite warm and confined sleeping areas and encourage her to nap there during the day and at night. Exercise the dog daily—but not strenuously. A mild, children's cough syrup will help soothe the cough, and that in turn may help your dog to conserve energy. Kennel cough without complications should disappear in about two weeks.

PREVENTION: Vaccinations effective against some of the kennel cough viruses are available. These include parainfluenza virus and canine adenoviruses types one and two. They will not prevent all cases, but they are recommended if you plan to board or show your dog, which could potentially expose her repeatedly to the virus.

LEPTOSPIROSIS

CAUSES: Leptospirosis is a highly contagious bacterial disease that can be transmitted from dogs to people. Usually a dog catches it from contact with infected urine. Because puppies and male dogs are less discreet in their urinating habits than are adult females, they have a much higher rate of infection.

SYMPTOMS: Signs of illness appear in five to fifteen days. In the early stage of the disease the dog will run a fever accompanied by listlessness, loss of appetite, excessive thirst, severe diarrhea, and vomiting.

Leptospirosis can affect many systems, but the primary signs are associated with the kidneys. The dog may move slowly with a hunched gait due to pain in the kidney area. She may also show signs of jaundice—the eyes, gums, and tongue may have a yellowish cast, which indicates a liver problem.

TREATMENT: Get professional treatment. Your veterinarian will probably give your dog the antibiotic streptomycin. In severe cases he or she will recommend hospitalization.

If your dog convalesces at home, good hygiene is essential to avoid catching the disease yourself. Wash your hands after touching the dog, and keep her out of the rooms in which you eat.

If the disease is recognized early and treatment is begun promptly, there is an excellent chance for recovery.

PREVENTION: Vaccinations are recommended, with a booster once a year—twice a year in regions where the disease is common. Consult with your veterinarian as to the appropriateness of twice-a-year boosters for your dog.

LYME DISEASE

CAUSES: Lyme disease, a newly recognized illness, is transmitted by the deer tick, which can infect both pets and their owners. The primary seasons for exposure to this disease are spring through fall.

Lyme disease appears most often in the northeastern and midwestern United States, but cases have been documented in more than forty states since 1975. White-footed mice and white-tailed deer are the main hosts for the deer tick. The ticks wait on low vegetation in wooded or long-grassed areas heavily populated by mice and deer and attach to anything that brushes them. Ticks do not fly or jump.

Deer ticks can attack a dog anywhere on her body, but most often bite her head, neck, ears, or feet. Unlike fleas, mosquitos, and bees, ticks cause little sensation when they bite. Animals can be covered with ticks and show no concern at all.

SYMPTOMS: Signs of Lyme disease in dogs include listlessness, fever, and sudden onset of lameness associated with pain, warmth, and/or swelling in one or more joints. A circular area of skin inflammation around the tick bite may occur, but it may be difficult to see because of the animal's fur coat.

TREATMENT: Any signs of Lyme disease in your dog should be reported to your veterinarian, since it can be more easily treated in its early stages. Your veterinarian may administer antitick serum. In the advanced stages of infection, your dog may suffer from paralysis that will initially attack the front and hind limbs and then the chest muscles, disabling the respiratory muscles and causing the dog to asphyxiate.

REMOVING A TICK

When removing a tick, grasp the exposed section of its body near the dog's skin with tweezers, forceps, or a gloved hand and pull with smooth, steady pressure. Avoid pulling a tick off with your fingers. If the tick is carrying a disease, it could be fatal to you. If the tick's mouth parts or head are still lodged in the dog's skin, do not worry. The leftover parts cannot continue to poison the dog. They may, however, cause a slight and temporary inflammation. Dabbing some antiseptic onto the bitten area after removing the tick will help prevent any inflammation.

Dispose of the tick by wrapping it in several tissues and flushing it down the toilet, or by dropping it in a small bottle of rubbing alcohol. Submerging the tick in water will not be effective because ticks don't drown. Do not crush, burn, or suffocate the tick, as this may release the infectious bacteria. Contact with the tick should be avoided.

If you suspect that the dog's infection is advanced, immediately contact your veterinarian. Hospitalization may be necessary.

PREVENTION: Tick repellents are available to ward off ticks. In areas where ticks are abundant, contact your veterinarian for advice on insecticidal bathing or dipping.

The risk of getting Lyme disease is directly related to the length of time the tick is attached. The best way to reduce the risk of infection is to remove ticks from the body as soon as possible (see box on page 114). Deer ticks look much like a mole or blood blister. The male is black and the female is dark red and black. An adult tick is only one tenth of an inch long, while a tick in its baby or nymph stage is much smaller. The tick becomes gray and can grow three to five times its normal size when filled with blood.

In July 1992, a Lyme disease vaccination for dogs was licensed by the United States government. Check with your veterinarian on the availability and use of this vaccine.

RABIES

CAUSES: The rabies virus occurs in nearly all warm-blooded animals. Meateaters, including raccoons, foxes, bats, and dogs, are its most likely victims. Humans are also vulnerable to the disease. It can be contracted only from an already afflicted animal. For the disease to develop, the saliva of the rabid animal must get into the victim's bloodstream through an open wound, mucus membrane, or bite.

The incubation period, which is the time between exposure and the development of symptoms, varies. The average incubation period is two to three weeks, but it can be as long as several months. Because the virus travels to the brain along nerve networks, the farther the site of infection from the brain, the longer the incubation period. After the virus reaches the brain, it then travels along the nerves to the salivary glands, where it multiplies.

SYMPTOMS: The symptoms of rabies are due to encephalitis, or inflammation of the brain. The most common early symptom of rabies may be simply an inexplicable change in the dog's behavior. A quiet, friendly dog may suddenly become aggressive and irritable, or a shy one may become overly affectionate. The dog may have a slight fever, along with diarrhea and vomiting.

As the disease progresses, the dog is affected by becoming either furious or paralytic—and a rabid dog may show signs of one or both behaviors.

The furious behavior is the "mad dog" type of rabies. The dog is frenzied and vicious and bites anything in her path. Eventually, convulsions occur, sporadically at first, then increasing in frequency and duration. Paralysis follows, and inevitably death.

In the paralytic form, the muscles of the head become paralyzed and cause the mouth to drop open and the tongue to hang out. The dog cannot swallow and is frantically thirsty. She often drools and paws at her mouth because of the paralysis, but contrary to popular myth, this behavior does not always occur. In later stages, paralysis overtakes the dog's whole body; death follows.

TREATMENT: There is no effective treatment for rabies in dogs. Euthanasia is the only possible procedure.

PREVENTION: Annual vaccination of all dogs is recommended, but check your local regulations. A puppy should be first vaccinated at three to six months of age.

WARNING: If you suspect rabies in your dog, or if you suspect that she has been exposed to a rabid animal, TAKE NO CHANCES. If the dog is in an area that you can easily close off, confine her. Otherwise, stay away from her. Inform your veterinarian immediately.

If you are bitten by your dog or you think that you have been exposed to rabies, contact your physician, who may have to administer an antibiotic or vaccination to treat you for rabies infection.

TUBERCULOSIS

CAUSES: The incidence of tuberculosis has risen dramatically in the human population over recent years. Unfortunately, tuberculosis not only affects people, but also dogs, as it can be transmitted from humans to dogs and vice versa. Contagion occurs through inhalation or ingestion of the infectious bacterium that causes tuberculosis.

Tuberculosis mainly attacks the lungs, causing an inflammation of the membranes around them and the sloughing off of dead tissue, which subsequently floats throughout the lung cavity.

SYMPTOMS: Your dog will have difficulty breathing, develop a chronic wet cough, and spit up a bloody or pussy material called sputum from the lungs.

DIAGNOSIS: The veterinarian will take an X ray and examine the sputum.

TREATMENT: Tuberculosis in dogs can be successfully treated with long-term hospitalization and antibiotics.

If you suspect that you have been exposed to tuberculosis, call your physician. You may have to receive a medication called isoniazid to prevent a full-blown outbreak of the infection.

10

HEAD AND NECK PROBLEMS

DOGS RELY upon the organs of the head and neck region to collect information on the sounds, tastes, sights, and textures that make up the world. This region of the dog's body has evolved into a warehouse of complex sensory organs, some of which are even more complex than those found in humans. You can help maintain and even sharpen your dog's already acute abilities to perceive the world by being alert to the signs of the various disorders outlined in this chapter and taking prompt action to remedy them.

THE EAR

Dogs' ears come in an array of shapes and sizes: The Afghan has long, flat ears that are covered with wavy hair, while the Chow Chow has short, alert ears that point toward you. The Italian Greyhound, on the other hand, has animated velvety ears that fall into the shape of extended birds' wings, and the Wire Fox Terrier has ears whose tips fall forward, making miniature tents atop the dog's head.

Despite the difference in the appearance of their ears, dogs share one thing—an excellent sense of hearing.

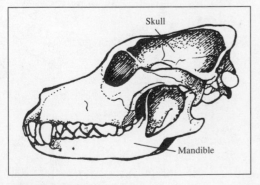

The canine skull.

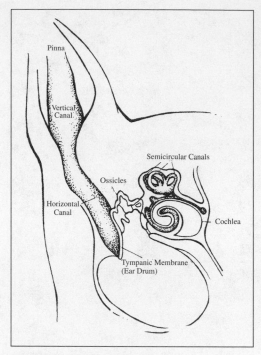

The canine auditory system.

Next to smell, hearing is the dog's most developed sense. A dog's hearing is about 140 percent sharper than ours, which means that he can not only hear sounds too faint for us to detect, but he can also hear noises pitched at frequencies much higher than we can hear.

The dog's superior capacity to hear begins with the pinna, the unique pink flap protruding from the dog's head that is in actuality a cartilage framework surrounded by muscles and skin. These muscles move to follow sound waves and to funnel them into the external ear opening, down the auditory canal, and to the eardrum, also referred to as the tympanic membrane.

By the time they have hit the eardrum, the sound waves have moved to the middle ear, where they are ampli-fied by three of the smallest bones in the dog's body: the hammer, anvil, and stirrup, also called the auditory ossicles. Once amplified, the sound waves are passed to the inner ear through a vibrating membrane, or the oval window. Within the inner ear is the spiral-shaped cochlea, which transforms sound waves into nerve impulses to be sent to the brain and to the semicircular tubes called the saccule and utricle, which are responsible for the dog's balance.

BLEEDING FROM THE EAR (see INTERNAL BLEEDING, p. 258)

BLOOD BLISTER IN THE EAR (HEMATOMA)

CAUSES: A hematoma, which can occur at any location of the body, is a swelling caused by an accumulation of blood under the surface of the skin. Dogs frequently suffer from hematomas in the earflaps as the result of a ruptured blood vessel. A hematoma is sometimes mistaken for an abscess, but it is firmer to the touch and occurs more suddenly.

The following are possible causes of hematoma in the ear: violent head scratching; head trauma caused by an accident or fight; a bite; ear mite infection; itchy, irritated area inside the ear.

TREATMENT: A hematoma needs veterinary attention. The veterinarian will drain the hematoma surgically and stitch the ear to prevent the swelling from recurring.

PREVENTING EAR PROBLEMS

Because the dog's outer and inner ear are such delicate structures, it is important to prevent ear problems before they occur. Here are some guidelines to help you do just that.

1. Gently wedge some cotton into the exterior ear opening before bathing your dog in order to ensure that no water drops into his ear.

2. Clean your dog's ears about once a month. Using a cotton swab dampened in mineral oil, alcohol, diluted peroxide, or a cleansing product suggested by your veterinarian, carefully wipe around the folds of the inner ear and the exterior ear opening, lifting away the wax buildup. Be sure not to bury the wax deeper into the ear. Also, in order not to damage the delicate inner ear structure, clean only those parts of the ear that are visible to you. Last, wax protects the ear canal. Therefore, it is beneficial to leave some behind and to postpone cleaning the dog's ears if there has been little wax buildup since the previous cleaning.

3. Some breeds, such as Poodles and English Spaniels, can have excessive hair in the ears that impedes air circulation and causes infection. Daily combing and regular trimming of the hair around the ears can prevent this. If the hair becomes too excessive, however, it should be removed. (See Ear Cleaning, p. 68.)

4. Always check under the earflaps when your dog has been running in tall grass and brush. Vegetative matter can affix itself to fur surrounding the ear. If this material is not removed, it can lodge inside the ear, irritating the membranes and causing infection.

5. Cuts and injuries under the inner earflaps can quickly become infected. Always check your dog's ears for any damaged tissue, especially if he has been involved in a dogfight.

DEAFNESS

CAUSES: While a person can communicate hearing loss, a dog's deafness must be observed. You have to be able to compare your dog's present response to certain sounds and frequencies to the reactions you have come to expect from him. Even then, it is hard to pinpoint hearing loss in dogs, because they are such resourceful animals. They may be using other senses to compensate for their damaged ears.

Some dogs develop deafness later in

life, while others are genetically predisposed to hearing loss—especially white dogs with blue eyes. Border Collies, Bull and Fox Terriers, and Dalmatians are especially vulnerable.

Many dogs lose their hearing as they age. This is because the nerve that controls hearing deteriorates over time. This type of hearing loss does not appear suddenly; rather, the sharpness of hearing dulls gradually, making the disability difficult to detect. Often, hearing loss is accompanied by a deterioration in vision—again, a common symptom of aging. Because the dog can no longer trust his ability to hear (and perhaps see), he must move more slowly and exercise greater caution. Often, people attribute this behavior to the generic cause "old age," rather than identifying the specific deterioration of the sense organs. Conversely, deaf puppies are difficult to diagnose because of their constant, rapid movement.

Other causes of deafness include acute ear infection, trauma caused by accidents or fights, reactions to drugs or toxic substances, and obstruction of the ear canal.

SYMPTOMS: Dogs who are deaf or have suffered significant hearing loss are less responsive than unimpaired dogs. They ignore commands, don't come when their names are called, seem confused or hazy, and are difficult to awaken. Their earflaps tend to hang limply. Their voices sound irregular.

TREATMENT: A veterinarian will determine if hearing is recoverable. In cases of acquired hearing loss, the underlying cause will be treated, if possible. A hearing aid made for a dog's ear may be suggested.

EAR MITES

CAUSES: Ear mites are specklike insects that feed on skin particles in the dog's ear. Their tentacles irritate the ear canal, making him vulnerable to infection from bacteria or fungi.

ABOUT HEARING-IMPAIRED DOGS

Many dogs lead happy, productive lives despite partial or complete deafness. As your dog's primary caretaker, you will be responsible for helping him to make certain protective adjustments. Never allow a dog who has lost his hearing to roam. He will no longer be able to hear the sound of an oncoming car or horn and is very prone to accidents. He also can no longer hear other aural signs of danger, such as a growling dog or another aggressive animal. Always walk a dog who has lost his hearing on a leash, to exercise maximum control over his safety.

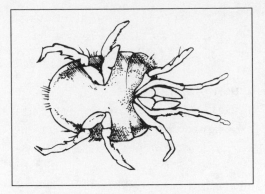

Enlarged depiction of an ear mite, the most common cause of ear disorders in younger dogs.

Mites are highly contagious, since they often wander from the ear, getting into the dog's coat and other dogs' ears. They are also easily transferred from mother to puppies, making it the most common culprit of ear infection in puppies and young dogs.

SYMPTOMS: Head shaking, rubbing the ear against objects, scratching at the ear, a waxy, dark-colored discharge. The ear appears to be dark and crusty, and emits a malodorous scent.

TREATMENT: After determining that mites are present, your veterinarian will wash out the debris with an insecticidal preparation that will kill the mites. He or she will ask you to continue daily home treatment for about three full weeks.

In addition to prescribing ear medicine, your veterinarian may instruct you to sprinkle flea powder on the dog's skin to kill leftover mites and to treat other dogs and cats in your household that may have become infected through contact. Since mites lay their eggs in the ears, a new crop will reinfect your dog if you stop the treatment too soon or fail to take the proper other measures.

FOREIGN BODIES IN THE EAR

CAUSES: An amazing variety of foreign bodies have been found in dogs' ears—everything from chewing gum to sticks and stones.

The foreign materials most often found in the dog's ear canal, however, are grass seeds, thorns, and ticks. They are not as innocent as they sound. They can often travel deep into the ear, causing infection or damaging the delicate structure of the ear.

SYMPTOMS: Shaking of the head, scratching at the ear.

TREATMENT: If the foreign object is visible, use tweezers to gently remove it. Treat remaining scratches or cuts by dabbing some antiseptic onto the injured area with a cotton swab. (See Removing a Tick box, p. 114.)

If the foreign body is deep in the ear canal or cannot be seen, take your dog to the veterinarian for removal of the foreign body.

OTITIS EXTERNA

While an outer-ear infection in itself may not seem serious, it must be diagnosed and treated early in order to

A dog with a middle ear infection will often shake the painful side of his head downward.

prevent a middle- or inner-ear infection from developing.

CAUSES: Wax buildup; matted hair lodged in ear; dried blood or mucus; mites; foreign objects including plant matter; water; soap; trauma caused by accidents or fights; bacteria; fungus.

SYMPTOMS: Tilting affected side downward, shaking head, frequent scratching of affected ear, malodorous discharge, redness and swelling of the skin folds in the canal.

TREATMENT: Veterinary care is necessary in order to determine the cause of the infection.

OTITIS MEDIA

Fortunately, middle-ear infections are not common in dogs. They are usually the result of originally minor ear problems left untreated.

SYMPTOMS: Severe pain, side of head with afflicted ear tilts downward, fever, lethargy, loss of balance.

TREATMENT: Immediate veterinary care is needed to stop the infection from spreading to the brain. Antibiotics will be administered, as will pain relievers. Surgery may be required to flush out the infected canal.

THE EYE

A dog's ability to see the world is different from ours. Dogs are not able to see things sharply, nor can they focus on distant objects. Their retinas also lack the cells responsible for distinguishing colors; therefore, dogs are only able to see black, white, and various shades of gray.

Despite these differences, however, the dog's eye is, in many respects, well developed. Unlike our eye, which is protected only by our eyelashes and eyelids, the dog's eye has added protection from a third eyelid, also called the haw or nictitating membrane, that is usually visible only as an outline around the bottom of the eye.

The way a dog sees is similar to the way we do. Light enters the dog's eye through the cornea, a transparent multicellular layer that covers the eye. After passing through the anterior chamber, it is received by the next layer of the eye, the iris, a colored muscular circle that controls the amount of light received by the pupil, and the sclera, the white area surrounding the eye.

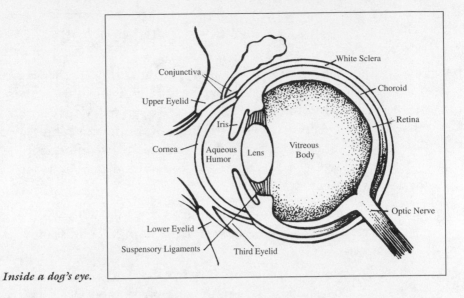

Inside a dog's eye.

Light then crosses the posterior chamber and goes to the retina, the inner layer of the eye consisting of rods and cones. The primary function of the retina is to convert light into nerve impulses that will travel through the optic nerve to the brain. The dog's retina, however, also enhances the dog's vision, allowing him to see well in the darkness. This is because the retina is comprised mainly of rods, which are capable of working well in low light levels, and because the retina is supported by a reflective layer that transmits light back through the rods, concentrating it. This reflective layer, the tapetum lucidum, gives the dog shiny green eyes during the night.

The way a dog's eyes are positioned in his head, and the strong muscles that move them around, give the dog a comparatively wide field of vision. Some breeds of dogs rely more on their eyes for hunting than other breeds do. The shape of the head, which alters the placement of the eyes, largely determines this.

The long-nosed "gaze hounds"—Greyhounds, Afghan Hounds, Deerhounds, Whippets, and Irish Wolfhounds—are dogs who hunt by sight. They have obliquely placed eyes and a narrow field of view directly in front of them. They can pick up quickly moving prey in the distance, but they perceive stationary objects poorly. This is why your graceful greyhound can trip over small obstacles when he is running at full speed.

BLINDNESS

CAUSES: If a dog suddenly loses his vision, it may be the result of a stroke, head trauma caused by an accident, or poisoning. Corneal disorders like cloudy eye (p. 126) can result in temporary blindness. Many dogs experience a gradual deterioration of vision

HELPING A VISION-IMPAIRED DOG

Most blind dogs have little trouble getting along in the world. Dogs learn to rely upon other senses like hearing and smell, which become far more acute once vision is lost. As far as we can tell, dogs are remarkably adaptable and simply get on with their lives after learning to make the physical adjustments necessitated by a disability like blindness.

To make life easier and safer for your vision-impaired dog, explore the following suggestions:

1. Shower your dog with attention. Praise him with words and gestures to reinforce the hard work he is doing in adjusting to a tough situation.

2. Speak to your dog frequently. Try working out a system of commands designed to help him through the new physical obstacles he faces.

3. Have his ears checked frequently, as blind dogs rely heavily upon hearing.

4. Avoid changing the orientation of your dog's surroundings. Maintain the familiar floor plan, and keep all the dog's belongings where they were prior to vision loss.

5. Never allow your dog out without supervision. Never allow him outside without a leash. Drivers can't differentiate between seeing and nonseeing dogs and will not be able to anticipate your dog's longer response time.

6. When you leave the house, turn on a radio. The sounds will be comforting to your dog and will ward off feelings of isolation.

due to aging (see Cataract, p. 125, and Glaucoma, p. 128).

SYMPTOMS: Dimming vision is often indicated by a change in the eye's appearance—it becomes blue-gray in color. Because dogs become so familiar with the "feel" of their home, vision loss may not become evident until the dog leaves his usual surroundings.

Then he may bump into things, walk with an uncertain gait, and carry his nose close to the ground.

STAINS IN THE CORNER OF THE EYE

CAUSES: Some dogs, especially Poodles, Maltese, and toys whose faces are white, sport darkly stained facial hair along the inside corner of their eyes. The stain is caused by tears, which should collect in the tear ducts but instead flow onto the face.

There are several reasons the tear ducts may not be draining all of the tears secreted. The ducts may be obstructed or too narrow to do their job properly. In some cases, the ducts themselves are properly formed and functional, but the tear flow itself is too excessive. This may be caused by conjunctivitis (see p. 126), allergies, entropion (see pp. 127, 140), infection of the Harderian gland, or an infection of the third eyelid (see p. 129).

TREATMENT: If you notice a new stain, or a stain that seems to be getting worse, consult your veterinarian; he or she will need to determine the underlying cause of the problem. If an infection is triggering the staining, antibiotics will be prescribed. Surgery may be recommended to remove the third eyelid, increasing the area into which tears can flow.

ELIMINATING THE STAIN AT HOME

1. Keep the hair clipped close to the face.
2. Mix two teaspoons of hydrogen peroxide in twenty teaspoons of lukewarm water. Gently rub some of the solution into the stained hair, taking pains to prevent getting any of it in the eye itself.
3. Carefully rinse with lukewarm water.

CATARACT

CAUSES: A cataract is a hardening of the lens that causes it to become murky and to eventually block light from passing through to the eye's retina. The most common cause of cataracts is old age. In fact, most dogs over eight years of age have some degree of haziness in their lenses. Other causes are diabetes (see Diabetes, p. 179), eye disease, inflammation, injury, and progressive retinal atrophy (see Progressive Retinal Atrophy, p. 128). Poodles, Cocker Spaniels, and Wire-Haired Terriers are considered to be genetically predisposed to cataracts.

SYMPTOMS: You will notice silvery flecks or a cloudy gray or bluish-white cast to the lens behind the dog's pupil.

TREATMENT: Your veterinarian may recommend surgical removal of the lens so that the dog can perceive light. Your dog's eyesight will not be perfect. While your dog may lose his ability to see sharp images, the surgery may enable him to perceive shadows and

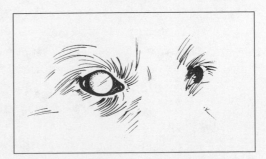

A cataract. Most dogs over the age of eight have some cloudiness in at least one eye.

distinguish the spatial relationship between itself and objects. This can increase his mobility.

If the cataracts are the result of diabetes, it is important to control the diabetes first. This will help ensure a successful operation if your veterinarian recommends surgery.

CLOUDY EYE (KERATITIS)

CAUSES: Keratitis is an inflammation of the cornea, or outside covering of the eye. It is usually caused by the presence of a foreign body in the eye, but it can also be brought on through vaccination with the live hepatitis vaccine.

SYMPTOMS: The cornea at first loses its shine, then appears hazy, then cloudy, and finally milky.

TREATMENT: Keratitis is serious because it may lead to partial or temporary blindness. Treatment will differ based on the cause of the inflammation.

COLLIE EYE ANOMALY

CAUSES: Collie eye anomaly is a congenital disorder that affects Collies and Shetland Sheepdogs. Dogs with this disorder are predisposed to changes in the optic nerve, the choroid, and the retina that can lead to blindness.

Collie eye anomaly appears at birth and can be recognized shortly after the bluish puppy film on the eye vanishes, or as early as six weeks after birth. Reti-nal degeneration may not be revealed until the dog is one to two years old.

TREATMENT: There is no treatment for collie eye anomaly. If you discover that your puppy is affected by this disorder, neither he nor his parents should be used for breeding. If you would like to someday breed your puppy, be sure to have him tested before you purchase him.

CONJUNCTIVITIS

CAUSES: Conjunctivitis is a painful inflammation of the conjunctiva, the membrane lining the eyelids.

Because the eyelids keep foreign matter from entering the eye, dogs whose lids do not cling tightly to the eye, such as Basset Hounds, Bloodhounds, and Newfoundlands, are susceptible to getting irritating matter in their conjunctiva and to developing chronic conjunctivitis.

Dog conjunctivitis is not contagious. It is caused by foreign debris in the eye such as dust, dirt, sand, and grit, or by allergies, overexposure to sunlight, chemicals, distemper (see Distemper, p. 110), or injury to the eye.

SYMPTOMS: Redness and discharge from the eye. If the discharge is clear or watery, the cause is most likely an irritant to the eye, such as a foreign body. If the discharge looks like pus and is so thick that it often encrusts the eyelids, the cause is most likely an infection and will require antibiotic treatment.

TREATMENT: Schedule an appointment to see your veterinarian, who will prescribe an eye ointment to clear up the conjunctivitis. Meanwhile, keep your dog's irritated eye clean. Remove any apparent foreign objects, gently bathe the area with a lint-free cloth moistened with warm water, and try to let the eye rest by keeping the dog out of direct sunlight or wind.

PREVENTION: The threat of conjunctivitis is another good reason to prevent your dog from sticking his head out the window when you take him for rides in the car. Road particles and even the wind can cause the eye to become severely irritated, which may eventually lead to conjunctivitis.

DRY EYE

CAUSES: Due to a shortage in or lack of tear production, the dog's eye dries out. This disease mainly affects older dogs.

SYMPTOMS: The shiny, moist eye will suddenly appear dull. The conjunctiva may become irritated and inflamed. A dense, sticky, stubborn yellow pus may cover the entire eyeball. In the advanced stages of dry eye, the dog's eye may become invaded by a black tint.

TREATMENT: Unless the condition is treated in its early stages, a serious deep-seated infection can result. Your veterinarian will aim treatment at reestablishing the flow of tears. In some cases this may be possible with antibiotics or anti-inflammatory drugs. In others, surgery may be necessary.

EYEBALL OUT OF ITS SOCKET (see EYE OUT OF ITS SOCKET, p. 252)

EYELID ROLLED INWARD (ENTROPION)

CAUSES: Entropion is a condition in which the eyelid rolls in, bringing the lashes into contact with the eye's surface. The abrasive action of the lid usually results in severe irritation and often corneal ulcerations.

Although either the upper or lower eyelid may be affected, it most commonly affects the lower eyelid. In breeds with large heads and loose facial skin, entropion may occur in the upper lid as well.

TREATMENT: In order to prevent permanent damage, surgery is usually

This dog's top eyelid is rolled inward (entropion), causing the eyelashes to rub against the eye's surface. Her bottom eyelid is rolled outward (ectropion), exposing the eye to irritants.

required. The veterinarian will adjust the eyelid so it remains in the correct position.

Lubricating the eye (according to your veterinarian's instructions) will give the cornea a layer of protection until the problem is corrected.

EYELID ROLLED OUTWARD (ECTROPION)

CAUSES: This is an inherited condition in which the dog's eyelids roll out, allowing foreign debris to easily irritate the exposed conjunctiva. Constant irritation due to ectropion may eventually lead to infection, the presence of discharge running from the eye, and severe conjunctivitis.

This condition is usually seen in dogs with loose facial skin and in older dogs in whom the facial skin has lost its tone and become saggy.

TREATMENT: Your veterinarian may advise plastic surgery to tighten the lid and protect the eye.

GLAUCOMA

CAUSES: Glaucoma is an enlargement of the eye. It is caused by a defect in the eye's drainage system that prevents fluid from properly nourishing the eye but instead allows it to build up pressure in the eyeball, impairing depth perception and vision.

There are two types of glaucoma: Primary glaucoma is hereditary and usually starts in one eye, but later affects both; secondary glaucoma occurs as a complication of an injured or diseased eye. Both are very painful to the dog and can result in blindness. Dogs especially susceptible to the inheritable variety include the American Cocker Spaniel, English Cocker Spaniel, Basset Hound, Malamutes, and Poodles.

SYMPTOMS: A dog suffering from glaucoma has a fixed blank look in his affected eye, which is usually red and cloudy. The affected pupil seems abnormally large, and often tears excessively.

TREATMENT: The goal of treatment will be to relieve pressure. Drops and/or diuretics may be administered. Surgery may be suggested, either to aid drainage or, in severe cases, to remove the afflicted eye. Your dog should adapt readily to life with only one eye—even blind dogs usually manage well.

PROGRESSIVE RETINAL ATROPHY

CAUSES: The retina is the eye's inner layer, which is highly sensitive to light. A dog's best vision occurs at the retina's center. Progressive retinal atrophy, a hereditary condition, kills off the pigment cells located in the middle of the retina, impairing the dog's ability to see fixed objects. The dog can still see moving objects, however, because he relies upon the outer rim of the retina to perceive motion.

The number of progressive retinal

atrophy cases has increased over recent years. By the time the condition becomes evident (usually around the fifth year of life), the dog is likely to have been bred, unless selective breeding practices have been employed. Dogs commonly affected include Collies, Irish Setters, Norwegian Elkhounds, Dachshunds, Labrador Retrievers, Shetland Sheepdogs, Welsh Corgis, and Poodles.

SYMPTOMS: Fear of the dark; reluctance to go outside at night; hesitation about or clumsy handling of stairs; bumping into objects.

As the disease progresses, you may notice that the pupils dilate. If you look inside, you can see the back of the eye, which appears brightly colored.

TREATMENT: There is no treatment. The disease will only be eliminated through selective breeding—i.e., not breeding dogs who have or whose parents had the disease.

SUDDEN SWELLING OF THE EYELIDS (CHEMOSIS)

CAUSES: If your dog's eyelids suddenly become swollen, chances are the condition is more frightening than serious. Chemosis can be triggered by an allergen like an insect bite or drug toward which your dog is particularly sensitive. Some other irritant may have made its way beneath the lid, causing the tissue to become inflamed.

The lids look like they're filled with

fluid, because water has passed out into the tissues in response to the allergy or irritant.

TREATMENT: This condition rarely lasts very long. The key is to remove the triggering factor and to keep your dog from pawing at the eye.

THIRD EYELID PROBLEMS

Unlike humans, dogs have a structure in the eye called the third eyelid, or nictitating membrane. This consists of protective tissue at the inner corner of each eye that helps produce and set tears flowing.

A gland located on the inner surface of the third eyelid also helps lubricate the eye. Because this gland is exposed to irritants and bacteria, it is more susceptible to infection than are the other tear glands, which are located farther inside the dog's head.

CHERRY EYE

CAUSES: Cherry eye is a term used to describe the pink, shiny, knotlike protrusion that appears in the corner of the dog's eye when the tear gland becomes infected. The condition is not dangerous. Cherry eye usually affects puppies of short-nosed breeds such as Cocker Spaniels, Beagles, Boston Terriers, and Bull Dogs.

TREATMENT: Antibiotics often cure this condition. Sometimes, however, surgery is required to reposition the

Cherry eye is the result of an infected tear gland.

gland. Because tears are essential for ridding the eye of harmful agents, the veterinarian will do everything possible to save the gland.

HAWS

CAUSES: Haws is a condition in which the third eyelid protrudes, or becomes more prominent, appearing as

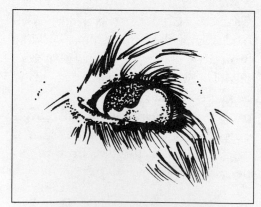

Trauma and foreign irritants are the two most common causes of ulcers in the eye.

a "skin" that may cover a quarter to as much as half of the inner part of the eye.

Although one breed, the Bloodhound, should have a visible haw, in other dogs a protruding haw can indicate that the dog is ill.

TREATMENT: Your veterinarian will need to determine the cause of the haw and recommend treatment.

ULCERS

CAUSES: The surface of the dog's eye is vulnerable to injuries and the ulcers that may develop from them. Since it can seriously impair a dog's vision, immediate attention to an ulcer is advised.

The most common causes are trauma caused by accident or a dogfight, or a foreign body in the eye. Other causes include infection, extra lashes, dry eye (see Dry Eye, p. 127), or a prominent eyeball.

SYMPTOMS: The color of the eyeball changes, becoming red or slightly blue. The dog will shed tears and may wink one eye. In the advanced stages of injury, a scar may form in the eye.

TREATMENT: See your veterinarian immediately. In a mild case, the veterinarian might prescribe a healing ointment. In more severe cases the veterinarian may create a kind of surgical bandage by stitching the third eyelid right across the eye and leaving it in place for up to a month.

THE MOUTH

By inspecting your dog's mouth, you can learn a great deal about his overall health. Signs of good health include firm, pink gums that, when pressed, change from white back to pink quickly. The gums should also be fairly smooth and not bloody or irritated. If your dog is infested with parasites or is suffering from anemia, the gums will appear to be very pale. If your dog has suffered a significant loss of fluids, is having difficulty retaining fluids, or is entering a state of shock, the gums will appear blue or gray. The tongue should be pink and free of blood or cuts.

In just three months, a puppy will progress from having twenty-eight baby teeth to forty-two adult teeth. All the adult teeth should be in place by about six months of age. This coincides with the point at which wild dogs leave the litter and become aggressive, hunting members of the pack.

Two types of canine teeth enable dogs to live in the wild. The carnassials are large, shearing teeth that can crush bones. The incisors, often called "dog teeth," are long, gently curved, and sharp. These teeth are excellent weapons, allowing the dog to puncture and carry his prey.

A dog's teeth are extremely strong—much sturdier than ours are. Because the enamel is comparatively thick, the tooth is well protected against decay. A good diet, including plenty of objects to chew on and biscuit if the dog's chief source of food is soft (see Feeding, p. 57, and Bones, p. 57), should be all a dog needs to prevent cavities.

Let's take a look at some of the problems that can occur inside a dog's mouth.

BITTEN TONGUE
(see INTERNAL BLEEDING, p. 258)

BURNS IN THE MOUTH
(see BURNS, p. 246)

DENTAL ABSCESS

CAUSES: An abscess is formed when bacteria-laden pus accumulates in a cavity. Dental abscesses form in the root of a dog's tooth. Common causes include tartar buildup left neglected, a cracked tooth, an oral infection that spreads to the root, or even an infection in another part of the body that makes its way to the mouth. Dental abscesses need to be taken care of quickly, to prevent the bacteria from spreading into the sinus cavity.

SYMPTOMS: The pain will force the dog to refuse food. The jaw will swell and may begin to envelop the affected area. If the infection has spread into the sinus cavity, pus will appear just below the dog's eye.

TREATMENT: In most cases, the afflicted tooth and root will have to be extracted.

FOREIGN BODIES IN THE MOUTH

CAUSES: Dogs are investigators and like to explore things by picking them up with their mouths. As a result, a wide variety of objects, from wood slivers to sewing needles, have been found in dogs' mouths. Often these objects get stuck there, either piercing the lips and gums, getting wedged between the teeth, or becoming caught across the top of the mouth.

SYMPTOMS: Licking the lips, drooling, shaking the head, pawing at the mouth, coughing.

TREATMENT: Foreign objects lodged in the mouth may be tempting to remove yourself. However, the veterinarian is best equipped to perform the procedure and may decide the situation merits the administration of a mild sedative.

If the foreign object has been in the mouth for a day or so, it may cause an infection. If the veterinarian thinks this is a possibility, an antibiotic will be prescribed.

GINGIVITIS

CAUSES: Healthy gums lie flush against the teeth. Problems arise when the gums swell, leaving space between the gum and the teeth. Inside this space, food debris and germs get trapped. When tartar (see Tartar, p. 133) builds up, the gums become even more aggravated, making it easier for infections to occur.

SYMPTOMS: Red, swollen, painful gums that may bleed.

TREATMENT: If gingivitis is advanced, the veterinarian will probably perform an intensive cleaning that requires anaesthesia. It is usually the only way to completely alleviate the problem. This treatment must be supported by good dental hygiene at home (see Dental Care, p. 68).

INFLAMMATION OF THE TONGUE (GLOSSITIS)

CAUSES: Dogs, who are inquisitive about new tastes and always searching for food, love to stick their tongues in garbage pails and empty cans. They also tend to play with objects regardless of the potential dangers they may pose.

A dog's tongue may become inflamed if it is scratched or cut by a foreign object such as a fishhook or a burr that may brush against the tongue when a dog cleans such objects out of his fur. A tongue may also become inflamed if the dog has ingested any corrosive poisons.

SYMPTOMS: The dog will refuse to eat because of the pain. He will drool profusely.

TREATMENT: If you suspect that your dog has gotten poison or a fish-hook in his mouth, take him to the veterinarian as soon as possible so the veterinarian can determine the cause and advise appropriate treatment.

LACERATIONS OF THE LIPS AND MOUTH

CAUSES: Your dog's mouth has delicate tissues that can easily become torn. Just the act of licking an opened can pulled out of the garbage or chewing on his favorite toy can develop cuts. In most of these situations, only minor wounds develop. Lacerations can sometimes be large and deep, however, bleeding profusely and becoming vulnerable to infection.

TREATMENT: If bleeding is profuse, control it with pressure (see Internal Bleeding, p. 258) and get the dog to the veterinarian.

If the cut is minor, cleanse it daily by dabbing a lint-free cloth moistened with an antiseptic such as Listerine onto the cut.

LOOSE TEETH

CAUSES: Other than trauma to the mouth, the chief cause of loose teeth is periodontal disease. The periodontal membrane is a fixative that holds the teeth in their sockets. The membrane can deteriorate due to tartar-induced infection. While the gums may only redden at first, the condition can progress to the point where the teeth are no longer held firmly in place.

SYMPTOMS: Periodontal disease leaves the mouth with a potently malodorous scent. You will see tartar (see Tartar, below) along the reddened and puffy gumline. The pain may cause your dog to salivate excessively, especially when he attempts to eat.

TREATMENT: If your veterinarian cleans your dog's teeth using an ultra-sonic tartar scraper and begins treating your dog with an antibiotic before periodontal disease is too far advanced, the dog's teeth may reset themselves to the bone. Otherwise, extraction of the teeth and portions of the infected gums may be necessary.

PREVENTION: Periodontal disease can be prevented by a good program of dental care (see Dental Care, p. 68).

TARTAR

CAUSES: Dogs develop plaque—the invisible mucus film that develops if you don't brush your teeth—just as humans do. Because very few owners brush their dogs' teeth, the plaque builds up. It starts out yellow-beige, then darkens as particles of food, salt, and minerals accumulate and harden along the surface of the teeth, usually next to the cheek. This calcified material is called tartar or calculus.

THE IMPORTANCE OF CHEWING

One easy way to avoid plaque and tartar buildup is to make sure your dog's diet forces him to chew. Soft food barely taxes your dog's mouth, raising the probability that food particles will remain behind after your dog has finished swallowing. Chewing helps to create a stream of saliva that ushers the food out of the mouth and down into the digestive tract. A rawhide or synthetic bone at least once a week will not only give your dog hours of enjoyment but also will help keep his teeth and gums healthy. Hard biscuits and dog "chews" are also good options.

TREATMENT: A veterinarian must remove tartar with a dental scraper.

PREVENTION: Good dental hygiene and a good diet are the keys to preventing tartar formation (see Dental Care, p. 68).

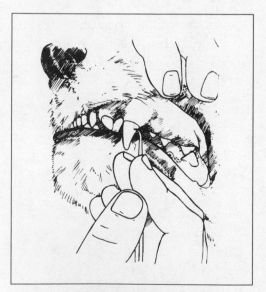

A veterinarian can remove tartar with a dental scraper. Because this is a delicate procedure, do not try it at home.

THE NOSE

The Bloodhound has achieved great fame for its famous tracking abilities. The truth of the matter is that, compared to humans, all dogs have an extremely acute sense of smell. In fact, on the average, the dog's complex system of smelling and identifying different odors is one hundred times more sensitive than ours, enabling him to "smell" the difference between thousands of different types of living organisms.

Why are dogs so adept at detecting scents? The olfactory area in a dog's nose is very large—about forty times larger than a human's. The sensory area is constructed of layered rolled cartilage connected to many blood vessels and nerves. Because the cartilage is rolled, the scents brought in through inhalation can be retained long enough for the brain to identify the stimulus.

When odors are detected, special cells are created that moisten the nose. The scents, which are actually composed of

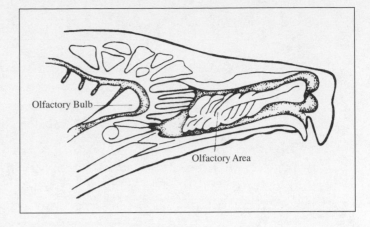

Inside a dog's nose.

tiny particles, become dissolved in this moisture and make contact with sensory cells. Through this contact, the scent is eventually detected. Smell is further aided by the vomeronasal organ, which is located in the roof of the mouth.

A dog hunts by scent, and he also comes to know his world by the odors he encounters. Dogs recognize other dogs by scent; in the dog world, a dog's scent becomes his chief form of identification.

Anatomical evolution has contributed to a dog's sense of smell. The dog's brain has forty times more brain cells involved in recognizing and distinguishing between different odors than the brain of a human being.

The dog's nose is a masterwork of physiology. Because scent is so important to a dog, it is crucial that you learn all you can about keeping your dog free of nasal problems.

FOREIGN BODIES IN THE NOSE (see INTERNAL BLEEDING, p. 258)

INFECTION

CAUSES: Any irritation of the nasal passages can cause an infection.

SYMPTOMS: Malodorous, viscous, creamy discharge from the nose.

TREATMENT: Your veterinarian will first try to determine the cause of the irritation, which can then be treated, along with the resulting infection.

NASAL POLYPS AND TUMORS

POLYPS

CAUSES: A polyp develops when one of the mucus glands within the membrane lining the nose becomes inflamed. It looks like a red, perfectly formed teardrop. The exact cause of polyps is unknown.

SYMPTOMS: Bleeding, obstructed air flow through the nostril.

SYMPTOMS OF NASAL PROBLEMS

1. **NASAL DISCHARGE:** A discharge from the nose that continues for several hours is a good clue that your dog has nasal irritation. Common causes are foreign bodies (see Internal Bleeding, p. 258), infections (see Infection, p. 135), and tumors (see Nasal Polyps and Tumors, p. 135).

2. **SNEEZING:** Because dogs rely on their nose to explore their environment, they often expose their nasal cavity to irritating matter including dust, bacteria, pollen, and viral bodies. Sneezing is one way dogs rid their nose of these irritants. It may, however, indicate a more serious problem.

   INTERMITTENT SNEEZING: If your dog appears healthy, but sneezes often or in a succession and then stops for several hours, he may be allergic to something in his environment. Try to determine the cause of the allergy. Your veterinarian may prescribe an antihistamine.

   PERSISTENT SNEEZING: If your dog is sneezing more persistently and there is a shortage of air from one of the nostrils or a blood-tinged pussy substance collects around the nostrils, your dog may have an infection. This infection could be directly in the nose (see Infection, p. 135) or could be caused by a nasal tumor (see Nasal Polyps and Tumors, p. 135) or irritated tooth root. See your veterinarian, who may take X rays to determine the exact cause of the sneezing and administer treatment accordingly.

TREATMENT: Polyps are not malignant and can be removed by your veterinarian.

TUMORS

CAUSES: Although rare, the nasal cavity can be the site of tumorous growths. The exact cause of these are unknown, but they can pose a threat to dogs.

SYMPTOMS: Discharge through one nostril.

TREATMENT: See your veterinarian as soon as possible. If tumors are immediately detected and are still small, they can easily be removed through surgery. Late treatment, on the other hand, may threaten your dog's life.

SINUSITIS

CAUSES: Sinusitis occurs when the mucus membrane lining the sinuses located in the front of the dog's head becomes inflamed. It can be caused by

PAROXYSMAL SNEEZING: If your dog experiences energetic bouts of sneezing, a foreign object may be stuck in the nose (see Internal Bleeding, p. 258).

3. **BREATHING THROUGH THE MOUTH:** Dogs naturally breath through the nose. This processes the air so that by the time it reaches the lungs, it has been filtered, warmed, and moistened.

   Your dog will breath through his mouth when the temperature is hot, or if both nasal passages are blocked by swollen membranes.

4. **NOSEBLEED** (see Internal Bleeding, p. 258)

5. **REVERSE SNEEZING:** A perfectly healthy dog may suddenly begin to snort loudly, acting as if he is trying to inhale an object caught in his nose. The attack may seem painful and dangerous, but it is most likely reverse sneezing, a harmless reaction brought on by a temporary spasm of the throat muscles. It does not require treatment.

6. **REGURGITATION THROUGH THE NOSE:** Sometimes the loss of a tooth can leave behind a passage in the hard palate of the mouth and the nasal cavity that allows food and water to pass through and causes the dog to regurgitate it through his nose. If you notice water or food coming out of the dog's nose and he has recently lost a tooth, suspect this problem, which is also referred to as an oral-nasal fistula. It can be treated with surgery.

any of several irritants: allergies, a stubbornly emplaced foreign object, an infected tooth root that punctures into a sinus, a tumor, or an infection in the nose that has spread.

SYMPTOMS: Discharge is usually evident in one nostril only; it is rare for two sinuses to be affected at once. If the dog has sinusitis, the nasal discharge will be persistent and chronic. The dog will also sneeze and sniffle.

TREATMENT: After determining the underlying cause, your veterinarian can prescribe the appropriate treatment. Depending on the cause, this may involve prescribing an antihistamine, extracting any foreign objects or tumors that are present, or administering antibiotics.

THE THROAT

Even though his throat has thicker walls and is more elastic than a human's, the dog still suffers from many of the same throat problems that we do. Let us take a look at some of them.

CHOKING (see CHOKING, p. 248)

SWALLOWING SHARP OBJECTS (see INTESTINAL OBSTRUCTION, p. 259)

TONSILLITIS

CAUSES: Like humans, dogs have two beanlike sacs at the back of their throat. These sacs, or tonsils, are responsible for defending the body against bacteria and germs. Tonsillitis occurs when tonsils become irritated and inflamed.

Tonsillitis is more common in young dogs and in some small breeds, such as toys. Puppies, whose susceptibility to disease is high because their immune systems are not fully formed, are vulnerable to tonsillitis. Dogs who weaken during changes in climate may develop tonsillitis after being outside in the rain or on a windy day. However, acute tonsillitis can usually be attributed to an infection.

SYMPTOMS: The dog may be disinterested in food, cough sporadically, and may vomit.

In a severe case, the symptoms are similar to those of a sore throat, except the dog runs a high fever (more than 103 degrees Fahrenheit). The dog refuses food, winces upon swallowing, and may salivate excessively. It may also gag, vomit occasionally, and cough intermittently. If you can see the tonsils when you look inside your dog's mouth, chances are they're inflamed.

TREATMENT: See your veterinarian, who will probably give your dog antibiotics.

While you are awaiting treatment, try putting a bit of honey on the dog's nose. Licking it will help soothe the irritated throat.

11

SKIN AND HAIR PROBLEMS

BECAUSE THE DOG'S COAT performs the protective function that our skin does, a dog's skin does not have to be as thick as ours. Like a person's, however, it consists of multiple layers. The epidermis is a scaly outer layer. It is protective and durable on the dog's nose and feet and vulnerable and delicate beneath the dog's front legs and around the groin.

The dermis is the inner layer of skin. The dog's hair grows from the many follicles embedded here. This layer is also responsible for providing nourishment to the outer layer of skin and to the dog's coat. The many blood vessels circulating through this layer, along with the sebaceous glands, which secrete an oil that coats the hair, perform this function. In humans, the sweat glands are located in the dermal layer. Dogs release sweat through other parts of their body, such as their tongues, and only have sweat glands in the dermal layer of their foot pads.

In human skin, the epidermis and dermis are linked together by ridges. This connective area makes our skin

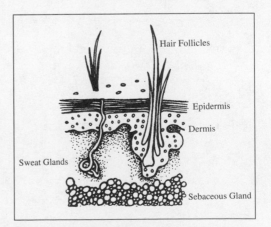

Cross-section of the skin.

139

flexible. Except on the thicker skin of her nose and footpads, the dog has very few of these ridges. The dog's numerous hair follicles help join the two layers.

Many dogs suffer from skin diseases, which tend to develop very rapidly. Frequent scratching, licking, biting, and rubbing are all signs that your dog is searching for relief from a skin disorder.

There are many different types of skin disorders. Some are hereditary, while others can be attributed to emotional factors. Allergies are often the culprit. Accidents, trauma, and environmental irritants such as chemicals and overexposure to light are common causes. Contagious skin diseases like mange are spread through direct contact with an afflicted animal. A dog may pick up an infectious skin disease like ringworm by coming into contact with infected fecal matter. If a dog's hormonal system is not working properly, she may develop certain forms of eczema.

ABSCESSES

CAUSES: Sometimes, after your dog has suffered a blow or has had an accident, the skin over the resulting wound closes before the injury has completely healed. Pus begins to collect beneath the new skin, resulting in a large, infected swelling called an abscess. Abscesses tend to be very painful.

SYMPTOMS: Fever, lethargy, reluctance to move because of pain.

TREATMENT: Veterinary care is required as soon as possible, for two reasons: The abscess is an infection that could spread if left untreated, and the abscess may be a symptom of a larger, more serious problem.

The veterinarian will lance the abscess, avoiding all blood vessels and arteries that may be located near the infection. After the abscess has been lanced, the veterinarian will remove dead material and clean out the abscess cavity by flushing it with an antiseptic solution. Antibiotics may be prescribed to prevent the growth of a new abscess.

ALLERGIES

For many years allergies have been recognized as a major cause of human discomfort. Only recently have we discovered that dogs suffer the same kind of annoying discomfort.

Allergic reactions in dogs can be caused by various foods, by certain insects, and by literally hundreds of specific irritants, including dust, molds, spores, pollens, grasses, smoke, and more.

Telltale signs of allergic reaction include lesions in the skin, hivelike swellings on the head and other parts of the body, a runny nose and eyes, coughing, labored breathing, vomiting, and diarrhea.

If your dog has allergic symptoms, the veterinarian can give her an allergy test. If the test is positive, the veterinarian will then correlate the results with your dog's history, surroundings, habits, care, and food. Once the causative agent is known, it can then be eliminated from the dog's environment. Or, if that is not possible because the cause is unavoidable, your dog can be vaccinated to desensitize her to the material (or materials) that produce the reaction.

ALLERGIC CONTACT DERMATITIS

CAUSES: Dogs, like people, are exposed to irritating chemicals every day. Sometimes contact with chemicals merely causes skin irritation. But a dog who is allergic to a substance and is repeatedly exposed to it will develop a condition called contact irritant dermatitis.

Chemical substances to which many dogs are allergic include flea sprays, poison ivy and poison oak, plastic and rubber dog bowls, and rug dyes.

SYMPTOMS: Contact dermatitis will most likely affect those areas that are vulnerable to chemicals such as the feet, skin, abdomen, groin, and scrotum, causing the skin on those areas to become bumpy, red, and inflamed. Wet pussy abscesses, scabs, blisters, and cuts may also develop in those areas. Your dog will most likely try to scratch the infection.

TREATMENT: After the allergen causing the problem is identified, your dog must be kept away from it. Your veterinarian may recommend cortisone to help relieve the itching and accompanying swelling.

BITES (see DOGFIGHTS, p. 250)

BRUISES

CAUSES: A bruise is formed when capillaries in the soft tissue rupture, often as the result of bumping into a hard object, a blow, or a bite.

SYMPTOMS: If a dog sustains a bruise in an area lacking hair, you should be able to see a blue-red-yellowish mark that is very sensitive to the touch. The dog's hair may conceal the bruise, however, and you may not even know the injury exists until you unknowingly touch it, causing your dog to draw back or wince.

TREATMENT: A bruise usually goes away on its own, with pain disappearing in about a week. For simple bruises, apply cold compresses. Treat any cuts accompanying the bruise (see Dogfights, p. 250). Be on the lookout for lethargy, painful movement, or loss of mobility. Sometimes, a bruise can be indicative of muscle damage, or damage to an internal organ. Seek veterinary treatment if a bruise lasts for more than two weeks, or if you notice any complications.

BURNS (see BURNS, p. 246)

CALLUSES

CAUSES: The bony protrusions at the dog's elbows, hocks (the joints of the back legs), and buttocks are exposed to constant pressure, especially in large,

---

PREVENTING CALLUSES

As calluses are often found on overweight dogs, be sure your dog stays lean. If necessary, put him on a diet (see Obesity, p. 59). This will not only stop callus buildup, but will also improve the dog's overall health.

---

heavy dogs who rest on concrete, tile, or other hard surfaces. Because there is very little tissue covering these protrusions, some dogs develop calluses.

SYMPTOMS: Hairless, thickened, bumpy, grayish patches of skin on any one of these areas that acts as a cushion to reduce the excess strain placed on it. Although calluses can be harmless, they often become infected, developing into oozing sores.

TREATMENT: Give your dog a soft, cushioned surface to sleep on. This may include rubber or foam pads, several layers of bedding, padded rugs, a dog bed, or a trampoline bed.

You may also rub some moisturizer onto the hardened skin. Keeping the callus smooth and elastic may prevent infection.

If the callus is infected, contact your veterinarian, who will prescribe antibiotics or, in extreme cases, perform surgery to remove the irritated tissue.

CHIGGERS

CAUSES: Chiggers, while very difficult to see, pack a wallop when they make contact with human or canine skin. The resulting irritation can be very unpleasant.

A "chigger" is actually a mite, usually yellow, orange, or red in color. A larval chigger feeds on dogs and other mammals—the blood enables them to mature into nymphs. The nymphs develop into adult chiggers, who then lay eggs and start the cycle anew. The adult chiggers feed on plants, so their larvae are usually encountered in wooded areas.

SYMPTOMS: Chiggers can be found almost anywhere on a dog's body, but most often they gravitate toward the head, neck, abdomen, ear canals, and earflaps.

TREATMENT: Your veterinarian probably will apply an insecticidal preparation to the affected areas and prescribe an antibiotic steroid cream to allay the itching and bring down the swelling.

PREVENTION: If your dog is going into the woods during warm weather, apply an insecticidal preparation (the same one as for Fleas, p. 143) before she leaves the house.

CUTS

TREATMENT: For simple, superficial cuts, first control bleeding (see Control of Bleeding, p. 240). When the bleeding has stopped, trim all hair away from affected area. Use tweezers to remove any foreign objects such as glass or pebbles. Run warm water over the cut, then clean it gently with a 3 percent hydrogen peroxide solution, applying it with a cotton swab. This should clear out all remaining dirt and bacteria. If the cut is in the footpad, finish the process by applying a bandage (see bandaging a paw, p. 86). Watch for bleeding.

DERMATITIS

CAUSES: Dogs experience hay fever just as humans do. Rather than becoming congested and sneezy after inhaling the irritating pollen, however, dogs come down with bothersome itchy skin.

The allergy is usually progressive. In a typical case the dog first starts itching in the ragweed season of August and September. As she becomes sensitized to other substances, she also starts itching in the tree-pollen season of March and April, and then in the grass-pollen season of May, June, and early July. Finally the condition becomes a year-round problem because the dog begins to react to other substances such as house dust and mold.

Dermatitis seldom occurs in dogs younger than six months old; it usually begins in dogs one to three years old.

Any breed can be affected, but some breeds are especially susceptible. These include West Highland White Terriers, Dalmatians, Poodles, and White-Haired Fox Terriers.

SYMPTOMS: Intensive scratching. Sometimes the scratching is accompanied by a runny nose, watery eyes, and the rubbing of bothered areas on a carpet.

TREATMENT: Ask your veterinarian to run a skin test on your dog to determine the cause of the allergy. Cortisone and a series of injections to stop the allergic sensitivity may then be administered.

FLEAS

CAUSES: Every spring since ancient times, fleas have welcomed dogs into springtime. The extremes of the flea's destructiveness are wildly varied—from the mild itching and irritation any well-groomed domestic dog may undergo to the unprecedented campaign of death that rat fleas waged on Europe during the bubonic plagues.

Today's dog is most likely to encounter the *Ctenocephalides canis*, a tiny, jumping organism that can easily land on your dog while she wanders through grass and bushes. The flea sees your dog as a source of blood, which is a prerequisite for the flea's egg-laying. Once the flea drinks its share, it will usually hop off the dog and land on a surface inside your house, such as a

Enlarged depiction of the flea most likely to affect your dog. You will be able to see the flea, its eggs, or both on your dog's skin.

stretch of carpeting or a bed, where it may lay some of its eggs.

SYMPTOMS: If you see your dog scratching, shaking, and biting as if it is trying to rid its fur of an irritant, chances are it may be playing host to fleas.

Start to look for fleas by pushing the fur back around the neck, along the back, and on the rear end and belly. You are looking for tiny brown bouncing specks. Another sign of flea infestation is black-and-white particles resembling sand. These are flea eggs and waste material.

TREATMENT: Before you start to treat your dog, you need to rid your house of fleas. Start by thoroughly scouring the area where your dog sleeps. Wash all bedding and place in a hot dryer. Then, vacuum every surface possible, including rugs, carpets, drapes, and furniture. Waxing the floors may increase the likelihood of killing stray fleas and their eggs.

Exterminators provide welcome relief if your own efforts are unsuccessful. It usually takes one spring and one mid-summer treatment to get the job done. If you live in a warm, humid climate, you should exterminate once a month.

As for treating the dog, the most effective action you can take is an insecticide dip. Do this about twice a month until you are certain there are no more fleas in your dog's coat. As further protection, spray short-haired breeds and apply powder to long-haired dogs in between dips.

Flea collars are not always effective, provide only local protection, and can actually cause significant discomfort to your dog's eyes and skin. Dogs who wear flea collars must have their necks checked for inflammation regularly. An inflamed neck indicates an allergy or severe sensitivity to the chemicals in the collar. Also, you will need to be sure that the collar is not too tight, impeding your dog's intake of air. Make certain the dog never chews the collar and that the collar never becomes wet. Wet collars must be replaced.

Keep in mind that puppies should never wear flea collars; nor should they be powdered until they are at least two months old. If your puppy has fleas, ask your veterinarian to recommend an effective treatment.

Treating older dogs for fleas is also problematic. They are prone to Flea Allergy Dermatitis (see p. 145). Certain physiological changes associated with aging make them poor candidates for common poisons used to kill fleas. Therefore, talk to your veterinarian before beginning any form of flea treatment for an older dog.

A NATURAL SOLUTION TO FLEAS

In keeping with today's interest in natural medicine, here is an approach that uses no chemicals. First, wash your dog in warm (but not hot) water, scrubbing her down with soap. Then, have her sit in the water for about a quarter of an hour. Be sure you keep her relaxed and preoccupied during this time; otherwise, you may have a hard time getting her to stay put. This stage of the process should eliminate all fleas that have thus far been submerged. Finally, wash all areas that have not been underwater with a cooled mixture of one teaspoon of dried rosemary boiled in a potful of water. This nontoxic herbal remedy is very effective and gives off a very pleasant aroma.

PREVENTION: There are many different "tricks" people have used over the years to ward off fleas. It is possible that one teaspoon of brewer's yeast (mixed into the dog's regular meal) may keep fleas away. Because this powdery substance is rich in various B vitamins, this treatment can be beneficial regardless of its effect on fleas. Also, ask your veterinarian about Proban, a product that can kill a flea once it has bitten your dog, thereby decreasing the rate of infestation in the house. Finally, check your dog for infestation every day during flea season, concentrating on her abdomen and inner thighs.

persisting even after the fleas have been expelled.

SYMPTOMS: Severe scratching around the back and the tail. Dogs often back up against something they can rub their bottoms against. If you observe the skin closely you will notice fleas and small, red bumps.

TREATMENT: You must, of course, rid the dog of the fleas that caused the reaction in the first place. Your veterinarian may then prescribe cortisone tablets or injections to prevent the allergic reaction and soothe the itch.

FLEA ALLERGY DERMATITIS

CAUSES: Some unfortunate dogs are allergic to flea saliva, and once bitten they will break out in an itchy rash.

An allergic reaction to a flea bite can be immediate or delayed, with itching

HIVES

CAUSES: Hives are most commonly caused either by an allergy to a food foreign to the dog, or by insect bites. Hives caused by insect bites usually disappear in twenty-four hours.

SYMPTOMS: In dogs, hives are fast-appearing welts that contain patches of hair. Facial hives are common and often involve the eyelids.

TREATMENT: Your veterinarian will probably prescribe antihistamines and cold packs to relieve the itchiness.

If the veterinarian is able to determine that the hives were triggered by a food allergen, an enema or laxative may be suggested. This will expel all traces of the irritating food from the body.

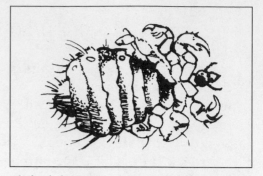

A single louse. You are more likely to see eggs in your dog's hair than lice themselves.

LICE

CAUSES: Lice infestation is uncommon among dogs, especially those who live in clean quarters and get consistent care.

Lice are flat, gray, wingless insects about a twelfth of an inch long. Lice move very slowly, if they move at all. There are two types of lice: One is content to chew on skin flakes; suckling lice, however, prefer a meal of tissue fluids. They cause more irritation because they must penetrate the skin in order to feed.

Animal lice carry disease and cause intense irritation. Their presence also may lead to complications such as anemia, so they must not be ignored.

SYMPTOMS: Intense scratching and irritation, often resulting in bald patches. Commonly infested sites include the ears, neck, shoulders, and anus.

Lice eggs (nits) are easier to see than an adult louse. Nits are attached to the hair and look like tiny white flakes of dust.

TREATMENT: Lice are relatively easy to treat, as they have not built up a resistance to insecticides. Cut off matted hair and wash the dog once a week in an insecticidal dip, such as one effective against fleas, until there is no more itching. For very young puppies afflicted with lice, see your veterinarian.

It's a good idea to discard the bedding your dog has slept on during infestation and to disinfect her sleeping area. This should prevent further infestation, and give you peace of mind.

LICK SORES

CAUSES: Large, short-haired dogs who are left alone for long periods of time or who have reached middle age and have become less active are vulnerable to lick sores. They are caused by anxiousness, when a bored dog begins to habitually lick a particular area, rubbing off her hair and irritating the skin.

A dog creates lick sores by continually licking a specific area, usually on one of his limbs.

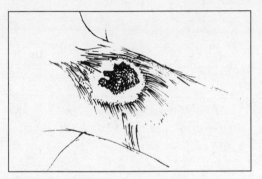

Close-up of a lick sore. Immediate at-home treatment is required to prevent infection.

SYMPTOMS: Lick sores begin as raised, thick, callused, bare patches of skin found mainly on the lower half of the forelegs, near the waist, or on the hind legs. Over time, the affected areas will turn gray.

TREATMENT: Because a deep lick sore is difficult to treat, it's important that you take action as soon as possible.

Start by bandaging the affected area (see Bandaging a Dog, p. 85). If your dog licks or chews through the bandage material, fasten an Elizabethan collar around her neck (see Elizabethan Collars box, p. 88). This should prevent your dog from disrupting the healing process. As a further precaution, coat the affected area with a bitter, nontoxic substance—one should be available at your local pet store.

If the sore isn't healing, your veterinarian may decide to inject the area surrounding the sore with cortisone or

PREVENTING LICK SORES

Sometimes, a lick sore is a cry for attention. Bored dogs crave more companionship. To prevent future lick sores from occurring, take your dog for more walks. Hold your dog more, and speak to her with love and enthusiasm. Make sure she has plenty of her favorite toys available when you are unable to provide her with human interaction.

cobra venom. Both have proven to be effective, safe remedies.

MANGE (DEMODECTIC)

The *Demodex canis* mite, an elongated, eight-legged creature, causes demodectic mange. It is commonly believed that most dogs carry around Demodex mites in their hair follicles. Puppies often acquire these mites from their mother. When the mites begin an intense period of propagation, demodectic (or "red") mange results. Demodectic mange takes two forms: localized and generalized.

LOCALIZED DEMODECTIC MANGE

CAUSES: Mostly affects dogs in their first year of life, and is confined to specific sites.

SYMPTOMS: Small bald patches on the face, forelegs, and around the eyes.

TREATMENT: While localized demodectic mange usually clears up by itself, it is wise to consult your veterinarian. It is possible for the layperson to confuse this disorder with ringworm (see Ringworm, p. 149). Also, an outbreak of demodectic mange in puppies could indicate a weakened immune system, which needs a veterinarian's attention.

GENERALIZED DEMODECTIC MANGE

CAUSES: Spreads throughout the body and can be acquired at any age.

Generalized demodectic mange causes patches throughout the coat, requiring immediate treatment.

It can be serious and even life-threatening.

SYMPTOMS: Rapid growth of patches throughout coat; infection of patches with pus formation.

TREATMENT: Seek veterinary help immediately. A skin soaping will reveal the presence of generalized demodectic mange. Antibiotics and anti-mite treatment will be prescribed.

MANGE (SARCOPTIC)

CAUSES: Sarcoptic mange is a parasitic skin condition commonly known as canine scabies. It is caused by a spiderlike mite called *Sarcoptes scabei*. This rapidly burrowing mite can spread from dog to dog and from dog to human. Mite eggs take three to ten days to hatch once the eggs are laid just a few millimeters under the skin.

SYMPTOMS: Intense scratching, biting, and/or licking. Loss of hair, reddened, encrusted skin. Irritated areas concentrated at edges of the ears, legs, elbows, lower chest, and face.

You may also notice small, red, raised bumps on the skin of those people who come in contact with your dog.

TREATMENT: If you suspect sarcoptic mange, seek veterinary care. Your veterinarian will perform a series of skin tests to determine if your dog is infested, direct you to topical medications that will kill the sarcoptic mites, and may provide an anti-inflammatory drug to relieve swelling and itching in the affected areas. If an infection has resulted from the scratching, an antibiotic may also be necessary. Be sure to change any bedding your dog has slept on during infestation.

NOTE: If you have been affected by your dog's bout with sarcoptic mange, ask your own doctor for treatment advice.

PORCUPINE QUILLS

CAUSES: A dog who has foolishly attacked a porcupine makes a sorry sight. The porcupine's powerful quills are an excellent weapon against predators. Most of the quills that are used on a dog will wind up on and around her mouth.

TREATMENT: Contact your veterinarian, who will give your dog a general anesthetic and remove the quills in such a way as to avoid infection. Do not try to remove the quills yourself. Your dog may experience acute pain when you pull the quill from the puncture wound. You may also accidentally break a quill, leaving behind a fragment and exposing your dog to infection.

RINGWORM

CAUSES: Ringworm is a fungal disease caused by *Microsporum canis* or *Microsporum gypseum*—it is not caused by a worm, as was originally believed. Dogs pick up the fungus from the ground, by sniffing around waste material, and even through contact with people. It is most common in hot, steamy climates like the American South.

SYMPTOMS: One or more hairless, flaky, reddish or grayish, one-half to two-inch-sized circular patches on the

Ringworm appears as a circular formation, usually in the head region.

dog's skin, especially on the skin around the head. Those patches may have scabs on them, but your dog generally will have no interest in scratching them.

TREATMENT: A veterinarian should be able to detect ringworm by using an ultraviolet light and will probably advise you to trim the hair around the affected area and use a special shampoo, as well as a topical ointment, for several months. More severe cases may require a prescription of griseofulvin, which is given orally for one to two months.

WARNING: Ringworm is contagious. Humans can pick up ringworm from dogs and vice versa. Children should *not* handle dogs with ringworm because their immature immune systems render them more vulnerable to the disease. Adults, it seems, are more resistant.

SEBACEOUS CYST

CAUSES: A sebaceous cyst is a growth that obstructs the sweat gland. Commonly found in older dogs, these cysts are harmless and frequently grow along the back.

TREATMENT: A sebaceous cyst usually takes care of itself. If it pops, a cheesy liquid will be released. To prevent recurrence or infection, squeeze the popped cyst free of all liquid, then flush the area generously with soap and lukewarm water. You can also apply a diluted antiseptic solution, such as hydrogen peroxide.

If the cyst does not heal and continues to discharge, your veterinarian will have to surgically remove it.

TICKS

CAUSES: Ticks are flat insects about the size of a small kernel of corn. Dog ticks live for anywhere from ten to twenty-three weeks, depending upon their ability to find a host upon which to prey. The female needs blood in order to mate and survive. Once it finds a host, it fastens its legs to a hair shaft and inserts its mouth through the skin, usually on the dog's underbelly, chest, front legs, or head. When it is securely fastened, it will mate with a male tick. A feeding female swells significantly.

After it has mated, it will lay eggs—often up to 5,000 of them. These eggs can incubate in crevices all over your house. Given a warm enough environ-

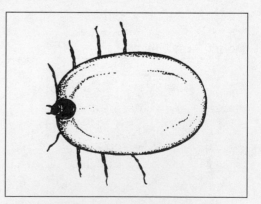

Enlarged depiction of a tick, which may carry one of several dangerous diseases including Lyme disease.

WHEN YOUR DOG ENCOUNTERS A SKUNK

Dogs frequently meet with skunks in rural areas. Surprisingly, skunks occasionally make their way into the suburbs and even cities. That's why the following remedy could be useful no matter where you live.

After putting on some rubber gloves, wash your dog with mild baby shampoo and warm water, then rub plain tomato juice or milk into her coat.

After soaking the dog in tomato juice or milk, thoroughly bathe her, again in mild shampoo and warm water. This will work—but you may have to repeat the washings several times.

---

ment, ticks can breed at any time of the year.

Ticks can be very dangerous creatures, posing a threat to both dogs and people. Rocky Mountain spotted fever, tularemia, Lyme disease (see Lyme Disease, p. 113), and encephalitis are all conditions that can be spread from ticks to humans.

Besides causing skin irritation and itching, ticks can do serious damage to a dog. Certain varieties of dog ticks, including the scrub and bush varieties, emit a poisonous substance that can actually paralyze their hosts.

SYMPTOMS: See Lyme Disease, p. 113.

PREVENTION: Before your dog goes into an area containing dense vegetation, use a veterinarian-approved flea-and-tick spray. Also, keep the grass and plant life around your house well groomed. This will cut down on the amount of ticks your dog may encounter. To remove a tick, see box Removing a Tick, p. 114.

WARTS

SYMPTOMS: Warts, common among geriatric dogs, are small, fleshy bumps appearing throughout the skin. They are harmless unless your dog scratches or bites them. The skin can form ulcers and become infected, requiring treatment.

TREATMENT: If you want to try to treat simple warts at home, try applying castor oil to the affected area.

Warts also can be easily removed surgically by your veterinarian. *Do not* try to do this yourself with scissors, because there can be profuse bleeding.

WOUNDS (see DOGFIGHTS, p. 250)

THE HAIR

Your dog's protective fur is actually a combination of two different coats. The rugged outer coat consists of primary or "guard" hairs; the fluffy undercoat consists of secondary hairs. Both these hairs grow together in complexes from follicles lining the dermal, or inner, layer of skin.

Each hair follicle is supplied by blood, which transports nutrition to the hair and sustains it. This is why the condition of your dog's coat can tell you a lot about her general health.

When a dog is feeling particularly aggressive, her hair will stand erect. Most of the hair follicles are attached to a tiny muscle that can pull the hair to a "standing" position.

Let's take a look at some of the hair problems that can afflict dogs.

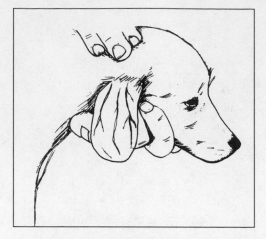

Some dogs are particularly susceptible to hair loss (alopecia) on the ear flap.

BALDNESS

CAUSES: Many dogs suffer some form of hair loss. Dietary deficiencies or hormonal disorders are common causes. External parasites can also trigger hair loss, which is literally scratched away by the irritated host.

SYMPTOMS: Spots of exposed skin, often but not always accompanied by scratching.

TREATMENT: See your veterinarian, who must determine the cause in order to treat the condition.

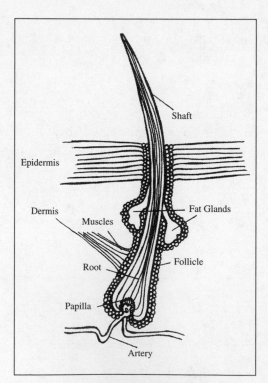

Cross-section of a single hair follicle.

Labels: Shaft, Epidermis, Dermis, Muscles, Fat Glands, Root, Follicle, Papilla, Artery

DANDRUFF

CAUSES: Dandruff, which looks like tiny white flakes, is usually caused by insufficient oils or fats in the diet. Dogs who rarely go outside, as well as those who get many baths, are also susceptible to the problem. Some dandruff is actually caused by a more serious problem—external parasites. Dandruff in puppies is commonly caused by worms.

TREATMENT: A veterinarian will first determine why the skin is flaking. Once the cause is determined (and treated, if necessary) you can begin to treat the skin. Your veterinarian might recommend first washing the dog with an alcohol solution to eliminate the excess flakes. Then a bland oil or hair tonic containing lanolin can be rubbed into the coat. Some veterinarians also recommend an oil rubdown once a week, with the oil being massaged right into the skin.

SHEDDING

CAUSES: Undomesticated dogs shed their coat twice a year, to help them cope with the elements. In spring, the coat begins to thin out to guarantee coolness against summer heat. In the fall, the thin summer coat falls out, to be replaced by the thick winter hair that protects against the cold. Nature's calendar triggers shedding; the dog's body responds to changes in the number of daylight hours. Shorter days lead to shedding in preparation for the thick coat's growth; longer days lead to shedding for summer. Dogs who stay inside under electronically produced light respond to this artificial stimulus by shedding more than they need to—some even shed throughout the year.

TREATMENT: If your dog is shedding large amounts of hair, first make sure that she is properly groomed. This is especially important in breeds with thick coats. The goal of grooming is to remove dead hair, which acts as an annoying abrasive when next to the skin (see Grooming, p. 61). First bathe, then brush.

12

RESPIRATORY SYSTEM PROBLEMS

AIR ENTERS THE dog's respiratory system through one of two openings: the nose or the mouth. At the back of the mouth, nestled in the throat, is the voice box, or larynx. The larynx is a cartilage-based structure that houses a dog's very prominent vocal cords. A dog produces his barking sound by forcefully pushing air from the lungs through the larynx.

Opening up from behind the larynx is the trachea, a tube made up of rings of cartilage. It leads down to the lungs, where it divides into the bronchial tubes. The bronchial tubes further divide into bronchi. From the bronchi, the air passes into tiny balloonlike sacs called alveoli, which are covered with tiny blood vessels. The blood absorbs oxygen and releases carbon dioxide through the walls of the alveoli.

Oxygen is moved in and out of the lungs by means of the ribs, muscles, and diaphragm. All must be working together in order for proper breathing to occur. Your dog's breathing should be even and free. Choppy, noisy, or obstructed breathing usually signals that something is affecting the complex respiratory system.

HOW TO RECOGNIZE PROBLEMS IN BREATHING

PANTING

While normal panting helps a dog lower his temperature, frantic, tense

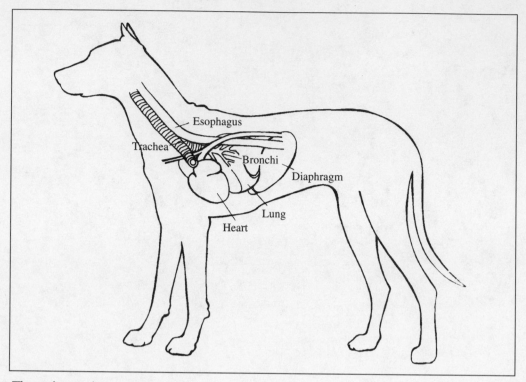

The canine respiratory system.

panting could indicate heat distress or respiratory problems.

LABORED BREATHING

An inflamed voice box can produce squeaky, forced breathing. This is usually due to laryngitis, but it can also be caused by the presence of a tumor or foreign object in the larynx area. Call your veterinarian if your dog demonstrates labored breathing.

SNORTING

If your dog is breathing loudly, something could be blocking his breathing passage.

RAPID RESPIRATION

Quick, forced breathing, sometimes heard while at rest, has many possible causes, including injury, anxiety, fever, heatstroke, shock, lung or heart disease, and dehydration. As it can indicate serious illness, contact your veterinarian if you notice your dog breathing rapidly.

FAINT BREATHING

A dog will breathe faintly if a full, deep breath inflicts pain. It usually indicates that the normal expansion of the rib cage is hindered. Pleurisy and rib fractures might be the cause of this type of breathing. Call your veterinarian.

UNDERSTANDING YOUR DOG'S COUGH

When an irritant disturbs a dog's breathing, the coughing mechanism is triggered, enabling the dog to force the irritant from his air passages. Persistent coughing may indicate an allergy, infection, or disease, indicating the need for professional attention.

Here are some tips on "translating" your dog's cough:

1. A low, wheezy cough suggests bronchitis.
2. A forceful, dehydrated, convulsive cough is symptomatic of kennel cough (see Kennel Cough, p. 112).
3. A wet, gurgling cough is caused by the presence of phlegm and may be a sign of pneumonia.
4. A persistent cough that occurs after exercise could mean your dog has heart disease.

Never ignore your dog's coughing, especially if it is persistent; to do so may compromise your dog's chances for treatment and recovery.

WHEEZING

Wheezing is strained breathing that involves a whistling sound. A dog's wheezing is usually a sign that something is wrong with his windpipe or bronchial tubes. Tumors, spasms, chronic lung disease, and congestive heart failure may be at the root of the problem. Call your veterinarian.

ASTHMA

CAUSES: Asthma is an allergic reaction primarily to pollen that irritates the dog's bronchial air tubes and can lead to lung disease. Fortunately, asthma is not common in dogs.

SYMPTOMS: Coughing and wheezing.

TREATMENT: In addition to removing your dog from an environment that is likely to cause attacks, your veterinarian might recommend liquid antihistamines, which can open the breathing tube and minimize respiratory difficulties.

BRONCHITIS

CAUSES: Bronchitis is a respiratory infection that attacks the walls lining the bronchial tubes, causing them to become inflamed and to cut off the regular oxygen supply to the dog. Dogs who have suffered from another respiratory illness are the most vulnerable to coming down with bronchitis, which typically attacks weakened immune systems.

SYMPTOMS: Dogs with chronic bronchitis cough persistently. The cough is deep and wheezy. If the dog is intensely aroused, the cough will be more exaggerated and the dog may retch up thick saliva. Fever may also be present.

TREATMENT: Seek veterinary assistance. The veterinarian may prescribe antibiotics after taking a culture of the dog's phlegm.

CHEST WOUNDS
(see CHEST WOUNDS, p. 248)

COLDS

Coughing, a runny nose, sickly eyes, and a fever may make you think that your dog has a cold. Don't be fooled, however. The common cold is not common in the canine kingdom. Such symptoms may indicate serious illness such as distemper. If the cold lasts for more than two days, or if the symptoms worsen, call your veterinarian as soon as possible.

KENNEL COUGH
(see KENNEL COUGH, p. 112)

PNEUMONIA

CAUSES: Pneumonia is an inflammation of the tissues in the lungs. It can be caused by the ingestion of bacteria, fungus, parasites, or any other viral agent. Pneumonia is uncommon in dogs because this disease is often a secondary infection that follows some other health problem, such as distemper. Pneumonia can be avoided by treating the primary illness quickly and efficiently.

SYMPTOMS: High fever; rapid breathing; a deep moist cough; rapid pulse; rattling and bubbling in the chest.

TREATMENT: Veterinary attention is required if your dog has contracted pneumonia. Once the veterinarian has determined the cause of the infection, he or she will administer antibiotics.

At home, encourage the dog to rest in a warm room. Run a humidifier in the area to ease breathing difficulties. Do not try to quiet his coughing by administering cough medicine. As discussed earlier, coughing is a reflex dogs use to clear their irritated airways and it may help them to get over the pneumonia.

13

MUSCULOSKELETAL SYSTEM PROBLEMS

THE SKELETAL SYSTEMS of humans and dogs have much in common. The main differences occur because humans evolved into two-legged creatures. Thus, for example, the dog's phalanges are analogous to a human's toes.

The 319 bones in the average dog's skeleton are of two major types: tubular bones, such as those located in the limbs, and flat bones, such as those that make up the shoulder blades. These bones vary in length and thickness within dogs of different breeds.

The outside of a dog's bone is called the cortex. It is composed of minerals and protein. It gives the bone its rigidity. Inside is bone marrow, which is important in red blood cell production.

The links between bones, or joints, act as shock absorbers. Each joint is surrounded by a joint capsule, which contains a substance called synovial fluid that lubricates and nourishes the joint. A protective layer of cartilage over the bone ends helps the joint move easily by keeping the bones from grating on each other.

The bones of the body are held together by connective tissue called ligaments. Ligaments stabilize joints and increase the mobility of limbs.

Surrounding the dog's bone and attached to it is the muscle. Muscles maneuver the bones, contracting in order to draw them together or relaxing to release them. The nervous system directs the muscles by carrying electrical impulses to them from the brain.

When a dog eats, gallops after a tennis ball, or even curls up in her favorite nap area, she is demonstrating musculoskeletal functions that have taken thousands of years to evolve. Any sign that this system is not properly operat-

159

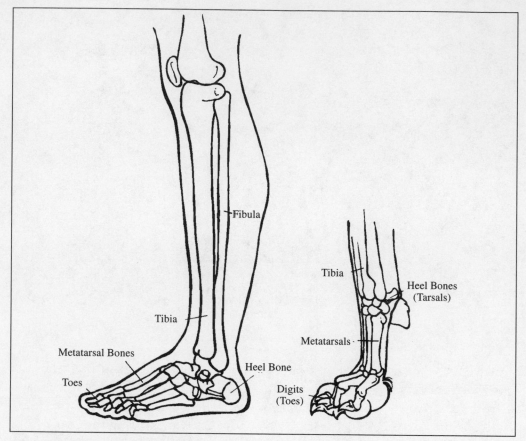

Comparing the human and canine lower limb.

ing may be cause for concern and should be regarded seriously.

AMPUTATION
(see AMPUTATION, p. 244)

ARTHRITIS

CAUSES: Arthritis is characterized by the inflammation of one or more joints. This painful ailment seems mainly to bother large, heavy dogs whose joints are under excess strain because of their weight. It also attacks any dog who has subjected her joints to abnormal wear and tear, has nutritional deficiencies such as a shortage of calcium, has inherited arthritic tendencies, has suffered accidental trauma, has a local infection that has spread into the joint, or is approaching old age.

SYMPTOMS: The symptoms of arthritis vary depending on the form. Dogs suffering from acute arthritis will limp and nurse their irritated limbs. The inflamed joint will be warm and soft to the touch. The pain may eventually subside.

A dog suffering from chronic arthritis will have trouble standing after periods of rest and may move around with more difficulty. The inflamed joint will be firm and less warm to the touch. The pain will persist.

TREATMENT: Ask your veterinarian to take X rays. If the cause of the arthritis can be pinpointed and is curable, your veterinarian may be able to treat it. For example, if an infection is at the root of the arthritis, antibiotics will be administered. If excess weight is putting undue stress on a joint, your dog will be placed on a diet.

If your veterinarian cannot cure the cause of the arthritis, he or she may prescribe painkillers like butazolidin or cortisone preparations. She will also advise you on how to enable the dog to lead a happy life. This will involve making sure your dog has warm quarters to sleep in and arranging her life so that she doesn't have to walk up and down stairs.

DISLOCATED JOINT

CAUSES: Trauma from a car accident, fall, or other forceful blow can dislocate and rupture a joint.

SYMPTOMS: Your dog will be in pain and will refuse to use the injured limb. In severe cases in which the dislocation is complete, your dog may also show symptoms of shock and internal bleeding (see Shock, p. 261, and Internal Bleeding, p. 258).

TREATMENT: Your veterinarian will reposition the joint in its socket and administer treatment for any additional injuries.

HIP DYSPLASIA

CAUSES: Hip dysplasia is a genetic disorder that causes the hip joint to degenerate rapidly. The joint should be a neatly fitting ball and socket; hip dysplasia loosens its fit, causing it to wear more rapidly than normal. Sometimes, this condition leads to arthritis (see Arthritis, p. 160), characterized by the erosion of the hip's soft cartilage, which is in turn replaced by bone. A dog with a full-blown case of hip dysplasia may lose mobility of the hind legs.

Larger breeds are particularly prone to this disease, especially those that grow fastest during the first four months of life. The powerful muscles of the Greyhound usually prevent this large breed from developing hip dysplasia.

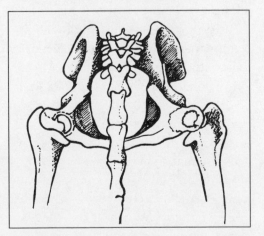

The right hip joint has deteriorated due to hip dysplasia, a genetic disorder.

HIP DYSPLASIA AND BREEDING YOUR DOG

Hip dysplasia can be eliminated only through selective breeding. If your dog has hip dysplasia, do not breed it. If you are purchasing a puppy and plan to breed it, always ask breeders for proof that she does not have hip dysplasia in her family.

SYMPTOMS: Hip dysplasia usually begins to appear during the first four to nine months, when a puppy grows most rapidly. The most obvious effect of this condition is pain in the hip, often evidenced by a limp or wavering gait. She may have difficulty running and jumping and may wince when attempting to rise from a sitting position. The position of the dog's hind limbs becomes distorted, with the knees meeting while the feet point outward.

TREATMENT: The veterinarian will use radiographs to make a definite diagnosis.

Because there is no cure for hip dysplasia, the goal of treatment is to help your dog adjust to her condition. The veterinarian may prescribe analgesics to relieve the pain.

At home, make sure your dog sleeps in a dry area free of drafts, as cold can aggravate this condition.

Dogs with hip dysplasia don't have to be sedentary; exercise is good for all dogs. However, your dog is the only one who can accurately measure just how painful movement is on any given day, so let her set the pace of exercise.

Watch your dog's weight. Even a few extra pounds can exacerbate this condition by putting extra stress on the affected joints.

Dogs with hip dysplasia can get on with their lives as long as they have support in adapting to the condition. Only if the pain is so unbearable that your dog is constantly suffering should you consider euthanasia (see Chapter Eight).

MUSCLE STRAIN

Just like humans, a dog can strain a muscle as the result of overexertion.

SYMPTOMS: Your dog will limp. The injured area will feel swollen and tender when you touch it.

TREATMENT: See Sprains, p. 164.

OSTEOCHONDRITIS DESSICANS (OCD)

CAUSES: Osteochondritis dessicans (OCD) is a condition caused by the development of abnormally thick joint cartilage that is highly vulnerable to damage. The actual cartilage cracks easily, causing pain and sometimes lameness. One or both shoulders is most often affected. Puppies who have excessive growth spurts between the ages of four and nine months are most vulnerable to this injury. Large breeds like the Saint Bernard, Doberman, Kuvasz, and Swiss Mountain Dogs are most susceptible.

SYMPTOMS: A dog afflicted with OCD will suffer pain in the affected joint and will eventually limp.

TREATMENT: Consult your veterinarian. Radiography will confirm if OCD is present. Surgery is often recommended, as are pain relievers.

PATELLAR DISLOCATION (SLIPPING KNEECAP)

CAUSES: Your dog's kneecap is held in a groove, called the patellar groove, by ligaments. When the kneecap is surrounded by weak ligaments, pulled by poorly aligned ligaments, or badly housed in the patellar groove, it can pop out. This condition is called slipping kneecap or patellar dislocation. It occurs mainly in toy breeds, such as the Maltese Terrier, the Toy Poodle, Pomeranians, and Chihuahuas due to hereditary defects.

SYMPTOMS: The dog will have difficulty straightening the knee and may whine with pain. The dog may seem to "present" the affected leg. The kneecap may then spontaneously fall back into its groove and the dog's leg will return to normal.

TREATMENT: If the kneecap remains out of the groove, carefully massage the knee while extending and flexing the dog's leg. If the condition persists, contact your veterinarian, who may recommend surgery to fix the kneecap.

RICKETS

CAUSES: This nutritional disorder is one very good reason not to feed your dog an all-meat diet. Meat is too low in calcium; when its level in the blood falls, calcium is reabsorbed from the bones, which results in their weakening. Such bones break easily and in some cases collapse.

SYMPTOMS: You may notice a swelling on the dog's underside caused by an inflammation of the joints connecting the rib bones to the cartilage of the sternum. The legs will appear deformed, bowed outward. Adult dogs may also have fractured bones.

TREATMENT: Your veterinarian will probably recommend a calcium carbonate supplement, along with a correction in diet.

PREVENTION: Be sure your dog is eating a balanced diet (see Your Dog's Nutritional Requirements, p. 54).

SPRAINS

CAUSES: Sometimes the ligaments surrounding a joint can suddenly become stretched or torn. This is called a sprain.

SYMPTOMS: Your dog will experience pain, will avoid putting weight on the injured leg, and may limp. You may notice swelling around the affected joint.

TREATMENT: In order to treat a sprain, you need to reduce the swelling it causes. Place a cold wrap on the injured area for a couple of hours, changing it every hour. To make a cold wrap, put crushed ice in a plastic bag. Close the bag and place it on the damaged limb. Secure it by loosely wrapping a stretchable bandage around it.

The dog should rest and enjoy minimal activity for a day or two. Do not give her aspirin or other painkillers, since this may reduce the pain and encourage her to move about.

Do not apply any liniments or preparations designed for human sprains. Your dog's skin is very sensitive and can be damaged easily by these preparations.

WARNING: Watch for complications like increased swelling or intensifying pain, or if your dog still exhibits severe difficulty in walking two days after the injury occurs. Those signs may indicate a more extensive injury—possibly a fracture. Seek veterinary assistance.

TENDINITIS

CAUSES: A tendon connects muscle to bone. It is dense and fibrous, and can become inflamed through injury or overuse. A sudden jerking motion can also cause a flareup.

SYMPTOMS: Pain, swelling, stiffness, possible lameness (indicates tendon rupture).

TREATMENT: Simple tendinitis usually goes away if the afflicted tendon is rested. Reduce exercise substantially and ask your veterinarian about suitable pain relievers if your dog is suffering. If immobility persists, consult your veterinarian. A more serious condition, such as tendon rupture, might be present, possibly requiring surgery.

14

CIRCULATORY SYSTEM PROBLEMS

THE DOG'S CIRCULATORY SYSTEM is like the human circulatory system in many ways. It is comprised of a complex network of blood vessels that lead to and from a powerful organ called the heart. As this circulatory system is crucial to your dog's vitality, it is important to understand how a healthy one works.

The heart, resting in the middle of the dog's chest, consists of two pumps. The left pump acts as a dispatcher, sending out oxygen-enriched blood to the aorta and then to the many blood vessels woven throughout the body. The blood nourishes the body's tissues with oxygen and, in turn, picks up the body's waste products, such as carbon dioxide.

The oxygen-poor blood then travels through the veins back to the heart, where it is received by the right pump.

The right pump sends blood into the pulmonary artery and then to the capillaries in the lung, where the carbon dioxide is exchanged for oxygen. From the lungs, a pumping movement sends the oxygen-rich blood back to the left chamber of the heart, thus completing the cycle.

The heartbeat—the heart's contractions that move the blood along—is what you are measuring when you take a dog's pulse (see How to Take Your Dog's Pulse, p. 84). The pulse rate should be steady, since it is controlled by the dog's internal nervous system. The pulse can vary due to exercise and excitement; too much variation, however, may indicate a problem. An increased heart rate, for example, could be caused by fever, heatstroke, anemia, blood loss, dehydration, shock, or

165

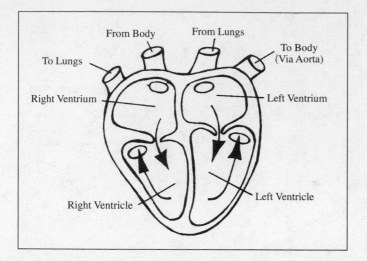

The canine heart is a four-chambered organ.

infection. A slowed heart rate, on the other hand, could be brought on by heart disease. An erratic heart rate suggests arrythmia or other serious ailments. Since the condition of a dog's heart is a good indicator of both illness and good health, read on to learn about the diseases and problems that can debilitate the circulatory system.

ANEMIA

CAUSES: Anemia is a condition occurring as the result of a reduced number of red blood cells and/or a reduction in the amount of hemoglobin in the blood. Hemoglobin is the red-pigmented part of the blood that carries life-giving oxygen.

Blood loss due to an accident or the presence of heartworm or hookworms can cause anemia.

When red blood cell production slows significantly, anemia can result.

This can be triggered by Vitamin E and iron deficiency, low-protein diets, infections, or possibly poisoning.

The destruction of red blood cells by poison, parasites, or defects in the immune system can also create an anemic condition.

SYMPTOMS: Lethargy, pale gums, listlessness, excessive sleeping, lack of interest in food, weight loss, emaciation, dehydration.

TREATMENT: Consult your veterinarian, who will probably take a blood sample to determine the cause of anemia.

The treatment will vary depending on the cause. The veterinarian will probably advise you to feed your dog large quantities of liver and red meat, along with supplements of iron and vitamins. She or he may also give your dog blood transfusions until his body can reproduce more blood cells.

HEART FAILURE

CAUSES: Heart failure occurs when the body demands more oxygen than the heart is capable of supplying. The pumping mechanism slows, and blood backs up.

SYMPTOMS: Symptoms differ according to whether the diseased heart begins to weaken on the right or left side.

LEFT-SIDE HEART FAILURE

When the left side of the heart starts to fail, there is a rise in pressure in the blood returning from the lungs, forcing small amounts of fluid out into them. This hinders the exchange of oxygen for carbon dioxide. Left-sided heart failure is usually caused by old age or a congenital heart defect.

Due to the lack of oxygen-enriched blood, your dog will experience shortness of breath. Exercise and other activities will be strenuous and the dog may tire easily. The dog will also be anxious and will have difficulty relaxing. He will develop a wet cough due to fluid accumulation in the lungs that will disrupt his nightly rest and exercise.

RIGHT-SIDE HEART FAILURE

When the right-side heart muscle begins to fail, the heart will stop pumping blood effectively. The amount of blood traveling through the body will decrease, leaving the body's tissues poorly nourished. It will also back up in the veins, causing swelling in various parts of the body.

Right-side heart failure usually follows left-side heart failure or is caused by an inherited heart defect, heartworm, or lung disease.

Your dog will experience fatigue and difficulty breathing. His pulse will be abnormally rapid. In the advanced stages of right-side heart failure, your dog will develop a pregnant-looking belly from the accumulation of fluid and the swelling it causes.

TREATMENT: If your veterinarian can cure the underlying cause of the heart failure, treatment will be directed toward that goal. If obesity is damaging the heart, your dog will be placed on a low-fat, low-salt diet. If heartworm is placing stress on the heart, the veterinarian will treat it (see Heartworm, p. 168).

Treatment will also be directed at

Right-side heart failure causes the veins to become backed up, possibly leading to swelling in the legs.

the symptoms. For example, diuretics will reduce fluid buildup. There are also several drugs that can control the heart's pumping capabilities.

HEART MURMUR

CAUSES: The two halves of the heart are each divided into two chambers, the atrium and the ventricle. Separating these chambers is a valve whose function is to close tightly, preventing blood from flowing back into the atria once it enters the ventricle. When the valve fails, blood seeps back, producing a swishing sound, audible through a stethoscope, called a murmur.

Some murmurs are natural to the individual heart and thus are harmless. Others, however, can be a serious indication of a birth defect, heart-valve disease, old age, or other circulatory system problem.

SYMPTOMS: A "shh" sound wedged between the normal "lub-dub" heartbeat.

TREATMENT: Not all heart murmurs are serious. Your veterinarian is the best judge. If needed, he or she can prescribe drugs similar to those used to treat human heart conditions.

HEARTWORM

CAUSES: As people have become more likely to travel, so have their companion dogs. In many cases, dogs

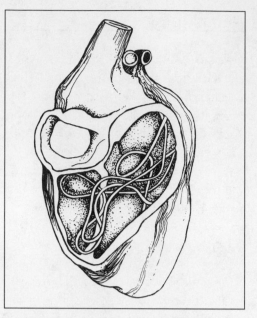

Heartworms can grow up to a foot long, residing in the right side of a dog's heart.

accompany their human friends to warm spots like Florida in winter.

Unfortunately, one consequence of canine travel may be the spread of heartworm. Heartworm (the worm itself is *Dirofilaria immitis*) was once confined to the tropics and semitropics but now has spread to temperate zones. Cases have been reported all over the U.S., including Alaska.

The heartworm can grow from six inches to a foot long. Adults live inside the right side of the dog's heart. An infected dog may host more than a hundred heartworms.

Mosquitos pick up heartworm larvae (*microfiloria*) from infected dogs. Two weeks of development inside the mosquito renders the microfilaria ready to invade a new animal. This occurs when the host mosquito bites a

---

PREVENTING HEARTWORM

Two heartworm preventative treatment programs are available to dogs: Diethyl carbamazine citrate in tablet or liquid form, administered daily, or Ivermectin, a tablet administered monthly. Both destroy the *microfilaria* before maturation occurs.

These drugs should be given only to dogs who are free of heartworm, so it is important that your dog be checked before a program of prevention is undertaken. If your dog already has heartworm, the preventative drug could kill him. The dead larvae must be removed from the system, a process performed by the body that may release poisons internally.

In states where cold winters kill mosquitos, you will have to give your dog the preventative drug only during mosquito season—from April to December.

If you live in (or visit) a warmer climate, your dog will need preventative heartworm medicine year-round because the mosquito population is never completely dormant.

---

dog. Once inside a dog's bloodstream, the *microfilaria* matures and settles in the dog's heart. It takes about three to nine months until the new heartworm can reproduce.

SYMPTOMS: Most of the symptoms of heartworm are due to the adult worms living in the heart, lungs, and large vessels. Because the adult worms obstruct the circulatory system, the heart and lungs are taxed as they attempt to compensate for the worm-caused blockage. The dog may cough, tire easily, and lose weight (even if he eats his regular diet). He may also suffer fainting spells from exercise.

As the worms multiply, anemia sets in (see Anemia, p. 166). The dog's immune system is no longer able to fight the ravages of other parasites, such as fleas.

TREATMENT: Heartworm can be diagnosed by examining a blood sample under a microscope. If worms are found, treatment will probably involve hospitalization; that, in part, depends upon the amount of destruction sustained by the lungs and heart, which can be determined through radiograph and an electrocardiogram.

The treatment itself usually consists of two parts. First, injections are given to kill the adult worms in the heart. The veterinarian will check the dog's liver and kidneys through blood tests because the drug can damage these organs and the dead worms can lodge there.

After several weeks, another drug is administered to kill the larvae moving about in the bloodstream.

15

NERVOUS SYSTEM PROBLEMS

THE BRAIN, the spinal cord, and the peripheral nerves—what is collectively referred to as the nervous system—are responsible for receiving stimuli from the outside world as well as for initiating, managing, and controlling all the functions of the body. Neurons, minute complex transmitters, receive and pass on nerve impulses that originate in the controlling part of the nervous system, the brain.

The neurons line all parts of the dog's brain, including the cerebrum (responsible for learning, judgment, and voluntary actions), the cerebellum (controls coordination and balance), the brain stem (responsive to primitive needs such as hunger, temperature control, and other involuntary life-sustaining functions), and the spinal cord (carries the messages from the brain to the body).

While the brain is protected by the skull, the spinal cord is protected by the many vertebrae known as the spine that line the back like guardrails, allowing nerve impulses to safely travel along a highway from the brain to the body. Coming off this highway are many exit ramps or nerve roots that further branch out into plexi that, in turn, further branch out into peripheral nerves. Peripheral nerves transport impulses to the muscles and also receive sensations from the body's tissues that can then be relayed back to the brain.

The main difference between the canine nervous system and the human lies at the center of the nervous system itself, the brain. Although both the human and canine brain are composed of the cerebrum, cerebellum, and spinal cord, pound for pound the human's brain is much larger. For example, a

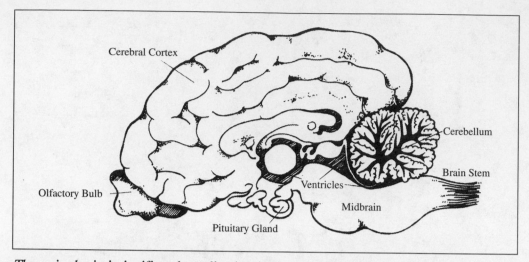

Cerebral Cortex

Cerebellum

Brain Stem

Olfactory Bulb

Ventricles

Midbrain

Pituitary Gland

The canine brain is significantly smaller than its human counterpart.

human who has the same body weight as a Saint Bernard has a brain weight that is 85 percent greater.

Also, the largest part of the brain in both dogs and humans, the cerebrum, is much more developed in humans than in dogs; it is composed of more gray matter, the material responsible for concepts and ideas, than the dog's is. This is why you can teach your dog to fetch the newspaper, but you could never teach her to understand the notions of politics or world crisis that the same newspaper discusses. Conversely, the area of the dog's brain used for the sense of smell, the olfactory bulb, which is located at the front of the brain just above the nasal cavity, has forty times the number of cells as the same area in the human brain. Thus, the dog's sense of smell allows her to be more sensitive and to have a more acute recognition of different smells than humans have.

Many of the ailments that can offset the delicate balance of the dog's nervous system are also different from those that affect the human nervous system. Let's take a look at some of them.

CERVICAL SPONDYLOPATHY

CAUSES: Cervical spondylopathy, also known as wobbler syndrome, is a life-threatening condition in which the vertebrae lining the spine become too narrow or suffer from a defect that causes them to injure the spinal cord. Although the condition may be either inherited or brought on by an injury, the exact cause of wobbler syndrome is not known. It is, however, more commonly seen in large breeds, such as the Great Dane.

SYMPTOMS: Cervical spondylopathy is called wobbler syndrome because its main symptom is an uncoordinated wobbling that can be slight or, in advanced cases, dramatic and similar to those of a drunk person. Partial or total paralysis will eventually set in, attacking the hind legs in most cases.

TREATMENT: Depending on the severity, surgery may be necessary.

CONVULSIONS
(see CONVULSIONS, p. 249)

ENCEPHALITIS

CAUSES: Veterinarians use the term "encephalitis" to describe a swelling in the dog's brain. The condition can be caused by distemper, canine parvovirus, rabies, the presence of bacteria in the brain because of infection or fracture, a parasite-induced disease such as Rocky Mountain spotted fever, or, in rare cases, a post-vaccination allergic reaction.

SYMPTOMS: Convulsions, stiff neck, pain when touched around the head.

TREATMENT: Encephalitis needs prompt veterinary treatment directed at the cause of the inflammation.

EPILEPSY

CAUSES: Epilepsy is the result of brain damage caused by a blow to the head, the presence of a brain tumor, hypoglycemia, poisoning, a heavy infestation of worms, a viral or bacter-

ial infection such as distemper, or an inherited disorder.

SYMPTOMS: Seizures often go through three phases. The first phase marks the onset of an attack. The dog will be restless, anxious, and her pupils will be dilated. In the second phase, the dog will foam at the mouth. Her face may twitch, her head will shake, and she will appear to be chewing on something. The third phase, which might last over three minutes, is characterized by collapse, rigidification, uncontrolled bowel movements, and a movement with the legs that resembles dog paddling. During recovery from a seizure, a dog will remain dazed, unresponsive, and wobbly.

TREATMENT: Epileptic seizures in dogs are controlled by the same drugs that are used for human epilepsy. Dogs, like humans, can readily adjust to epilepsy if the condition is properly treated.

HEAD INJURIES
(see SKULL FRACTURES, p. 255)

HERNIATED DISC

CAUSES: Cushioning the bony vertebrae protecting the spinal cord are discs. When a dog herniates or slips a disc, she has pierced the cartilage surrounding it, allowing the gelatinous fluid within this cartilage to seep out and put pressure on the spinal cord. The result is an inflammation of the spinal cord that is painful to the dog and hinders her normal movement.

A slipped disc can occur over time or suddenly due to trauma, athletic activity, or everyday exercise. Dogs who have an extended back and short legs, such as the Corgi and the Dachshund, are especially vulnerable to slipped discs due to their elongated spinal column.

SYMPTOMS: Symptoms vary because the rupture can vary in size and location from dog to dog.

If the herniated disc is in the back, your dog will arch her back, walk with a clumsy gait that will appear especially exaggerated in the hind legs, and whimper. In certain cases, paralysis of the hind legs may occur.

If the herniated disc is in the neck, your dog's neck will stiffen and she will avoid moving it. She will whimper, especially if you pat her on the neck or head.

TREATMENT: Take the dog to a veterinarian, who will most likely inject a dye into the spinal cord that highlights the herniated disc and then take an X ray to properly diagnose the problem and prescribe treatment.

If the slipped disc is a minor problem, treatment will involve up to two weeks of rest in a cage or other confined area, painkillers, drugs to reduce the swelling, and tranquilizers to keep the dog relaxed.

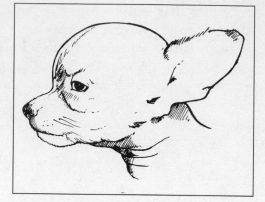

A general swelling of the head can indicate hydrocephalus.

If the slipped disc will not respond to this type of treatment, surgery may be necessary.

HYDROCEPHALUS

CAUSES: Brain infections, tumors, a blow to the head, or a hereditary defect can damage the brain's drainage system, causing cerebrospinal fluid to accumulate. As pressure increases, the brain's tissues are forced against the skull.

SYMPTOMS: Blindness, dizziness, convulsions, or the presence of a domelike bulge on the dog's head may result. Chihuahuas and Poodles are prone to this condition.

TREATMENT: Successful treatment depends on early diagnosis and surgery.

16

DIGESTIVE SYSTEM PROBLEMS

THE TASK OF TAKING in food, breaking it down, and converting it into the energy essential to your dog's vitality is handled by the canine digestive system, a long tract that spans the body and includes the mouth, esophagus, stomach, small and large intestines, liver, and pancreas.

The digestive process begins whenever your dog becomes hungry, is reminded of food, or eats. Glands nestled in the back of the mouth secrete saliva, an enzymatic fluid that moistens the mouth and helps the teeth to break down food and swallow it. Swallowing is actually a complex process in which many muscles roll the broken-down food, or bolus, past the larynx and into a long narrow tube called the esophagus.

Once in the esophagus, peristalsis, a rhythmic muscular contraction, moves the food down the tube, through a valve called the cardiac sphincter, and into the stomach. The stomach is lined with muscles that churn to further grind down the food and with glands that secrete the acidic gastric juices responsible for breaking down proteins in the food. Food can remain in the stomach for up to four hours before being released into the elongated tube called the small intestine.

The small intestine is actually divided into three parts: the duodenum, the jejunum, and the ileum. The duodenum is the upper section that receives the food and triggers two nearby organs to begin their task in the digestive process. The first organ, the pancreas, is responsible for manufacturing three important digestive aids. One of these aids neutralizes the acids forced into the small intestine from the stom-

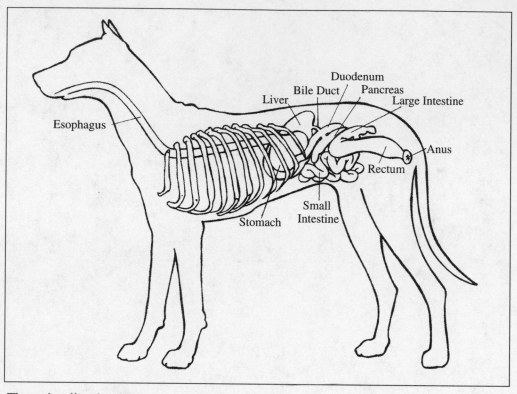

The canine digestive system.

ach. Another, pancreatic juice, seeps into the duodenum through a duct in order to break down and make more absorbable the sugars, fats, and proteins in the digested food. A final important pancreatic digestive aid is insulin, which passes directly into the dog's bloodstream in order to ensure that his cells get enough glucose, a simple sugar essential to maintaining energy levels.

The second organ triggered by the entry of food into the duodenum is the liver, which has several important functions. It releases bile, a fluid containing cholesterol and acids that further assists in breaking down fat so that it can be absorbed into the bloodstream; the liver also converts digested material from the bloodstream into proteins, necessary fats, and sugars, it purifies toxins and drugs, it recycles dead red blood cells, and it helps to determine the amount of nutrients that will be sent into the body. By the time the small intestine, pancreas, and liver have performed their functions and passed the food on to the large intestine, all the nutrients from the food have been absorbed into the body.

The large intestine's task, then, is only to remove what is considered waste. Some of this waste is reabsorbed for use by the body. The rest is processed into feces and passed along until it exits the anus.

In order to maintain a healthy digestive system, it is important to recognize the ailments that can affect it. Read on to see what those ailments include.

ANAL GLAND BLOCKAGE

CAUSES: When dogs meet, they identify each other by smell. They sniff each other's rear ends to take in the scent emitted by the anal glands. These glands, in a sense, are like identification badges for dogs. In skunks, the same glands serve as the source of defense against predators and attackers.

Normally, the fluid of the sac drains into the rectum, but sometimes the duct through which these sacs empty becomes obstructed. The fluid within the sacs accumulates and causes discomfort to the dog. Infection can follow.

SYMPTOMS: The dog rubs or licks the anal area and may rub his rear end along the ground, an action that is called "scooting."

TREATMENT: The anal sacs must be emptied. It's possible for the layperson to perform this technique at home, but to be sure your method is correct, ask your veterinarian to walk you through it once.

Surgical removal of the sacs is often recommended in chronic cases. Domestic dogs have no use for their anal glands, so removal will not be debilitating.

HOW TO EMPTY A DOG'S ANAL GLANDS

There are two anal sacs, each located below and slightly to either side of the anus.

If your dog's sacs are swollen, you can feel them beneath the surface of the skin, bulging like soft marbles.

Hold a pad of cotton across the palm of one hand and raise the dog's tail with the other. Put the pad on the dog's rear. Gently grasp the gland between your thumb and forefinger, aiming for the area just behind the sacs. Squeeze gently, applying pressure upward. Look for slightly brown or yellow, thick liquid to emerge.

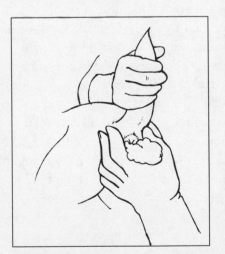

Clogged anal glands may be emptied at home using sterile gauze and direct pressure.

ANAL GLAND ABSCESSES

An anal gland infection may lead to the development of an abscess, a soft, red, hairless, swollen area at the side of the anus. If an infection develops in the anal glands, the area will become swollen. If you touch the gland, it may cause your dog pain.

TREATMENT: It's usually wisest to let the veterinarian take care of an anal sac abscess, since infection is involved. Often it will have to be lanced or surgically drained, and antibiotics will be administered.

If it bursts on its own, clean it with water and hydrogen peroxide. Keep it as clean as possible over the next week, flushing it with fresh water regularly.

APPETITE FLUCTUATIONS

Normal appetite fluctuations can be caused by changes in the weather or in your dog's exercise. However, if your dog's appetite suddenly becomes voracious or disappears, or if you notice diarrhea, dramatic weight gain or loss, or other changes in his health, a more serious cause may be involved.

If your dog has an *increased* appetite, the following could be at fault:

- pregnancy
- pancreatic, liver, or intestinal problems
- diabetes (see Diabetes, p. 179)
- tapeworm (see Tapeworms, p. 185)

If your dog has a *decreased* appetite, the following may be the root of the problem:

- eating at your neighbor's house or from neighborhood garbage cans
- gum or tooth abscess
- gastritis (see Gastritis, p. 181)
- advanced, untreated diabetes (see Diabetes, p. 179)
- distemper (See Distemper, p. 110)
- parvovirus (see Canine Parvovirus, p. 109)
- hepatitis (see Infectious Canine Hepatitis, p. 111)
- pancreatitis (see Pancreatitis, p. 183)

Consult your veterinarian if you suspect your dog may be ill.

BLOOD IN STOOL

CAUSES: A bloody stool could be caused by trauma, poisoning, infectious canine hepatitis, rectal tumors, or the presence of particles of bone in the food matter.

A small amount of blood in the stool is common from time to time in all meat-eating animals. If you notice large amounts of blood in the stool, however, you should immediately consult your veterinarian. A stool tainted with bright-red blood could indicate that your dog's colon is damaged, while a stool tainted with dark-black blood could be a sign that your dog's upper digestive tract is bleeding.

TREATMENT: Your veterinarian will determine the cause of the bleeding and direct treatment toward eliminating it.

CONSTIPATION

CAUSES: A dog who has repeated difficulties passing a stool or is completely unable to defecate is constipated.

Constipation is caused by a low-fiber or high-meat diet, by the intake of objects that cannot be digested such as bone particles, thread, paper clips, and wood, or by weak abdominal muscles resulting from old age and trauma.

TREATMENT: Mild constipation may be relieved by adding an over-the-counter laxative such as Metamucil to your dog's food.

To add moisture to the stool, you can also try spooning some mineral oil into your dog's food. Use one teaspoon per ten pounds of body weight twice daily. Mineral oil will act as a mild laxative, but it can also inhibit the absorption of important nutrients, so don't use it for more than three days. Also, be sure to put the oil in the food. Don't put it directly in your dog's mouth because he may inhale it and get it into his lungs, which could result in pneumonia or other respiratory distress.

If the constipation is severe, take your dog to the veterinarian. The doctor may recommend or administer an enema, or may even have to anesthetize your dog and then instigate the final states of digestion from within your dog's intestinal tract.

NOTE: Sometimes the problem may not be rooted inside the digestive tract, but at its exit. Pseudocoprostatis, or false constipation, is a frequent problem in long-haired dogs. Expelled fecal matter sticks to the hair surrounding the anus, blocking the opening through which bowel movements are released. The treatment is fairly routine: Taking great pains not to cut the skin, cut the matted hair with scissors. Gently rub some Vaseline or baby oil over the affected skin. Consult your veterinarian if the skin's appearance or odor suggests infection.

DIABETES

CAUSES: Diabetes is a condition in which the pancreas fails to release proper levels of insulin needed to force the body's cells to absorb the digested sugar, or glucose, necessary for maintaining energy. The unabsorbed glucose accumulates and eventually drains into the kidney, causing excess urination and other symptoms.

The exact cause of diabetes is still unknown. It is commonly believed to be an inherited disorder, however. It is therefore advised that you not breed a dog diagnosed with diabetes.

SYMPTOMS: Excessive urination, abundant thirst and appetite, decrease in weight, and fatigue are the signs of diabetes. Some more severe cases may also involve cataracts (see Cataract, p. 125), vomiting, breathing difficulties, and coma.

TREATMENT: Diagnosis is made from an analysis of the dog's urine and blood for excess sugar. Treatment typically involves daily insulin injections, a high-fiber, low-fat diet, and regular monitoring of your dog's blood-sugar levels with tests that your veterinarian will supply.

DIARRHEA

CAUSES: Diarrhea is very common among all dog breeds. Most of the time it is not serious, but it is important to remember that diarrhea is a symptom, and a symptom shouldn't be dismissed before the cause is known. Diarrhea can be caused by a number of problems.

TREATMENT: If your adult dog has diarrhea but is otherwise healthy and energetic, put him on a water-only fast and give him some Kaopectate (fol-

CAUSES OF DIARRHEA

1. **INDIGESTION. The ingestion of milk, greasy foods, foods that are high in fat, or scraps from the garbage is often the cause of diarrhea. It can also be brought on by changes in diet, excessive eating, and intolerance to particular foods.**

2. **WORMS. The presence of round, whip, hook, or tapeworms in the body can result in diarrhea (see worms sections, pp. 182, 184, 185).**

3. **LIVER DISEASE. The liver is a key organ in digestion. If it is diseased and is not producing enough bile and digestive enzymes, diarrhea can result (see Infectious Canine Hepatitis, p. 111).**

4. **PANCREATIC DISEASE. When an infected pancreas cannot produce the enzymes essential to digestion, diarrhea will result (see Pancreatitis, p. 183).**

5. **OBSTRUCTIONS. Diarrhea followed by no bowel movement at all can indicate that some foreign object has become lodged in the dog's digestive track (see Intestinal Obstruction, p. 259).**

6. **POISONING (see Poisoning, Chapter Twenty-two).**

7. **ENTERITIS. Bacterial infections, such as leptospirosis, or viral infections, such as canine parvovirus, can result in diarrhea.**

8. **NERVES. Upset, nervous, or anxious dogs are often afflicted with diarrhea.**

lowing the dosage requirements for humans) until he passes a firmer stool or for up to twenty-four hours. Gradually wean him off the fast by providing small snacks of boiled white chicken or lean grilled hamburger and boiled rice or potatoes. Increase the amount of food over the next three days. Gradually change the dog over to his normal diet after that.

If your dog is a puppy, appears dehydrated, is also vomiting, has a bloody stool, or experiences diarrhea for more than twenty-four hours, consult your veterinarian. Tests and prescribed treatment may be necessary.

ENTERITIS

CAUSES: Enteritis is an inflammation of the bowels due to an infection, a foreign body in the bowel, distemper, hepatitis, leptospirosis, a severe worm infestation, poisoning, or a twisting of the bowels.

SYMPTOMS: Cramps and intestinal spasms; a painful abdomen that is extremely sensitive to the touch; diarrhea, sometimes accompanied by vomiting.

TREATMENT: Take your dog to the veterinarian, who will have to determine the underlying cause.

FLATULENCE

CAUSES: Gas is a natural product of the digestion process. Some gas is expelled through the anus, while most goes into the blood and is released through exhalation. However, certain conditions lead to the overproduction of gas, resulting in an abnormally frequent emission of odorous gas from the anus.

TREATMENT: Dogs who are permitted to pick through garbage often suffer from bouts of flatulence.

Some foods tend to produce more gas than others. These include vegetables, uncooked carbohydrates, legumes, and milk. Some dry foods contain large amounts of soybeans and cornmeal, which in some dogs produces excessive gas. Diets too high in carbohydrates, protein, or fat often result in flatulence. Lactose intolerance is yet another cause.

If your dog's usual dry food contains large amounts of soybeans and cornmeal, cut back on it by substituting dry canned food or trying a new brand. You can also give your dog mild home-cooked food such as boiled chicken and rice for one or two days.

You can also try feeding your dog small amounts frequently rather than one large meal. Discuss the problem with your veterinarian, who may be able to recommend a safe medication that will cut down the flatulence if changes in diet don't do the trick.

GASTRITIS

CAUSES: Gastritis is a condition in which the dog's stomach lining becomes irritated and inflamed. Vomiting and, in some cases, diarrhea and a loss of appetite result.

The ingestion of foreign objects, grass, unnutritional foods, and other stomach irritants are the most common cause of gastritis. Other causes include poisons (see Poisoning, Chapter Twenty-two), worms (see individual worms), distemper (see Distemper, p. 110), hepatitis (see Infectious Canine Hepatitis, p. 111), parvovirus (see Canine Parvovirus, p. 109), and leptospirosis (see Leptospirosis, p. 113).

TREATMENT: If your adult dog has an upset stomach but is otherwise healthy, put him on a water-only fast and give him some Kaopectate (again, following the dosage requirements for humans) for twenty-four hours. After that, feed your dog small amounts of boiled white chicken or grilled lean hamburger and boiled rice or potatoes. Gradually reinstate your dog's normal diet after two or three days.

HEARTWORM
(see HEARTWORM, p. 168)

HOOKWORM

CAUSES: Hookworms are very small bloodsucking worms that grow to about a quarter of an inch in size. One end is bent in the shape of a hook.

Hookworms attach themselves to the intestinal lining via structures similar to teeth. These teeth hold them in place, allowing them to feed off your dog's body, wreaking severe damage

to the intestine's walls. The worms make sure the blood keeps flowing by secreting a substance that inhibits coagulation. The severe blood loss can cause life-threatening anemia and hemorrhaging if the worms are present for a long time.

The adult hookworm lays its eggs in the stomach and intestines. The eggs are passed out in the dog's feces and hatch outside in about a week. Dogs swallow the infected feces and the larvae make their way to the intestine, where they hatch into worms after a few weeks.

The larvae can also penetrate the skin, usually through the feet, and eventually make their way to the stomach. Once inside the skin, they travel through the bloodstream to the lungs, where they dig through the alveoli walls. They're expelled through coughing and then are reswallowed, thus ending up in the stomach.

A mother can transmit worms to her litter through nursing. The infection can even occur in the womb before the puppies are born.

SYMPTOMS: Diarrhea, bloody stool, emaciation, anemia, weakness, red and swollen skin.

TREATMENT: Veterinary care is essential. The veterinarian will first kill the worms by injections or tablets. Then, if the dog is suffering from anemia or malnutrition, the veterinarian will treat these conditions.

The veterinarian will ask you to set up regular appointments to guard against another infestation. Also, you will have to treat the soil in your yard if that is the likely source of worms. Your veterinarian should be able to recommend products suitable for your climate.

NOTE: If you allow your dog to roam around or defecate on your property, remove waste products at least once a week. Also, keep the grass well groomed and water infrequently—just enough to keep your grass healthy. These steps will help prevent infestation.

HICCUPS

Puppies are more prone to hiccups than adult dogs, but adult dogs do occasionally get them. A common cause is eating too quickly. A puppy can also get hiccups if his stomach is empty.

Hiccups usually go away as spontaneously as they begin. For an adult, you may want to administer one teaspoon of a mild antacid to cure persistent hiccups. A puppy can be relieved through gentle burping—rub his abdomen gently. If hiccups persist in any dog for a day or longer, however, consult a veterinarian.

MOTION SICKNESS

CAUSES: Motion sickness is caused by a disturbance in the balance center in the brain. It usually affects puppies during their first few car trips, causing them to become queasy and some-

times to vomit. Dogs usually outgrow motion sickness, although some continually experience difficulty when traveling.

TREATMENT: You can give dogs motion-sickness pills. Give an adult dose for dogs weighing more than forty pounds and a child's dose for smaller dogs. If this does not help, see your veterinarian, who will probably prescribe a tranquilizer.

PANCREATITIS

CAUSES: Pancreatitis is an infection of the pancreas that causes it to release its digestive enzymes into the bloodstream rather than into the small intestines. The outcome of pancreatitis can vary from vomiting to death (which is caused by the pancreatic enzymes digesting the pancreas).

The cause of pancreatitis is unknown, but it typically attacks middle-aged, overweight dogs.

SYMPTOMS: High fever, abdominal pain, vomiting, weight loss, diarrhea, listlessness, lack of appetite.

TREATMENT: Your veterinarian will first confirm a diagnosis through examination and blood tests. Treatment will vary according to the severity of the infection. Conservative treatment may involve pain relievers, drugs to stop the vomiting, intravenous fluids, a low-fat diet of boiled white chicken and rice, and antibiotics. A more aggressive treatment may also include enzyme supplements.

ROUNDWORMS

CAUSES: No worm is more familiar to dog owners than the roundworm. Resembling the earthworm, these organisms are most likely to be found in puppies and can grow up to about a half foot in length.

The cycle of destruction begins with the worm feeding on food in the stomach and intestines. Then it digs through the organ walls and enters the bloodstream. From there, it makes its way to the liver and later to the lungs. Eventually, it enters the trachea, is expelled into the mouth through coughing, and is sent back to the stomach and intestines through swallowing.

Roundworms that are left unchecked may migrate to a growing puppy's muscles. There, the worms form cysts and vegetate. If the host becomes pregnant, however, her whole litter can be infected by the worms, which will travel to and settle in the puppies' lungs.

Fortunately, dogs naturally develop an immunity to roundworms over time. However, some dogs come into direct contact with infested food or feces and then develop the condition.

SYMPTOMS: Upset stomach, loose stools, pain and discomfort, loss of shine in coat. Puppies with systemic infestation may have distended abdomens or appear potbellied. If there is significant lung involvement, respiratory problems

will ensue. Puppies can get pneumonia from roundworm migration, since the alveoli become damaged.

TREATMENT: Your veterinarian will request a stool specimen in order to check for worms. There are a variety of effective drugs your veterinarian may prescribe to defend your dog against roundworm infestation. Your dog's stool will be examined for worms at various stages of treatment.

PREVENTION: It is especially important that a female with roundworm be thoroughly treated for the condition before you breed her.

To be certain that all worms are found early, every dog should have stool specimens examined twice a year.

One very good way of keeping your dog out of the trash (where roundworms may be waiting) is to be certain his regular diet is complete and filling.

WARNING: Roundworms pose a serious danger to children, so it is important that you keep infested dogs away from youngsters until treatment has ended.

SORE BOTTOM

CAUSES: The skin surrounding the anus can become irritated and inflamed by persistent diarrhea, passage of hard, dry stools, the presence of bone fragments or other sharp objects in the feces, false constipation, worms, or insects. Puppies are most vulnerable to infection of the anus, but all dogs are susceptible.

SYMPTOMS: Scooting.

TREATMENT: Treatment should be directed at the cause of the inflammation. Relieve the soreness by applying an ointment such as Vaseline, or a human hemorrhoidal preparation, on the anal area. Discourage your dog from licking the ointment.

SWELLING OF THE ABDOMEN (see BLOAT, p. 246)

TAPEWORMS

HYDATID DISEASE

CAUSES: Hydatid disease is caused by the only variety of tapeworm that poses a threat to people. This worm can be found in the uncooked innards of cattle and sheep. The adult version of this tapeworm is relatively short—approximately five millimeters in length.

SYMPTOMS: None.

TREATMENT: The veterinarian will detect the presence of tapeworm by examining a stool specimen. If tapeworm is present, veterinary care will be required.

PREVENTION: Don't feed your dog uncooked meat. Keep children away from untreated rural dogs, who often pick up the worm through contact with the remains of dead livestock.

DIPYLIDIUM CANINUM

CAUSES: Transmitted by fleas, this cucumber-shaped organism is the most common form of tapeworm to affect dogs. The flea larva ingests rounded tapeworm segments filled with eggs or the actual eggs themselves. Once the flea matures, it lands on a dog. The dog then eats the flea and, in turn, the tapeworm egg.

As the flea passes through the dog's digestive system, the tapeworm egg affixes itself to the intestine, hatches, and matures. The mature segments, packed with eggs, pass out of the dog's anus. The segments, if moist, can move about for a while. The eggs contained in the new segments are then eaten by fleas, thus beginning the cycle anew.

Humans cannot acquire this type of worm from dogs. It is very difficult to treat fully, because the head separates from the body and remains affixed to the intestinal wall.

Tapeworms can grow to an astounding length of two feet inside a dog's body.

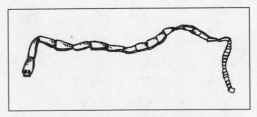

The common tapeworm. Each segment may contain eggs, which are eaten by fleas.

SYMPTOMS: When tapeworms leave the body, they sometimes affix themselves to the outside of a dog's anus, leaving the dog scratching itself for relief. The dog may stop gaining weight because he is unknowingly sharing his food with the worms. The stool itself will reveal tapeworms, which will appear as tiny white grains that perhaps move about in the folds of the stool.

TREATMENT: Veterinary care is required, since deworming agents are extremely potent and must be administered with great care.

You must take steps to rid the house of the fleas that carry tapeworm eggs (see Fleas, p. 143).

THIRST FLUCTUATIONS

Your dog's need for water can vary depending on the weather and how much he exercises. Certain medications or pregnancy can also make your dog thirstier than usual. Be aware, however, that excessive thirst accompanied by vomiting, diarrhea, excessive urination, dramatic weight loss, or other signs of illness could indicate that your dog is sick. Some causes of excessive thirst can include:

- dehydration
- liver or kidney disease
- diabetes (see Diabetes, p. 179)
- in female dogs only, an infection of the uterus.

VOMITING

CAUSES: Dogs sometimes vomit without being ill. Spoiled dogs, for example, vomit simply to get attention, while other dogs can vomit from becoming excited.

Dogs sometimes regurgitate their food after eating it and then turn around and eat the vomitus. Although this is a disgusting sight, it is a dog's way of predigesting his food.

A dog can sometimes vomit up a yellow, foamy substance that appears to be a symptom of sickness. It is really only bile thrown up as a result of hunger.

Some vomiting can indicate gastritis and other stomach problems. If you are going to proceed with treatment, however, be sure your dog's vomiting is abnormal, occurs more than once in a day's time, and is accompanied by other signs of sickness, such as slight diarrhea or fatigue.

TREATMENT: If you suspect that your dog's vomiting is a symptom of a slight illness, administering Maalox, Mylanta, Kaopectate, or Pepto-Bismol and putting your dog on a water-only fast is the best solution. Once the vomiting has stopped, or after twenty-four hours, feed your dog small snacks of boiled white chicken or lean grilled hamburger and boiled rice or potatoes. Reintroduce the dog's normal food after a day or two.

If the vomiting persists or if your dog has a fever, black or bloody

WHEN VOMITING IS SERIOUS

If your dog vomits more than three times within a twenty-four-hour period or vomits persistently over a period of days and has a fever, black or bloody vomit, severe abdominal pain, difficulty urinating, bloody stools, or excessive fatigue, he may be seriously ill.

Causes of serious vomiting include a brain injury (see Skull Fractures, p. 255), diseases such as distemper (see Distemper, p. 110), hepatitis (see Infectious Canine Hepatitis, p. 111), leptospirosis (see Leptospirosis, p. 113), and pancreatitis (see Pancreatitis, p. 183), the presence of foreign objects in the body, intestinal obstruction (see Intestinal Obstruction, p. 259), heatstroke (see Heatstroke, p. 256), poisoning (see Poisoning, Chapter Twenty-two), tonsillitis (see Tonsillitis, p. 138), and worms (see individual worms in this chapter).

If your dog vomits persistently, consult your veterinarian. Immediate care and long-term treatment will vary depending on the cause of the vomiting.

vomit, lethargy, severe abdominal pain, frequent unsuccessful attempts to urinate, or bloody stools, consult your veterinarian.

WEIGHT GAIN

If your dog has gained weight, immediately suspect that you are simply feeding him too much. Be cautious, however: A circulatory or liver problem may be at the root of the weight gain.

To be certain, have your veterinarian examine the dog to rule out any serious health problems. If overeating is the culprit, you and your veterinarian can work out a weight-loss program for your dog.

WEIGHT LOSS

Often, a dog's weight loss can be attributed to psychological factors. If you have moved recently, brought a new pet into the home, or had a baby, your dog may not eat well. Dogs tend to eat less when they are uncomfortably warm, so a heat wave might lead a dog to shed a few pounds. Also, if you've suddenly started to take your dog on long hikes or runs, he may be burning up calories faster than normal.

However, weight loss not attributable to the above factors may be caused by a more serious problem such as diabetes, liver disease, cancer, or worms.

Because the list of medical problems that can cause it is endless, it is a good idea to take your dog to the veterinarian for an examination if he's losing weight. Bring along a fresh stool sample when you do.

WHIPWORMS

CAUSES: Whipworms are such hearty organisms that they can survive outdoors for long stretches of time. They resemble a whip in that they are thin on one end and thicker on the other. Their width is comparable to that of a thick thread.

Dogs ingest the eggs or the immature form of the whipworm, which reaches maturity as it moves through the digestive system. The adult worms fasten themselves to and draw blood from the cecum, a pocket between the small and large intestines. The mature female lays her eggs inside the host. The eggs are then excreted in the feces.

SYMPTOMS: Loose, bloody stool, dull coat, weight loss, vomiting yellow-green bile, anemia.

TREATMENT: Veterinary care is required. Your veterinarian will determine the presence of whipworms by examining your dog's stool specimens. Several attempts may be necessary, since whipworms are sometimes difficult to detect.

Your veterinarian will administer a potent deworming agent. Ask her or him to recommend a product that will help you combat whipworms that may be living around your house.

PREVENTION: Because whipworms require moisture to survive, outdoor dogs should be kept in dry quarters that are regularly exposed to the sun.

17

URINARY SYSTEM PROBLEMS

THE DOG RELIES upon her urinary system, which is composed of the urethra, bladder, ureters, and kid- neys, to rid her body of toxic waste products.

The two kidneys hang inside the

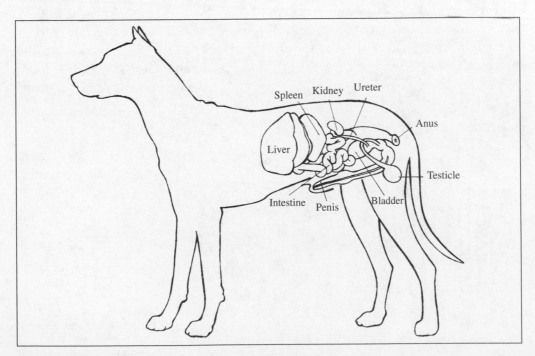

The male canine urinary system.

dog's abdomen close to the bottom set of ribs. As in humans, a dog's kidneys strain poisons from the blood. They also respond to the body's demand for salt, potassium, and water. Two tiny tubes called the ureters siphon off extra water and waste produced by cellular reactions. This fluid is sent to the bladder, which stores it. When the bladder is full, a message travels along the nerve network to the brain, telling the dog it is time to urinate. The urethra, a slender vessel leading to the penis or vulva, carries the urine out of the dog's body.

BLADDER INFECTION (CYSTITIS)

CAUSES: Cystitis is an inflammation or infection of the bladder. Female dogs, whose urethra is shorter than that of males, are more prone to bladder infections. The longer the urethra, the farther the bacteria has to travel before it can settle in the bladder.

The burning sensation caused by cystitis makes the sufferer feel as if she needs to urinate frequently, regardless of the amount of urine stored in the bladder.

SYMPTOMS: Frequent urination, burning, bloody urine, pain which causes the dog to hunch while walking.

TREATMENT: Your veterinarian will take a urine sample to test for bacteria. If cystitis is present, she or he will prescribe antiseptics to soothe the bladder lining and antibiotics to fight the infection. Cystitis must be treated quickly and thoroughly to avoid spread of infection throughout the urinary system.

BLADDER STONES

CAUSES: Kidney stones are rare in dogs, but dogs do suffer from bladder stones or stones in the urethra. Stones form when salts present in the urine crystallize and form lumps called calculi. If the crystals lodge in the blad-

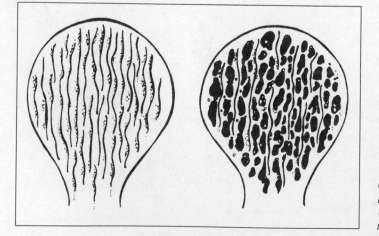

Comparing the mucosa lining a healthy bladder (left) with that of a dog suffering from cystitis.

WARNING ON URINATION

If your dog is straining to urinate and there is no urine, this is an emergency. Get immediate veterinary help.

---

der, they rub against the lining and cause irritation.

Because stones can block the passage through which urine flows, this condition can place the dog in grave danger. It is particularly dangerous for male dogs, whose narrower urethra makes them easy candidates for blockages. Obstruction of the passageway can cause toxic waste products to accumulate and poison the bloodstream, a condition known as uremia.

Stones can affect dogs of any age, but middle-aged dogs are most commonly afflicted.

SYMPTOMS: A dog with bladder or urethra stones may have some or all of these symptoms: painful, difficult, and/or unusually frequent urination, abdominal swelling and tenderness, dribbling of urine.

TREATMENT: In some cases, depending on the type of stone, your veterinarian may recommend surgery. In others, medications and diets low in magnesium ammonium phosphate may be sufficient.

PREVENTION: In many cases, by strictly watching your dog's diet and using medications you can avoid a recurrence. Discuss this with your veterinarian.

KIDNEY DISEASE

Once dogs reach eight years of age, their kidneys are less likely to function as well as those of younger dogs are. Diseased kidneys have sustained damage that inhibits their ability to strain and eliminate waste products. Kidney disease can be sudden (acute) or long-term (chronic).

Acute kidney disease is the result of a potent underlying cause, such as a significant drop in blood pressure, loss of fluids or blood, shock, ingestion of a toxic substance, heart failure, or infectious disease. In treating a dog with kidney disease, the goal is to first deal with the underlying cause. Usually, such treatment results in the restoration of urine production.

Chronic kidney disease is a much slower, degenerative process, with subtle signs that can often take years to surface. Common causes include infection, heart disease, diabetes, poisoning, or physical trauma. Because the kidneys contain plenty of reserve tissue normally capable of toxin disposal, about two thirds of the organ must be damaged before symptoms can be detected. However, it is essential that the disease be checked as early as possible.

SYMPTOMS: A dog suffering from chronic kidney disease may finish her water bowl more quickly than usual and look to you for refills. She may urinate more frequently than normal, and may begin to accidentally urinate in inappropriate places because the kidneys are no longer capable of holding urine.

As the disease progresses, uremia will develop, characterized by lethargy, poor appetite, dull coat, darkening of the tongue, diarrhea, vomiting, and anemia. You may also think you are smelling ammonia on her breath.

TREATMENT: With chronic kidney disease, while he or she will not be able to restore the kidney itself, there are several steps your veterinarian will recommend to keep your dog as healthy and functional as possible.

Strict attention to diet will help the kidney work as well as possible. You will have to reduce the amount of protein your dog ingests. Nitrogen waste is the by-product of protein metabolism. This waste leaves the kidneys as urea. If the kidneys are faulty, urea will back up and enter the bloodstream. However, your dog needs protein for cell production, so you must work with the veterinarian to create a diet (perhaps a specially packaged food program acquired through veterinary hospitals) that will be beneficial to your dog.

This diet will include proteins that are easy to digest, and may be supplemented by foods like cooked eggs and cottage cheese. Carbohydrates will also be suggested. Useful supplements include pasta, potatoes, whole-wheat bread, and oatmeal.

Vitamin supplementation may be necessary. Also, be sure that your dog is able to drink freely—always have water available.

NOTE: Domestic dogs usually only need about a quarter of the amount of protein their diets provide. It is possible that by reducing the amount of protein an older dog receives in her diet, you may delay the onset of chronic kidney disease.

CANCER

18

THANKS TO DECADES of veterinary advances, domestic dogs now live longer than ever before. Research has been widely disseminated to veterinarians and dog owners alike, resulting in the use of new medicines, treatments, techniques, and preventive strategies. Thankfully, all of this research can add up to more years for you to share with your pet.

However, now that dogs live longer, they become more prone to diseases and conditions that occur later in life, perhaps naturally, perhaps as a result of years of interaction with the environment. Cancer is one such disease.

Cancer is the word we use to describe a series of illnesses characterized by the rapid reproduction of abnormal and destructive cells. It is thought that individuals may be genetically predisposed to certain forms of cancer, and that this hereditary risk may combine with environmental and viral factors to instigate cancer's development. A failure in the immune system may also play a role.

The abnormal cell growth associated with cancer can manifest itself in one of two ways: by clustering in the blood, as in leukemia, or, more commonly, by developing into rapidly-growing, palpable masses called tumors. Tumors are more common in dogs than in any other animal. The most common

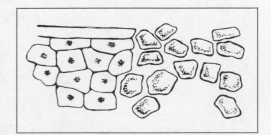

Cancer cells reproduce rapidly and destroy healthy cells.

canine tumors affect the skin and the mammary glands.

TYPES OF TUMORS

There are two classifications of tumors, benign and malignant. Benign tumors are noncancerous. They don't spread or kill tissue, although they may exert pressure on nearby organs or other structures, causing pain. Benign tumors are surrounded by a layer of fibrous or membranous tissue, called a capsule, that keeps the tumor safely contained. If a tumor is known to be benign, it can be removed without fear of recurrence.

Malignant tumors, on the other hand, are cancerous. They lack a capsule, and represent the uncontrolled reproduction of cancer cells. You may be able to see a malignant tumor through the skin. Malignant tumors spread to other places in the body through the blood or lymph system, a process called metastasis. If your dog is to survive cancer, metastasis must be stopped.

Two of the most common types of tumors are lipomas and mammary tumors. They grow anywhere there is fibrous connective tissue, and, when touched, often feel as if they are floating beneath loose skin. They can sometimes be detected in the abdominal cavity as well. They vary in size from half an inch to ten inches long.

Mammary gland tumors are quite common in female dogs, especially in those who have not been spayed before

An ulcerated mammary gland tumor. Close to fifty percent of all canine mammary gland tumors are malignant.

GENERAL SYMPTOMS OF CANCER

A dog suffering from cancer will gradually begin to lose weight. He may shun his food, and suffer from fatigue and general malaise.

Here are some more symptoms that, when appearing alone or in combination, should prompt you to further investigation:

- growths or bumps that increase in size
- wounds that never seem to heal
- bleeding from any cavity
- inability to finish walks or routine exercise
- abnormal gait
- emission of an unfamiliar foul odor
- pain upon eating or swallowing
- painful or obstructed breathing, urination, or defecation

---

two years of age. This provides strong incentive to spay your female early. Mammary gland tumors are small, hard lumps under the skin, detectable near the nipple. Sometimes, the tumor will become ulcerated and may bleed. Close to half of these tumors are malignant.

TREATING CANCER

If cancer is suspected, your veterinarian will conduct a complete physical examination. Blood tests will be taken as well as radiographs and possibly a biopsy. A dog can be treated for cancer just as a human can. Surgery, chemotherapy, hormonal and nutritional therapies, and radiation are all strategies that have been successfully utilized to fight cancer in dogs.

Treatment depends upon a number of factors. Your veterinarian will determine what form of cancer your dog has and how extensive it is, meaning whether or not it has metastasized. He or she will explain the modes of treatment available for your dog's specific form of cancer, as well as the prognosis for recovery. Before treatment begins, you will need to consider carefully whether treatment is likely to prolong your dog's life, maintain or improve the quality of his life, or extend his suffering. You will also have to think about the cost of treatment. As difficult as it may be to ponder, sometimes the expense of prolonged treatment may be too high to make some therapies worthwhile for dogs. If the cancer is unlikely to respond to treatment (or is already responding poorly), it may be best to euthanize your dog (see Euthanasia, p. 99).

Just as people can survive and live productive lives with cancer, so can dogs. With proper treatment, cancer's spread and its painful effects may be kept in check. Early detection is the most productive cancer intervention you can undertake. Make sure your dog gets regular veterinary examinations. Between visits, check your dog's body for growths regularly. Pay particular attention to the mouth, skin, mammary glands, and testicles.

19

FOR MALES ONLY

THE MOST VISIBLE physical feature of the male dog is the penis, which protrudes from the body in between the hind legs. The penis is protected by the prepuce or foreskin. Starting at puberty, sperm is produced by the coiled tubes known as the testes.

Every time a dog ejaculates, millions of sperm travel through the vas deferens to the urethra. There, the sperm combine with fluid secreted by the prostate gland. This fluid, composed of enzymes, fats, proteins, and sugars, gives sperm cells the nutrition and protection they need in order to make their way out of the penis and toward the female reproductive tract.

Male dogs are prone to a number of urogenital problems, as described below. This chapter also contains important information on neutering your male dog.

DISCHARGE FROM THE PENIS

It is important that you learn to differentiate between the normal, light-colored discharge that may normally accumulate around your dog's foreskin and the discharge that signals urogenital trouble.

Bloody discharge from the penis could indicate urethral or prostate inflammation. Seek veterinary assistance if you notice this problem.

Also, be on the lookout for bloody discharge from the penis coupled with straining to urinate. The dog needs to be able to thoroughly empty his bladder of urine; inability to do this could indicate a serious urogenital disorder. Seek immediate veterinary care.

ENLARGED PENIS

CAUSES: Sometimes a dog's penis stays erect or inflamed after a period of sexual excitement. For hygienic reasons, you may need to guide the penis back into its correct position.

TREATMENT: First, lubricate the penis's shaft and head with warm petroleum jelly. Then, gently push the penis in while pulling the sheath out.

Paraphimosis, or an enlarged penis that fails to retract.

HERNIA, PERINEAL

CAUSES: Perineal hernias become evident when a dog is defecating. You will be able to see a bulge near the anus. Dogs over the age of seven are prone to perineal hernias, especially if they suffer from an enlarged prostate, which can block off the anal canal. As they try to push waste material out of the rectum, they exert great force upon the tissues of the rectum. Eventually, the tissues start to rupture, leading to perineal hernia.

TREATMENT: Seek veterinary care. Perineal hernias are usually corrected through surgery.

INFECTION OF THE FORESKIN AND THE HEAD OF THE PENIS

CAUSES: Hair or other debris can become caught in the area between the foreskin and the penis's head. Irritation of the penis's skin can eventually lead to infection.

SYMPTOMS: The penis may protrude from the foreskin, accompanied by green, thick discharge, pain, licking of the area, and inflammation of the penis. The dog may attempt to avoid pain by refusing to urinate.

TREATMENT: Wash with warm water and soap twice a day. Apply an antibiotic ointment. To avoid the spread of

SOME IMPORTANT REASONS TO CONSIDER NEUTERING

Neutering is an important tool to control the pet population. Fortunately, people no longer believe that neutering is unfair to the male dog, a theft of his masculinity. We have come to understand that allowing male dogs to roam unchecked results in thousands of the unwanted puppies that inhabit animal shelters. It also creates a population of puppies who are abandoned in remote areas or cities and left to starve, suffer, or be killed in accidents or dogfights.

infection, consult your veterinarian if the condition lasts for more than three days.

PROSTATITIS

CAUSES: The prostate of some dogs over the age of five becomes enlarged, resulting in a condition called prostatitis.

SYMPTOMS: The swollen prostate impedes the proper elimination of solid waste by exerting pressure against the rectum; it also pushes against the urethra, making urination difficult. Often, a dog with prostatitis will release urine in dribbles rather than in a steady stream. The pain associated with prostatitis may cause your dog to walk awkwardly.

TREATMENT: Prostatitis is diagnosed through a rectal examination. Hormonal treatments involving estrogen are given to reduce the size of an enlarged prostate.

NEUTERING

If you do not plan to breed your dog, you should strongly consider neutering him. A neutered dog has had his testicles removed. Once the operation has been performed, he will no longer produce sperm, and his testosterone level will be reduced significantly.

Neutering, which is usually performed after puberty (once the body has had the chance to develop fully), may have benefits beyond birth control. It may prolong your dog's life by preventing testicular cancer and decreasing the chance of prostate problems and perineal hernias.

By about a month after the operation, a neutered male will probably be less interested in roaming and will spend more time with his human companions. Neutering may make a vicious dog friendlier. Eventually, a neutered dog will be far less likely to indulge in mounting legs, furniture, and female dogs than before the operation. However, neutering should not rob your dog of his protective instincts. If you have already relied on your dog to watch your home and ward off burglars, chances are he will continue to do so.

If you notice that your neutered dog has gained weight, don't blame it on the operation. Obesity is the result of dietary problems and lack of exercise. Ask your veterinarian about changing your dog's diet (see Obesity, p. 59) and establishing a solid exercise program.

Neutering is a relatively simple operation. General anesthesia is adminis-tered, which veterinarians stress is safely done only when the stomach is empty, so it is important to withhold food and water from your dog the evening before the procedure. The testicles, the site at which testosterone is produced, are removed via an incision in the scrotum. Your dog should be home the next day.

Once home, make him as comfortable as possible and feed him his regular diet unless he shows signs of intestinal distress. After recovering from the day's events, he should be back to speed in no time.

20

FOR FEMALES ONLY

THE FEMALE'S TWO OVARIES, each about three quarters of an inch long, are suspended from the top of the abdominal cavity and rest near the kidneys. The ovaries have two main functions: to produce and release eggs, and to create hormones that will eventually make the womb hospitable to a developing embryo.

The bursa, a fatty sac, envelops the ovaries. This structure receives the eggs and sends them to the uterus by way of the fallopian tube. The uterus, a structure with thick walls, actually looks like a pair of horns joined together.

The cervix protrudes from the uterus into the vagina. It opens only during birth (whelping) and estrus. The vestibule is at the entrance to the vagina. The vestibule's walls form the vulva, the lips of the vagina's opening. The vulva also serves as the outlet for the bladder.

BIRTH CONTROL

If you are planning to breed your dog, consult with your veterinarian about using some kind of birth-control device—pills, liquid contraceptives, and IUDs (intrauterine devices) are all effective—until breeding is to take place.

If you are not planning to breed your female, you should strongly consider spaying her. Even if you keep your dog fenced in your backyard, she is still vulnerable to roaming males, who could easily climb over and mount her when she is in heat (see p. 203).

In the past, people erroneously believed that spaying would cause a female dog to become lethargic and prone to excessive weight gain. We now know that diet and exercise are essential to keeping a dog energetic and trim. Most seeing-eye dogs are spayed females and are sleek and brimming with energy.

Ovariohysterectomy is the medical term for the process you know as "spaying." In this routine procedure, an incision is made in the abdomen and the uterus and ovaries are removed through it. General anesthesia is administered.

It is wise to have the operation performed when your dog is a young pup—six months old, before her first heat. Your veterinarian will want to examine your dog prior to the operation to make sure her health is good enough for her to withstand an operation (just like humans).

While it is understandable that the idea of putting your precious pet into surgery may frighten you, keep in mind that thousands of dogs successfully undergo this procedure each year. Contemporary anesthetic techniques will not harm your dog, nor will the surgery—in fact, you can expect her home in a day or so.

Your veterinarian will give you specific instructions to follow in preparation for surgery. This procedure is safest when your dog's stomach is empty—no food or water the night before surgery.

After your dog comes home, make her as comfortable as possible. Discourage her from jumping on or off furniture, since this may cause her pain at first. Check the incision for signs of infection (irritation and the emission of pus are strong ones). Your veterinarian may want to remove the stitches in a week to ten days. Some sutures are absorbable and do not have to be removed. (See Nursing a Sick Dog at Home, p. 87.)

YOUR DOG'S REPRODUCTIVE CYCLE

A dog reaches puberty sometime between her sixth and eighteenth month of life, although occasionally it may take longer. Smaller toy breeds mature early, while larger breeds may take as long as two years.

Heat usually occurs once every six months, but some dogs experience more while others go into heat only once a year (i.e., the Basenji).

The heat cycle lasts for six to seven months—again, variations are possible.

MATING

The time to mate is during the estrus phase, when the female is obviously receptive to the male. If the female stands still and shifts her tail to the side, the male will first lick her vulva and then enter her from behind. He will grasp her sides to help her adjust to the position. The penis will be thrust into the vagina repeatedly for about twenty-five thrusts before ejaculation. The male will dismount.

At this point, a strange but entirely natural thing will occur. The male will turn around, remaining connected to the female even though the two are facing opposite directions. This position is called the "tie" and is caused by a

---

PHASES OF THE HEAT CYCLE

I. PROESTRUS

DURATION: Seven to nine days

In this initial phase, hormones produced by the ovaries trigger a swelling of the womb. The womb then creates a lining, which it prepares for possible pregnancy.

The vulva swells, stiffens, and emits a bloody discharge. The amount of discharge varies from dog to dog, with larger breeds often not showing any signs at all.

During this period, the female draws the male in by emitting pheremones. However, she will not yet allow the male to mount her.

II. ESTRUS

DURATION: Nine to eighteen days

Ovulation can occur during this phase. The vulva becomes softer, and the bloody discharge may change to a clearer color.

This phase is often called "standing heat," because the female will stand still and present her rear end to the male. She will raise her tail and shift it to one side, displaying her vulva. The more blatant these actions are, the more likely it is that the female is ready to breed.

III. METESTRUS

DURATION: Two months

If the female doesn't breed, metestrus sets in. She rejects the male, her vulva returns to normal, and all discharge ceases. The uterus begins to return to its preheat condition. Egg production has ceased.

IV. ANESTRUS

DURATION: Three to five months

The system rests during this period.

---

swelling at the penis's foundation, known as the *bulbis glandis*. The vagina clasps this swelling, leaving the male and female in a fixed position until the swelling subsides. The tie can last up to a half-hour and should not be disrupted.

TO BREED OR NOT TO BREED

Nearly twenty million dogs are put to sleep each year because no one can find homes for them. This statistic alone strongly underscores how impor-

SOME ERRONEOUS ASSUMPTIONS ABOUT BREEDING

1. As a female, my dog *needs* to have a litter.

   Untrue. People are socialized to believe that women should become mothers. Dogs don't experience that kind of social pressure or internalize similar expectations. There is no evidence that a female dog needs to give birth in order to feel physically or psychologically fulfilled.

2. Breeding will prevent illness later on.

   Untrue. Recent studies actually suggest that unbred females are less prone to developing growths than those who have had litters.

3. Breeding will lead to easy profits.

   Doubtful. Breeding is an expensive proposition. Look at the following costs per litter:

   - stud fee (owner of male purebred will charge for services)
   - box in which mother will give birth
   - veterinary examinations
   - vaccinations
   - food
   - advertising the pups as being for sale
   - registration of puppies
   - worming

   On top of this, there is no guarantee that your female will give birth to pups who will fetch a high price on the market.

4. Even if I can't get my asking price, I'll still be able to find homes for the puppies.

   Untrue. This kind of thinking results in unwanted puppies taking up residence in local pounds.

tant it is that all pet owners think very seriously about the reasons why they want to breed their dogs.

FINDING THE RIGHT MATE

The goal of breeding is to improve the bloodline by producing strong, healthy animals featuring the very best qualities of the breed. In order to accomplish this, you'll need to research the breed standards, which will give you the profile to which to aspire. You should also study the congenital deformities (for instance, hip dysplasia) associated with the breed you are considering.

Ask your veterinarian to refer you to

breeders or call the local kennel club for referral. They should be able to lead you to an ethical, well-informed professional who has a healthy male dog suitable for your female. Another source is the breeder from whom you purchased your female.

Once you zero in on a potential male, study him and hold him to the breed standards you've researched. Study his bloodlines, looking closely at the dogs from whom he is descended. Examine, if possible, the dogs he has sired. Know all the faults of your own dog and those of the potential male. *Never breed two dogs who share the same faults.*

Sexual Maturity

Male dogs reach puberty from six months to one and a half years of age. As a general rule, the larger the breed, the longer it takes to become sexually mature. The female's first heat occurs at about the same age, but it is not advisable to breed a female until at least her second heat. While she may be anatomically capable of being mated, a female this young has not had time to develop physiologically or psychologically to adequately support a litter. She

may not be able to spare the nutrients puppies will demand, and she may also be traumatized by whelping.

A good age range for breeding the female is from eighteen months to seven years. For males, the range is about fifteen months to eight years. In general, the best age to breed dogs is two to five years.

A Clean Bill of Health

Once a potential male has been selected, it is important to be sure both dogs are in excellent health just prior to breeding. At this time, all hereditary breed defects will be revealed. Vaccinations will be checked, uterine infection and parasites discovered, and stool samples taken. Both dogs should be given blood tests for canine brucellosis, a sexually transmitted disease that should preclude breeding until it clears up. This is a serious bacterial disease that can diminish fertility.

The Best Time to Breed

The best time to breed the female is during estrus, nine to twelve days after

VACCINATIONS AND BREEDING

Female dogs should have their DHLPP booster shot *before* being bred. This booster will protect her and her litter against distemper, hepatitis, leptospirosis, parainfluenza, and parvovirus (see Vaccinations, Chapter Five).

bleeding has started. An excellent indicator is a change in the blood's color from deep red to pale red or yellow. By that time, the vulva has softened and become less congested. For a more scientific approach, a veterinarian can take vaginal smears during heat to determine when ovulation is occurring. Smears can also help predict when a pregnant dog will give birth. Once your dog has started to bleed, take her to the veterinarian to have this procedure undertaken.

GETTING IT RIGHT

Many breeders recommend introducing the male and female weeks before breeding. Some say that the female should spend her entire heat period near the male. Both are good suggestions, as long as the two are well supervised during their interaction.

When the time has come to breed, experienced dogs will know exactly what to do. It may be necessary to help in some cases, however, especially with novices.

An inexperienced male may need you to place him in the mounting position. Once you have accomplished this, allow him to finish the job. If the male becomes overly (perhaps brutally) excited, carefully take control of the situation so as not to make the situation completely unpalatable for the female.

The shy or nervous female can be helped along by a mild tranquilizer. If she becomes too aggressive, you may have to separate them temporarily to prevent injury. However, after mating has occurred, do not break apart the "tie" (see p. 202).

Sometimes the female seems very willing to mate, but refuses the male repeatedly. This could indicate a physical problem or a miscalculation in

REASONS WHY A BRED FEMALE MAY NOT BECOME PREGNANT

- The heat cycle has been miscalculated, and breeding has taken place prior to ovulation
- Poor nutrition
- Emotional instability caused by a change in surroundings
- Poor hormonal production (this condition is often responsive to hormone therapy)
- Blocked fallopian tubes
- Impenetrable hymen
- A serious disease like distemper can result in temporary infertility (up to two years)
- Obesity

THE SIGNS OF PREGNANCY

Here's a rough timeline describing the physical signs of a normal pregnancy:

25 DAYS	Veterinarian can sense enlargements in the uterus through palpation.
30 DAYS	Mother will gain weight; abdomen has visibly enlarged, although this isn't necessarily noticeable in large breeds or if the litter is small. Increase in appetite.
35 DAYS	Nipples grow large, pink, and hard.
45 DAYS	Nipples grow still larger but have become softer.
50 DAYS	Breasts begin to produce milk, as evidenced by swelling.
55–60 DAYS	Nipples emit a watery liquid. Subtle, visible uterine movement. Decrease in appetite, leading to refusal of food. Birth is about to occur.

determining what phase of heat she's in. Call your veterinarian for assistance.

It's a good idea to mate your dog twice during this period, over a course of about forty-eight hours. Don't wait more than four days between matings, because this could result in two separate conceptions, which increases the chances of premature births.

ACCIDENTAL PREGNANCY

A female dog in heat will not discriminate between breeds—she is likely to mate with any male who shows interest. That is why it is crucial to keep your dog confined or under close supervision when she goes into heat.

If an accidental and unwanted pregnancy does occur, it is possible to prevent the birth by injecting the female with the female hormone estrogen. However, this should be performed within forty-eight hours after mating, and it is very difficult to determine exactly when an unplanned mating has occurred. Also, estrogen may be unsafe for dogs, so most veterinarians will only use this method once or twice per animal.

PREGNANCY

Canine pregnancy is often determined by what may seem like primitive methods. A veterinarian generally judges by external features, though Ultrasound and X rays are sometimes used, and can now detect pregnancy very early on. The gestation period is between fifty-eight and sixty-eight days, with the average falling at just about nine weeks.

FALSE PREGNANCY (PSEUDORYSIS, PSEUDOPREGNANCY)

Sometimes, a dog may believe she's pregnant even if she actually isn't. She may exhibit the physical signs of pregnancy: lactation, nipple enlargement, abdominal distension, and personality changes. She may create a warm, cozy space to house her potential litter and may even exhibit maternal, protective behavior toward household objects like socks, soft shoes, or bones. This all adds up to false pregnancy, which is believed to be caused by post-estrus hormones.

This can occur regardless of whether the female has actually been bred.

Some painful symptoms occasionally surface, including cramps and mastitis (see Mastitis, p. 214). The "pregnancy" begins at about five weeks, following the end of estrus, and can last for another three or four weeks.

It's possible to relieve symptoms of false pregnancy with hormone injections, but usually rest and the application of hot and cold packs to enlarged breasts will suffice.

If several false pregnancies occur in a row, it may be wise to consider ovario-hysterectomy (see Birth Control, p. 201).

EXERCISE DURING PREGNANCY

Exercise during pregnancy is beneficial, as long as it isn't excessive. Keep to your dog's daily routine up to the last three to four weeks of pregnancy.

FEEDING DURING PREGNANCY

28 DAYS   Normal diet.

35 DAYS   Feed twice a day, increasing protein, iron, and calcium. Add cheese, yogurt, eggs, and muscle meat.

50 DAYS   Feed several meals throughout the day, to avoid anorexia and malnutrition.

The goal is to increase the level of nutrients, especially protein, without drastically increasing the amount of food you give your pregnant dog. You'll only want to give your dog about 50 percent more food than normal during this period. Obese dogs often birth overweight puppies and undergo difficult labor. Ask your veterinarian about vitamin and mineral supplementations.

THE WHELPING BOX

Like the human delivery room, the whelping box provides a special, clean place for the mother to birth her litter.

Whelping boxes can be purchased or made. The best are composed of strong, smooth wood, with sides high enough to prevent puppies from crawling out but low enough to allow the mother easy entry and exit. The interior sides of the box should be lined with a narrow ledge to prevent the mother from squashing her puppies against the wall. The ideal box should be large enough to hold the mother when she is fully elongated or stretched out. Keep it elevated a few inches off the ground to prevent chilling.

Place the whelping box in a peaceful area near the mother's sleeping space. Scrub it with disinfectant and line it with plenty of newspapers. The mother may scratch and dig at the newspapers before giving birth, heeding her evolutionary call to create a nest.

Make sure to keep the whelping box warm—eighty-five degrees Fahrenheit for the first week after the puppies are born. Each week after the first, lower the temperature by five degrees until you level off at seventy degrees. Monitor the temperature regularly and use a heat source to maintain warmth.

Some examples of a heat source include setting up a spare heater in the whelping-box room, keeping the whelping box near a temperature-controlled radiator, or placing hot water bottles or heating pads one or two layers beneath the puppies' bedding.

Chances are, she'll know when enough is enough. If her weight gain or discomfort slow her down, follow her lead. Avoid rigorous exercise like hiking and climbing.

COUNTDOWN TO DELIVERY

TWO TO THREE WEEKS BEFORE:

Take the mother-to-be for a veterinary examination. Ask for tips on delivery and get an emergency phone number from the veterinarian if you don't already have it.

TWO WEEKS BEFORE:

Make the whelping box (see box above).

ONE WEEK BEFORE:

Trim the hair away from the mother's nipples, which will make nursing easier.

Check for infection. To avoid the transmission of parasites from mother to brood, wash each nipple with warm water and a mild antiseptic soap. Soften with baby oil.

Prepare the whelping quarters with the following:

    newspapers
    plastic garbage bags
    clean towels
    white thread
    scissors
    rubbing alcohol
    surgical gloves
    water for mother
    a safe heat source
    a scale
    a pad or notebook where you can
        record names and weights of
        puppies

THE BIRTH OF A LITTER

Your goal during whelping is to allow nature to take its course, but to also step in promptly should something go wrong.

UNASSISTED DELIVERY

Your dog will show several key signs just prior to giving birth. She'll start to dig and paw in one area, as if she is trying to make a nest. Take her to the whelping box if she doesn't go there on her own. Her temperature will start to drop to about ninety-nine degrees Fahrenheit. She may also have a sticky fluid coming from her vagina.

Make sure the area you have designated for delivery is serene. Keep all but the necessary people out of the area and avoid loud noises and bright lights. Also, try to restrain your own tension and excitement. You want to create as stress-free an environment as possible. Keep in mind that should something go wrong, you'll certainly have enough time to get veterinary help, either in person or, if necessary, over the phone.

As labor begins, your dog's "water" may or may not "break." Each puppy is surrounded by a water bag. While you will see the bag beginning to appear from the vulva, it might stay intact until the puppy has completely emerged, depending upon the forcefulness of the uterine contractions. Rhythmic panting will also be a telltale sign that the litter is about to be born.

Once labor begins, the mother will stretch out on her side or her front—it varies from dog to dog. You will be able to observe the tensing and relaxing of her abdomen and diaphragm, which is caused by contractions. The time between these contractions will diminish as birth approaches.

Pups are most likely to appear head-first. However, in many cases the hind legs are the first part of a puppy to see the world. This should not pose any threat to the mother or litter.

It's the mother's job, according to nature, to rid the puppy of the gelatinous material known as the amniotic

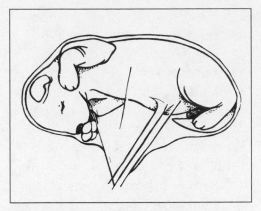

A pup is born in its amniotic sac, which the mother should remove by licking it.

sac and the fetal membranes covering it. She'll usually accomplish the latter by licking the pup, which also helps it to breathe. If she doesn't do this, step in. Pick the puppy up carefully, breaking the amniotic sac if it hasn't already burst during delivery. Holding him gently in both hands, with his head up, swing him in a small arc. This will clear the mouth, throat, and lungs of mucus and other fluids. Then, using a towel, rub the puppy vigorously, making sure his nose points downward. This will help him to start breathing.

Mouth-to-nose resuscitation is necessary if a puppy doesn't start breathing on his own. Be sure to blow with less force than you would use on an adult in distress.

As the mother nuzzles and cleans her puppy, she will sever the umbilical cord with her teeth. The puppy can continue to draw useful blood from the placenta through the umbilical cord, so it's fine for the cord to remain intact for about fifteen or twenty minutes after delivery. If the mother doesn't show any interest in cutting the cord herself, do it for her. Take some dental floss and tie a knot around the cord about an inch away from the puppy's body. Make another knot about one more inch away. Cut between the two knots.

An important fact to keep in mind is that nature doles out one placenta per puppy. Each placenta must be expelled

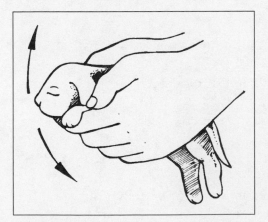

If the mother hasn't assisted her pup's breathing by licking it, swing the puppy gently in a small arc, clearing its airways.

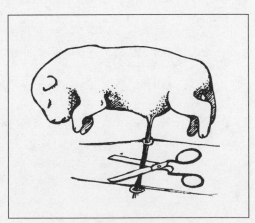

If the mother has not chewed through the umbilical cord, sever it yourself using dental floss and scissors.

either at birth or within fifteen minutes of it. Count placentas after delivery. Placentas that are not expelled from the uterus can cause serious infections (see Metritis, p. 215). Mothers usually like to eat placentas, which is fine as long as she doesn't go overboard. Discourage her from eating more than two in order to avoid gastric upset.

The average time between births varies anywhere between ten minutes and two hours. It's a good idea to temporarily transfer the newborn to another box just long enough for the rest of the litter to be born. This will avoid accidents and unneeded distractions that can be magnified by the confining nature of the whelping box.

Make sure the newborn's temporary shelter is warmed by a heating pad or hot water bottle wrapped snugly in a towel. There should be enough room in the box with the heating pad so that the puppies can move away from the heat if it is too intense.

Give the mother an opportunity to drink some water several hours into the delivery process. All the straining she will be experiencing may leave her very thirsty.

By the time the final puppy has been delivered, the mother will seem very fatigued, but relaxed. Transfer the puppies back to the mother after gently cleaning her nipples with soap and warm water. Put the puppies to her nipples if they don't go automatically.

PROBLEM LABOR:
WHEN TO CALL THE VETERINARIAN

Labor is a complicated process. If you sense something's going wrong, call the veterinarian immediately. Here are some indicators of problem labor:

1. Thirty hours have passed since the mother's temperature dropped, yet labor hasn't begun.
2. Two hours have passed since the onset of moderate contractions but no hard contractions have begun.
3. More than thirty minutes of hard contractions occur without any sign of the puppy emerging.
4. Thirty minutes have passed since the membranes ruptured, yet the first puppies haven't arrived.
5. More than three hours have passed in between the arrival of puppies.
6. Initial contractions are followed by the discharge of a dark or bloody substance.
7. Your dog is in extreme discomfort.

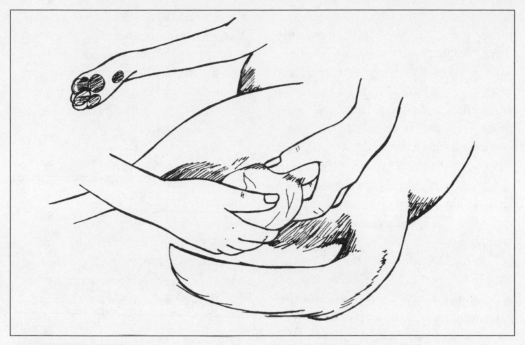

When assisting a delivery, try to match the force and speed with which you pull the puppy to the mother's natural contractions.

ASSISTED DELIVERY

If you think the puppy is stuck in the birth canal, it may be time to step in—taking great pains to be gentle. Follow these steps:

1. Wash your hands with a strong disinfectant.
2. Spread the vulva apart to expose puppy.
3. Using a sterile towel, grasp the puppy and pull, matching your force with the mother's contractions. In doing so, try to pull the puppy by the shoulders; avoid favoring a single limb.
4. Avoid the amniotic sac that envelops the puppy.
5. If a retained placenta blocks the way, remove it with a clean cloth.

AFTER THE DELIVERY

It's a smart idea to take mother and litter for a veterinary examination about a day after delivery.

In the first twenty-four hours after the litter is born, the mother will respond to the puppies' demand for food by producing a watery milk product called "colostrum." This will help the puppies fight off disease. The amount of colostrum produced depends upon the demand.

That first week, the mother will probably be most interested in caring for her litter and will be very protective. Unless the puppies are being ignored or harmed, leave them alone as much as possible, allowing the mother to meet their needs.

During the first week of motherhood, check the mother's temperature daily, making sure it doesn't go above 102 degrees. Also, check for vaginal discharge. While it's fine for her to emit some fluid for a few days, heavy or brown discharge usually indicates complications. All discharge should stop within one week. Finally, make sure the mother relieves herself regularly while nursing. Gently coax her away from her litter if she seems reluctant to leave.

During the first week, you will probably find your dog's appetite close to normal. Feed her her prepregnancy diet for seven days. However, she'll need plenty of extra nutrients to keep her litter healthy. After seven days, feed her the regular diet plus an extra 100 calories per pound of puppy. If you follow this rule, the dog will be eating about three times her normal diet three weeks into motherhood. The extra calories should come from high-protein food such as milk, egg, meat and liver. Ask your veterinarian if vitamin and mineral supplementation is also recommended. When weaning begins (see Weaning, p. 221), start to decrease the mother's food intake; by the time the puppies are about six weeks old, the mother should be close to her normal diet.

POSTPARTUM PROBLEMS

MASTITIS

CAUSES: Mastitis is an inflamed or infected mammary gland or breast. Infection, a cut or bruise, or milk backup can cause this painful disorder.

SYMPTOMS: Lumpy, painful, unusually warm, purplish-blue breasts; fever; diminished appetite; discolored milk; lack of interest in nursing.

TREATMENT: Seek veterinary help. If an infection is detected, antibiotics will be administered to curb its spread. The gland may require drainage. Your veterinarian may advise you to apply cold

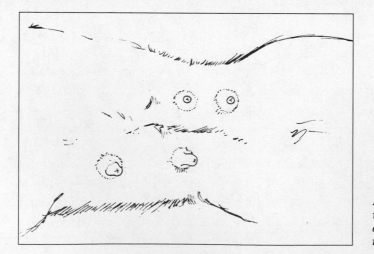

Many mothers with mastitis will avoid nursing because of the pain associated with this condition.

WARNING ABOUT NURSING DOGS

A dog with infected mammary glands must not nurse her puppies. Her milk may be toxic. The puppies will have to be hand-fed (see Hand-Feeding Your Puppy box, p. 219).

---

packs temporarily to the affected region to soothe pain and reduce swelling.

PREVENTION: While your dog is nursing, make sure the surfaces she comes in contact with are clean and smooth, to avoid both infection and physical damage.

METRITIS

CAUSES: Metritis, an infection that spreads upward toward the uterus, can be attributed to a number of labor-related causes. Membranes or fetal tissue may be stuck in the uterus, or the delivery condition might have been unclean, leading to infection. These conditions include unsterile instruments, hands, or cloths. Chronic vaginitis is yet another cause.

SYMPTOMS: Lethargy and depression, fever, disinterest in food, vomiting, malodorous, thick red-brown discharge from vulva.

TREATMENT: Immediate veterinary care is required. Prevent puppies from nursing, since the milk may be toxic (see Hand-Feeding Your Puppy box, p. 219).

MILK FEVER

CAUSES: Milk fever usually arises about two weeks after birth if the mother isn't getting enough calcium to support herself and her puppies. This is an emergency situation because the dog's heart requires calcium in order to keep pumping properly. She can die within four to six hours after the first symptoms appear.

SYMPTOMS: Listlessness, abnormally fast breathing, whining, stiff, spastic walk, possible convulsions.

TREATMENT: This is an emergency. Notify your veterinarian at once. Treatment consists of intravenous calcium solutions to restore normal calcium levels. Puppies should be taken off the mother for at least the first twenty-four hours.

MOTHER DOGS WHO IGNORE THEIR LITTER

Instinct usually takes over immediately after delivery, and mothers begin to care for their puppies without any help from their human caretakers.

Occasionally, the mother may put up some resistance or show indifference, especially if the delivery was a surgical one. Even a mother who delivered naturally may shy away from her very first litter during the first few hours. In both cases, she may be traumatized or exhausted by the experience. She may just need a little help, perhaps to be shown how to nurse her puppies by having the newborns nuzzled to her nipples. Spend some time with her and the puppies to reinforce the connection between them. If she leaves the whelping box for long periods, take her back and stay with them for a while.

Sometimes a spoiled female will not eat for a few days after her first litter. Try indulging her with her favorite treats.

Everyone wants to cuddle puppies, but this can cause the mother great distress. She may become so upset that she will actually injure her puppies in a flight of rage. If the mother seems very agitated, keep people away from the puppies and watch the litter closely.

SORE NIPPLES

CAUSES: Puppies, eager to get their share of milk, may claw at their mother's nipples, causing irritation. To avoid pain, the mother may not allow the puppies to suckle.

TREATMENT: You can solve this problem by clipping the puppies' claws—but be very careful only to take the very tips, or you may cause bleeding (see Nail Trimming, p. 67).

21

CARING FOR PUPPIES

IT'S HARD TO ARGUE with the adjective "adorable" when it comes down to a puppy. But proper care for that irresistible creature demands time, money, and patience. This chapter welcomes you to the world of puppydom, and shows you what you need to know in order to raise healthy puppies.

THE NEWBORN

At birth, puppies are not nearly as developed as their human counterparts. Many scientists believe that puppies are born so early because their mothers couldn't afford to be slowed down by pregnancy. If they remained pregnant for longer, they would lag behind the pack in which they traveled.

Newborn puppies can neither see nor hear, as their sense organs are not yet functional. It takes a little more than a week before puppies will respond to aural stimuli. Full hearing develops by about six weeks.

The eyes open long before the brain is ready to control vision. Look for puppies' eyelids to separate at about ten days to two weeks. This enables them to differentiate between light and dark. The eyes will focus on images about a week later. Keep the puppy in

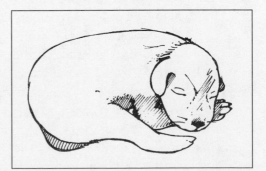

A healthy newborn rests.

dim light until she has time to adjust to her newfound vision.

A puppy has a strong sense of smell from birth—she first encounters the world and satisfies her needs through her ability to smell. The puppy finds the mother's nipple by way of the pheromones emitted from the mammary glands. The scent is strong enough to attract the puppy to this initial source of food. Quickly, the puppy learns to associate this scent with feeding—i.e., warm milk.

WARMTH

Whether in a cozy home or out in the wild, puppies need to be kept warm in order to survive. A newborn puppy lacks the ability to generate her own heat. The blood vessels normally produce and maintain heat, but a newborn's circulatory system has not developed enough to carry out this function. As a result, the newborn must turn to an external source of heat.

The heat emitted by the mother's body can keep the puppy's temperature at about 96 to 100 degrees. To avoid chilling, which can kill a puppy, keep the whelping box (see Whelping Box, p. 209) at about 85 degrees during the first week of a litter's life. If the puppies have thick coats, set the box a few degrees cooler; if their bodies are not yet protected by hair, raise the temperature a few degrees.

Always watch the temperature of the box closely. Just as chilling can be very dangerous, so can overheating. Puppies exposed to too much heat can suffer severe loss of fluids. This can result in death.

WEIGHT GAIN

A healthy newborn may lose weight in the first few days of life but should start to gain weight by the time she is forty-eight hours old. In fact, she

Normal weight gain and developmental advances during the first two weeks of life.

should double her birth weight in eight to ten days. A good indicator of a pup's potential to put on healthy weight is to see if the mother is gaining weight, as this is a sign that she has the nutritional support available to pass on to her litter.

A puppy that loses 10 percent or more of her birth weight in the first two days of life and does not start gaining by three days probably will not survive unless she is hand-fed (see Hand-Feeding Your Puppy box, below).

A puppy who at birth weighs about 25 percent less than her litter mates should be placed in an incubator (see Making an Incubator box, p. 221) and hand-fed. Many underweight puppies can be saved if quick action is taken and their weakness is not complicated by disease or hereditary defects.

HAND-FEEDING AND REARING

The mother of a litter may become ill, develop an infection dangerous to her puppies, have toxic milk or no milk at all, or just be unable to handle so many puppies. In those situations, it is ideal to have a foster mother care for your needy pups. If your veterinarian cannot suggest a foster mother, however, you will have to take over the nursing responsibilities. This includes hand-feeding, cleaning away the urine and feces from especially young pups, and ensuring that the litter stays warm.

Your veterinarian can suggest the most appropriate feeding formula for your litter. Be sure to prepare a fresh formula every day and to store it in the refrigerator. When you are ready to feed it to the puppies, heat it up so it is warm to the touch.

Weigh your puppy on a daily basis not only to be sure that she is maintaining healthy weight gain, but also to figure out how much food is nutritionally sound for her. Also monitor pups' food intake to determine when you should feed them. If a puppy has a very small appetite or is weak, you may want to feed her less food more frequently.

HAND-FEEDING YOUR PUPPY

This chart, along with your own calculations, can help you to devise a good puppy diet.

AGE IN WEEKS	AMOUNT OF FOOD (IN OUNCES) PER POUND OF DOG	AMOUNT OF FOOD (IN TABLESPOONS) PER POUND OF DOG	NUMBER OF FEEDING TIMES PER DAY
1	2	4	7–12
2	2 1/3	4 2/3	7–12
3	2 2/3	5 1/3	3–6
4	3	6	3–6

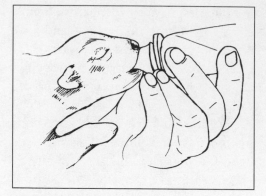

The proper method for bottle feeding.

A puppy with a robust appetite, on the other hand, can have larger amounts of food fewer times a day.

Avoid feeding your puppy with an eyedropper as you could unintentionally force milk into her lungs and cause pneumonia. The best feeding container is a bottle: a regular baby bottle, a doll bottle, or a bottle purchased from a pet store or your veterinarian. Before feeding your puppies, be sure your bottle and your hands are clean and that the fluid flows easily. Enlarge the hole on the nipple if necessary by inserting a boiled, sterilized needle into it.

You may want to place the puppy on a table or on your lap, facing forward, when you are ready to feed her. Elevate the puppy slightly by placing your hand or a small towel under her front legs. Gently wedge the nipple of the bottle into the puppy's mouth and over the tip of the tongue. Hold the bottle at about a forty-five degree angle and allow the formula to run slowly into the puppy's mouth. The puppy may want to "knead" as she would on her mother's teat to stimu-

late its milk production, so allow her front legs to move freely.

Unsuccessful feeding is a danger to a young puppy, especially if she is weak or small. Try dabbing a spot of milk on the puppy's lips, right at the opening of the mouth. Sometimes this will stimulate a poor appetite. If this method fails, do not force the puppy to eat. Consult your veterinarian, who will feed the puppy by inserting a long tube into her belly. The veterinarian may show you how to do this at home, but it is a delicate procedure and you should be thoroughly familiar with it before you attempt it.

Always be careful not to overfeed your puppies. While some may refuse the bottle, others will take advantage of your hospitality. Runny stools and excessive bloating may result. If you notice such symptoms, cut back slightly on your doses or dilute the doses by adding some water.

After successful hand-feeding, two important procedures must follow. First, hold the puppy up to your shoulder and pat her back. Burping the puppy much like you would a human baby can release excess air that was swallowed during feeding. After burping, you need to encourage the puppy to go to the bathroom. The canine mother would do this by licking the abdomen and anal area. You should do this by rubbing a cotton ball or towel moistened with warmed water over these areas. You may also use this procedure to clean the puppy, wiping away any milk, urine, or feces that may be on her fur. (Note: If your puppy's feces are

MAKING AN INCUBATOR

Incubators provide necessary warmth for puppies who have been orphaned. Place a heating pad over the side of a small cardboard box. Cover part of the bottom of the box with the pad, leaving plenty of room for the puppies to move to the other side should they find the warmth uncomfortable. Cover the pad with a thick towel, as puppies have very sensitive skin. Turn the pad on low.

Measure the box's temperature with a thermometer. The incubator should be kept at 85 degrees to 90 degrees for the first week, 80 degrees for the second week, 75 degrees for the third and fourth weeks, and 70 degrees thereafter.

runny and messy, reassess her diet. If this doesn't stop the problem, or if the stools are white in color, consult your veterinarian. An infection or some other illness may be to blame.)

Between feedings, you may want to allow the puppies to return to the care and warmth of their mother. Before you do this, however, consider some potential problems. The mother may become upset when she smells a foreign scent on the puppies. As a result, she may obsessively clean the puppies and, in the process, hurt them. Other mothers may simply reject their puppies. You are the best judge of how your dog will react.

A trusting dog may want you, as her human best friend, to help her with the litter. If your dog is slightly suspicious, be sure to wash your hands without soap and then to pet the mother before touching her puppies. Not only may this reassure your dog that you are coming in peace, but it will also mask your scent by replacing it with hers.

Even if you trust your dog, be sure to closely monitor her relationship with the puppies' the first few times you return them to her. Maternity can bring out new behaviors in your dog and you should always be cautious and patient with her.

WEANING

The process of weaning should begin when the puppies are between three and five weeks of age. Exactly when you begin weaning is your decision. A mother's shortage of milk could also become a factor in your decision.

BEGINNING THE WEANING PROCESS:

1. Prepare a soupy meal consisting of oatmeal, baby food, or commercial

Start weaning by extending a fingerful of soupy meal to your puppy.

dog food heavily diluted with warm water.

2. Dip your clean finger in the soupy meal and introduce it to each of the puppies. They may immediately lick it off. If they don't, however, dab some on their lips. It may take them a day or two to get used to this new food.

3. The puppies should continue nursing. You may want to gradually decrease the mother's food intake and vitamin supply, however, so that her milk production begins to slow down.

TWO DAYS LATER:

1. Pour a small amount of the soupy meal onto a couple of saucers or shallow dishes. Place them in the whelping box.

2. If the puppies are reluctant to eat their new food:

- Place the puppy before the dish. Once again dip your clean finger into the mixture and wipe it on the dog's lips.
- Remove the mother from the whelping box at least two hours before feeding the puppies so that they develop an appetite. Keep the mother away from the whelping box so that she doesn't interrupt the puppies' meals.

3. Your puppies will spill most of the food you give them. Much of the rest will end up on their fur. Be sure to clean the puppies after their new meals by wiping them down with a warm, moistened washcloth. You may also have to wipe around the abdominal and anal area, as their new food could induce slight diarrhea.

4. Your puppies should continue nursing, although now about twice a day.

FOUR TO SEVEN DAYS INTO THE PROCESS:

Puppies will begin to adapt to their new task, lapping up the food from a shallow dish. Diarrhea should stop.

1. Begin feeding the puppies about four times a day, always being sure to provide some water as well.

2. Slowly thicken the consistency of the mixture by adding less and less water to it. You may also want to mix one or two tablespoons of cottage cheese or lean grilled hamburger into the mixture for added nutrition.

3. Your puppies will still nurse. They may, however, be too full to want much milk. The mother may also not have enough milk to feed them. Don't worry about this; it is part of the process of weaning.

A WEEK AFTER THE PROCESS OF WEANING HAS BEGUN:

1. As your puppies continually improve in their ability to eat the new food, you should begin introducing solid foods to them. Since they do not have teeth yet, moisten some dry dog food with warm water and add it to their mixture. Continue to feed them four times a day.

2. Once you are confident that your puppies are eating solid foods, discourage them from nursing. If you spot a puppy nursing, remove it from the mother. Allow the mother to get away from her puppies more often and to exercise. The mother may help you out with the process, since her puppies may have begun to teethe and the tooth buds popping out of their gums hurt her when the pups try to nurse. She may even get up and leave just to avoid what she may feel, at this time, is a tiring task.

When your puppies are eight weeks old, the process of weaning should be complete. Continue to moisten their dry food until their teeth are fully developed.

YOUR PUPPY'S GROWTH AND DEVELOPMENT

In raising a puppy, your goal should be overall good health. Physical well-being is but one dimension of that objective. A puppy's socialization is another important dimension.

WEANING TO THREE MONTHS

The seeds of socialization are planted during this early period. One important step you can take to help ready your puppy for domestic life is to give her plenty of affection while she is with the litter. Young puppies respond well to gentle strokes and cuddling. It shows them that humans are their friends.

Try to keep a puppy with the litter for about two months. This will help her adjust to being with her fellow dogs. It's a good idea to separate the litter by twelve weeks—more than that will lead to pups who are very comfortable with other dogs but who probably will be reluctant to be with people. By being removed from the litter at around eight weeks, a puppy will know how to behave around other dogs and will also be secure enough with humans to respond well to training.

THREE MONTHS TO FIVE MONTHS

By this stage, puppies want to know the world they live in. Expect a puppy to be into everything, and support this

Hard rubber toys are great for teething and provide puppies with hours of fun.

need by providing plenty of protective supervision.

At about this age, puppies start to chew. Of course, they do not have the ability to differentiate safe objects to chew on from those that could cause them problems. You will want them to chew on acceptable toys, but they might become interested in furniture, cords, and even draperies. If a puppy's chewing habits get out of hand, the first step you need to take is to determine what motivates the chewing.

Puppies begin to lose their baby teeth at about four months. They teethe in response to the arrival of adult teeth. Supply a puppy with plenty of hard rubber toys and rawhide bones. Do not give her meat bones or soft rubber toys. Soft rubber can easily be ripped apart by young teeth, and meat bones small enough for a puppy to play with can splinter. Either can result in intestinal damage or blockage. Safe toys can also ease boredom, which can result in destructive chewing.

During this period, look for internal parasites by having a stool specimen checked by your veterinarian. Your veterinarian should also begin vaccinations (see Chapter Five).

FIVE MONTHS TO SEVEN MONTHS

A puppy moves into a transitional "juvenile" stage at this age. This is the

THE IMPORTANCE OF PLAY

It is crucial that you make a strong effort to satisfy your puppy's desire to play. While playing with a puppy is great fun, it is far from mere frivolity. Rather, playing with her helps you become close to your puppy, and will allow you to show her both that you care for her and that you are her master. Showing a puppy love, attention, and a sense of fun will most likely result in a warm and affectionate adult dog.

most comprehensive period of development.

Even if it looks like your dog has finally developed a full coat, she really hasn't yet. Don't start clipping the coat of a long-haired dog yet, for her growing fur will protect her, even in summer. If your dog stays inside most of the time, you will need to protect her from the elements during her trips outdoors. A warm sweater will protect her from the cold, while brisk rubbing with a towel will keep her from becoming chilled after a rainstorm.

Since dogs should have been housebroken prior to this period, ask a veterinarian if your dog still has constant accidents. Professional training is probably the answer, but you will first need to rule out any significant physiological disorder that may be causing the problems.

Begin to look into obedience classes at this age, if this is the route you have decided to take. After the initial round of classes has been completed, consider enrolling in a refresher course about a half a year later.

At six months, a dog should get a rabies vaccination.

Housebreaking or paper training should also occur between three and five months (see Toilet Training Your Puppy, this page, and Paper Training, p. 226).

SEVEN TO TWELVE MONTHS

Inquisitiveness mixes with confidence at this age, creating a pet who can be as delightful as she may be exasperating. Indulge your dog in her curiosity and newfound fascination with the world, but exercise firm discipline when she steps out of line.

By the end of the first year, your dog will have reached her full height and weight (larger breeds take slightly longer). Her fundamental temperament and basic responses to people will be rather firmly set. She understands and does her best to live up to her role in the home she shares with you.

A dog at this age has her full set of adult teeth. Her adult digestive system can well accommodate two meals a day. Since her reproductive system is now mature, you must decide whether or not you plan to breed your dog. If the answer is no, this is an excellent time for spaying or neutering (see Birth Control, p. 201).

Apply at this time for any necessary licenses, such as the ones smaller towns require in order to monitor the canine population.

TOILET TRAINING YOUR PUPPY

Puppies need a great deal of support during housebreaking or paper training. In order to be supportive, you will need to exercise great patience.

Puppies love to please and will respond to your lessons with great enthusiasm. Do not punish your puppy unless you are sure she understands what you are trying to tell her, but is wilfully disobeying you.

Four to six weeks are needed to housebreak the average dog. But remember, that is the average. Every dog is unique, so give your puppy a break if she learns a little more slowly than anticipated.

PAPER TRAINING

You may want to paper train your dog until she is fully housebroken, especially if you will not be around to take her out every couple of hours.

Designate an area in the house that can be closed off and easily cleaned. You don't want this area to be too remote, as your puppy will be lonely when you leave her there. If you plan to leave the puppy in her paper training area for a day, be sure it is kept warm.

Cover the area with newspapers and close it off with a gate or a door, if possible. Your puppy will typically soil the same area of the paper. As the habit develops, remove some of the papers until they eventually cover only a small surface of the floor.

If the puppy continues to soil only one newspaper, you can pull it toward the door you use to take the puppy for its bathroom walk. A properly housebroken dog will sit at the door when she needs to go to the bathroom. At that time, you can remove the newspaper.

When the dog has an "accident," immediately scrub the area with a disinfectant and deodorant. Otherwise, the puppy may be attracted by the scent and repeat the behavior in the same spot.

Your pet store may carry some commercial aids to help paper training.

They have an odor of urine that draws the puppy to the spot you have deemed acceptable for urination and defecation.

HOUSEBREAKING

Housebreaking a puppy can be painless, with a little patience.

A good way to begin housebreaking is to feed the puppy at designated times, removing food in between meals. Expect the puppy to need a bathroom run between fifteen to thirty minutes after eating. At that time, take the puppy outside for a walk.

You should also take the puppy outdoors after she takes a long nap, has a drink, or if she looks anxious and is wandering around the house sniffing in certain spots.

A routine walk will at first help the puppy develop proper habits. Always go out the same door. Walk the same route and remember where your puppy last went to the bathroom; the lingering scent could encourage her to do her business there. Always be sure to lavish praise on her when she does her business outdoors.

You may find housebreaking tedious. At first your puppy may need to go out every two hours. As she matures and learns, however, you should only have to take her out every three or four hours. A fully housebroken puppy should be able to hold her bowel movement for up to eight or nine hours.

Disciplining your dog while you are housebreaking her is almost useless unless you catch her in the act of going to the bathroom indoors. If you do catch her, say a firm "No, no" or "bad girl" to her and immediately take her on her routine walk.

COMMON BEHAVIOR PROBLEMS AND HOW TO CORRECT THEM

Puppies will be puppies, but when your puppy misbehaves and you do not correct her, ask yourself if the same behavior will be as "adorable" when the dog is an adult. Will you really enjoy a needy German Shepherd pouncing on your dinner guests?

Here are some common behavior problems and some good methods to correct them.

AGGRESSION

It is difficult to think of a tiny puppy as aggressive. If she snaps or growls at you when you interrupt her meals, however, she could be displaying an aggressive character that could grow worse with adulthood.

Discouraging this behavior sooner than later through a role-playing exercise could be one way to save a great deal of aggravation down the road. When you see your puppy eating or shortly after you have fed it, take the dish away. If the puppy snaps or growls at you when you do this, tell her that she is a bad girl. Wait a minute or two before replacing the dish of food.

Repeat the exercise. When she stops growling or snapping, lavishly praise her and allow her to continue eating. Of course, the exercise may have to be repeated a couple of times before your puppy understands courtesy and equality. If it persists, however, consult a dog trainer for suggestions on how to curtail the aggression.

BARKING

Excited puppies often bark to get their caretaker's attention. Unfortunately, this method of communicating with you can develop into an annoying habit once your puppy becomes a dog and barks incessantly to keep you nearby.

Stop this habit at an early age by discouraging barking. If your puppy barks to be let out, to make you play with her, to get food or table scraps, or for any other type of attention, tell her to stop. Say a sharp "no" with every bark she makes. Praise her when she stops barking.

If a neighbor complains that your puppy is barking or crying while you are away, purposely leave and quietly return to discipline your dog, following the same procedure.

BEGGING

No matter how endearing the look, do not capitulate to a pleading pup. Feed the puppy before you eat. Leave her food out for an hour. If the puppy hasn't eaten, throw the food out. After a few days of unfulfilling begging and seeing her own food disappear, the puppy will learn when and what she is supposed to eat.

Give edible treats only as a reward for a job well done. Otherwise the puppy will have difficulty identifying her own good behavior and may come to expect food all the time.

BITING

Puppies bite and nip at you when playing. Often they do this with the onset of teething to soothe the ache. They may also do it as a way of establishing dominance over you. Neither purpose is acceptable behavior, as their sharp young teeth can eventually hurt you and their habit could develop into an adult problem.

Discourage playful nipping and biting by telling your puppy "no" when she does it. Introduce a toy and encourage the puppy to bite that toy. Playing tug-of-war with an old towel is a wonderful way to continue playing with a nipping puppy while focusing some of her natural aggressive energy on one of her toys rather than on you. Biting and nipping should stop quickly. If it does not, say "no" and get up and leave. Refuse to play with the puppy until she behaves.

CHASING CARS

Dogs have always chased moving objects. That ability has enabled them to be excellent hunters. On the other hand, chasing also leads the modern dog right into the path of fast-moving automobiles. While chasing a car can be habit-forming fun, it is one game that poses a clear threat to a dog's life. It is also antisocial behavior in that grave injury to people can ensue as the caring driver swerves to avoid the reckless dog.

If your exhortations do not work, here's a technique that sounds brutal but is definitely harmless and highly effective. Ask someone your dog has never encountered to drive by in an unfamiliar car. Tell the person to "arm" herself with a water gun filled with a weak ammonia solution (one teaspoon of ammonia to at least a pint of water). If the dog starts to chase the car, have the person "shoot" the dog directly in the face. Repeat this several times by the car. Your dog will be unhappy about being squirted with this stinging (yet safe) solution, and will remember from then on that chasing equals pain.

CHEWING (see YOUR PUPPY'S GROWTH AND DEVELOPMENT, p. 223)

DIGGING

Dogs have always burrowed through soil, both as hunters and to create cool areas in which to rest. However, this evolutionary asset doesn't necessarily mesh well with domestic life, especially if you have a garden.

Digging is an instinct and instincts are always very strong. Your goal will be to get your dog to adapt to your needs. If you know your dog is a digger, try to catch her in the act. Shout at her and throw objects—near the dog, but not at her, to scare her. Don't let her escape without a firm reprimand. Lead her by the collar to the spot she dug up and say "bad!" firmly while shaking her by the collar. Repeat each time you catch her digging. You may not be able to stop the behavior completely, but you may keep it within acceptable limits.

JUMPING UP

An excited puppy may jump on you to greet you. While the dog is not intentionally trying to misbehave, this action can develop into an annoying habit, especially if your puppy grows to become a large dog.

Discourage this behavior by telling the dog "no" and commanding her to sit or lie down. Use a hand signal to reinforce the command. If your dog does not obey, then you need to follow the steps taken in obedience training to make your dog learn how to respond to the command (see "Sit!", p. 78). Do not pet your puppy until she has followed your instructions and is sitting or lying down. Lavish praise on her and perhaps give her a treat to let her know she is a good dog.

If your puppy continues to jump on you or other visitors, be more firm in your discipline. If you see her beginning to jump up, stick your knee out. The puppy will either see the obstacle and decide not to jump on you or she will jump and get a knee jammed into her chest. Continue to say "no" and follow this with a stern "bad dog!" The behavior should become less frequent.

SUBMISSIVE URINATION

Some shy puppies may squat and urinate at the sight of you or anybody else. You may misinterpret this as a housebreaking problem. It is, however, the result of being intimidated.

The worst thing you can do to an insecure puppy is to yell at him for such behavior. Have patience and let your puppy know she can trust you. Approach her quietly and slowly and speak to her in a happy, soothing tone. You may also want to squat low or bend down so you are on a more equal level with the puppy. With trust and maturity, the problem should disappear.

URINATION WHEN EXCITED

This problem requires patience and understanding. Bladder control comes with time. If urination is triggered by excitement, assume the puppy is still maturing. Most likely, the problem will go away by adulthood.

Punishment in such cases is not only useless, it may be harmful and actually lead to poor bladder control later in life. Instead, mitigate your own annoyance by playing only in areas where accidental urination won't do damage to carpets, drapes, bedding, or furniture.

PUPPY DISEASES AND HEALTH PROBLEMS

The following conditions and diseases can occur in newborn puppies, so take a moment and read through them to familiarize yourself.

BLEEDING

CAUSES: Puppies who are less than a week old may have a tendency to bleed easily. This tendency is caused by a lack of vitamin K, a vitamin responsible for manufacturing the blood clotting agent prothrombin. A lack of vitamin K can be passed on by a poorly nourished mother.

SYMPTOMS: Bleeding from body openings.

TREATMENT: If one puppy bleeds, all puppies in the litter should be injected with vitamin K by your veterinarian.

BLOOD POISONING (PUPPY SEPTICEMIA)

CAUSES: Navel infections or an infected mother's milk can transmit

---

INDICATIONS THAT A PUPPY MAY BE ILL

Contact your veterinarian if you notice any of the following:

1. **Diarrhea.** If left unchecked, diarrhea can kill a puppy due to extreme loss of fluids.
2. **Excessive crying and whining.** Sick puppies, like ill babies, will cry continuously, much more than their healthy littermates.
3. **Lethargy and weakness.** Healthy puppies seem to have plenty of energy, while sick ones have difficulty moving and are unresponsive.
4. **Grayish gums.** Any deviation from healthy pink gums may be evidence of illness.
5. **Dehydration.** Severe fluid loss causes a lack of elasticity in the puppy's skin (see Dehydration, pp. 87–89).
6. **Bloat.** If the abdomen is visibly distended or tender, the puppy may be bloated. Other related problems are constipation and parasites.
7. **Red-blue skin.** Look at the puppy's stomach. If it isn't a healthy pink, she is probably ill.
8. **The mother ignores the puppy.** For survival purposes, mothers tend to neglect sick puppies and focus on the healthy members of the litter.
9. **The puppy refuses to nurse,** thereby cutting off the supply of nutrients.

bacteria to the puppy. Once it is in the puppy's digestive tract, bacteria can spread quickly through the body, causing symptoms that will typically appear in the abdomen.

SYMPTOMS: Whimpering, pain, bloating. As the condition advances, the abdomen becomes taut and stretched, and the skin becomes bluish or dark red.

TREATMENT: Get immediate veterinary help. The veterinarian will give your puppy a potent antibiotic.

CIRCULATORY FAILURE OF THE NEWBORN

CAUSES: Sleeping quarters that are too cold or too hot, breathing difficulties, or improper care can inflict stress on a puppy less than a week old. The result is a cyclical degeneration that may include a decrease in the body temperature, a slowed heart and breathing rate,

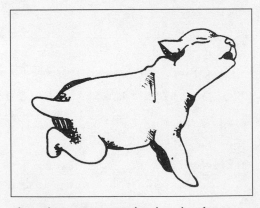

A newborn puppy experiencing circulatory failure may lose its balance and become immobile.

weakness, difficulties in feeding, spasms, shock, and death.

SYMPTOMS: Early signs include drooling, crying, and excessive swallowing. Later the pup loses her crawling and balancing ability and lies on her side. The puppy may pass bloody stools.

TREATMENT: Consult your veterinarian. Early treatment consisting of oxygen, adrenaline, and temperature monitoring may be able to save the puppy.

FADING PUPPY SYNDROME

CAUSES: Fading puppy syndrome can quickly rob a newborn of her life. It is actually the name given to any number of debilitating factors working in conjunction against the puppy. Some of the causes of this condition include bacterial or viral infections transmitted by the mother, worms, immaturity, birth defects, a harsh environment, lack of maternal care, lack of food, and chilling.

SYMPTOMS: A fading puppy begins life with energy and vigor. Within the first week, however, you'll notice that she hasn't gained weight. She begins to lose strength, stops nursing, and, if left alone, quietly dies.

TREATMENT: Seek veterinary assistance. Antibiotics, oxygen, fluids, electrolytes, and monitoring the puppy's body temperature may treat the underlying cause and restore the puppy's health.

PUPPY DEATH

Roughly one in three puppies does not survive past the weaning stage. This unfortunate statistic may result from inadequately vaccinating or feeding the mother, or from wet whelping quarters. If you have carefully attended to the birth and the litter, however, puppy death is most likely caused by another factor. Some puppies, for example, can sustain fatal injuries during their expulsion from the birth canal. Others become infected with life-threatening diseases passed on to them by their mother. A mother's tainted milk could also diminish a puppy's chances of survival, as could maternal neglect.

Hereditary defects are one of the most frequent causes of puppy mortality. Cleft palate, for instance, is a congenital defect in which an opening in the roof of the mouth allows milk to seep into the puppy's nasal cavity and, thus, makes it impossible for her to receive proper nourishment. Another hereditary defect is umbilical hernia, a condition in which the intestine or fatty tissue penetrates the abdominal lining and pushes against the puppy's skin. The result is a dangerous swelling. Circulatory system defects such as hemophilia and heart disease are also common in puppies. Other causes of puppy deaths are circulatory failure of the newborn, fading puppy syndrome, and physical immaturity.

HERPES VIRUS OF PUPPIES

CAUSES: Puppies between five to twenty-one days old may suddenly lose their appetite, experience a drop in body temperature, begin whimpering, pass discolored diarrhea, lose coordination, become bloated, and die within a day due to the herpes virus of puppies.

This disease, transmitted from an infected mother to a puppy during its passage through the birth canal or through the puppy's contact with an infected dog or a human who has touched an infected dog, can wipe out whole litters.

SYMPTOMS: Pups will stop nursing and cry, be unable to settle, and will show abdominal pain. Autopsy will reveal a kidney marked with red spots.

TREATMENT: One or more of your puppies will usually become ill and suddenly die, making it unlikely that you will be able to diagnose the disease in time to even try the typically unsuccessful incubation treatment available. If any of the pups from the litter are still alive, consult your veterinarian for advice on what to do for them. If they are infected, euthanasia may be your best option.

NOTE: Subsequent litters whelped by the same mother do not necessarily become sick. The herpes virus that afflicts puppies is not the same herpes virus that humans get, and it is not transmissible to humans.

HYPOGLYCEMIA (LOW BLOOD SUGAR)

CAUSES: Hypoglycemia is a condition in which the liver is not sufficiently providing the sugar needed for maintaining your puppy's energy level. As a result, exercise, inadequate heating, a missed meal, or any other stress can result in a hypoglycemic attack. Toy breeds are particularly susceptible during the first two to four months of life.

SYMPTOMS: The symptoms of an attack can vary. Your puppy may become fatigued, droopy, and clumsy. Spasms or convulsions may follow. Coma and death affect severe cases. Sometimes a puppy is found in a semi-comatose condition with the usual signs of shock (see Shock, p. 261).

TREATMENT: Immediate treatment is required to restore the proper sugar levels. If the puppy is awake, give her honey or sugar in water orally (see Force-Feeding, p. 89). If the puppy is unconscious, the veterinarian will have to administer an intravenous solution.

In either case, call the veterinarian at once.

NAVEL INFECTIONS

CAUSES: After the puppy's umbilical cord is severed by the mother, it shrinks and falls off. The scar that remains is called the navel.

If the mother has dental disease, she can transfer bacteria to the umbilical cord when she cuts it, causing an infection. A dirty whelping box can also cause an infection in the navel.

SYMPTOMS: The navel is inflamed and red, with a small amount of thick liquid oozing out.

TREATMENT: Gently flush the infected area with lukewarm water and soap. Apply an antiseptic cream.

WARNING: If the infection does not clear up within twenty-four hours, consult your veterinarian immediately.

PHYSICALLY IMMATURE PUPPY

CAUSES: Almost all litters have their runts: the one or two puppies who are always last in line to be fed or who are pushed out of the warmest sleeping spots. This is usually the result of overcrowding in the uterus and a placental inadequacy to fully nourish every pup.

An entire litter of small puppies may result from inadequate nourishment in the uterus.

SYMPTOMS: While some runts quickly catch up with their littermates and survive beautifully, other runts can be more severely handicapped due to low birth weight, underdeveloped musculature, breathing difficulties, and, in some cases, lower thinking capacities.

TREATMENT: The affected puppies must be separated from the mother and raised by hand (see Hand-Feeding Your Puppy box, p. 219).

Rectal Prolapse (see Rectal Prolapse, p. 261)

Toxic Milk Syndrome

CAUSES: Due to mastitis, metritis, an infection in the uterus, or some other cause, the mother's milk may contain toxins unsettling to your puppies' digestive systems.

Puppies usually affected by toxic milk syndrome are between three and fourteen days old.

SYMPTOMS: Your puppies will become anxious and cry. You may notice diarrhea and bloating.

TREATMENT: Puppies should be taken off their mother's milk and handfed until your veterinarian determines that the mother's milk is free of toxins. A bandage or other barrier placed on the mother's chest can allow the puppies to remain with her for warmth.

Umbilical Hernia

CAUSES: Sometimes the intestine or some fatty tissue penetrates the puppy's abdominal lining and pushes against its skin. This is called an umbilical hernia.

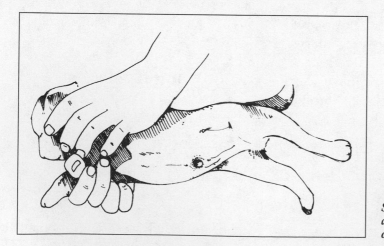

Small umbilical hernias can be ignored, but larger ones may require surgery.

TREATMENT: Small protrusions can be ignored, as they often disappear within a year. If the hernia is larger—about the width of your finger—it may, however, need surgical correction. The puppy will not have to stay at the hospital overnight, and should be fine within a day.

If the pup is a female and you plan to have her spayed, you can postpone the surgery until that time.

WORMS (see INDIVIDUAL WORMS in Chapter Sixteen)

22

FIRST-AID GUIDE

IT'S A BEAUTIFUL DAY for a walk. You and your dog are meandering blissfully along when suddenly a squirrel darts across your path. The leash is yanked from your hand and your dog gives chase. Tires screech. Your dog has been hit by a car.

Or you arrive home from work to find your puppy gnawing on that lamp cord you forgot to unplug.

Emergencies are by their very nature unexpected. In an emergency your quick action can save your dog's life. This chapter will help you make on-the-spot decisions that may let you do just that. It is divided into three sections:

Emergency Procedures
Common Emergencies
Poison Control

Part One explains how to perform lifesaving techniques such as cardiopulmonary resuscitation, heart massage, and controlling bleeding. It will also show you how to approach an injured dog, and how to safely transport him to safety.

NOTE ON EMERGENCIES

In an emergency, the best way to ensure your dog's survival is to get him to a veterinarian as quickly as possible.

Part Two provides step-by-step first aid techniques that will help you through emergency situations common to dogs, including dogfights, electric shock, and frostbite.

Part Three focuses on poison control, outlining the many substances toxic to dogs and detailing procedures for aiding a dog who has come into contact with them.

EMERGENCY PROCEDURES

This section outlines basic procedures. Because an emergency calls upon you to act decisively and efficiently, learn and practice these procedures at home. If you have taught yourself how to perform these techniques, you will be better able to remain calm and think clearly in the face of a real emergency.

RESUSCITATION

ARTIFICIAL RESPIRATION

The purpose of artificial respiration is to simulate the work of normal breathing in an unconscious dog. Determine whether your dog is unconscious and has a heartbeat, and then act quickly—if a dog's brain cells go without oxygen for five to ten minutes, permanent damage will result.

TECHNIQUE:

1. Check for any material inside the dog's mouth that could obstruct airflow. Open his mouth and check to make sure there is nothing inside. If

there is, gently pull it out with your finger. Make sure that the tongue is as far out of the dog's mouth as possible.

2. Place both hands on the dog's chest and press sharply. Release quickly. You should be able to hear air moving in and out.

3. Repeat every five seconds in a rhythmic manner timed to the normal breathing rate of the dog, which is twelve to thirty times per minute. Don't give up. Remember, there is always hope of reviving the dog as long as there is a heartbeat.

4. As soon as the dog starts breathing on his own, let him sniff some spirits of ammonia. Then treat him for possible shock (see Shock, p. 261).

If the chest-compression technique does not work, try mouth-to-nose resuscitation.

MOUTH-TO-NOSE RESUSCITATION

TECHNIQUE:

1. Be sure the dog's mouth is clear of any foreign material. Pull the tongue forward and close the mouth.

When performing mouth-to-nose resuscitation, cup the snout to prevent air from escaping.

2. Cup your hands around the snout to prevent air from escaping. You may have to place your mouth completely over the nose of your dog.

3. Blow gently into the nostrils for three seconds. Do this at a rate of eight to ten breaths per minute. The chest will expand. Let it fall back naturally. Continue this until a breathing response or coughing occurs.

CARDIOPULMONARY RESUSCITATION (CPR)

Heart massage (see p. 240) combined with artificial respiration is called cardiopulmonary resuscitation or CPR. Because cessation of breathing is soon followed by cardiac arrest—and vice versa—the combined technique frequently is required to save a dog's life. The goal of CPR is to get your dog to resume breathing *and* to stimulate circulation of freshly oxygenated blood. Once you have determined that the heart isn't beating and the dog isn't breathing, begin CPR.

TECHNIQUE:

1. Lay the dog on his right side. Try to elevate and support his chest slightly with a folded cloth placed under his right side.

2. Open the dog's airway by pulling out his tongue and checking for obstructions. Remove any foreign matter than might impede breathing.

3. Perform mouth-to-nose resuscitation with three to four quick breaths (see Mouth-to-Nose Resuscitation, p. 238).

4. Check for heartbeat. If there is none, place the heel of your hand on the side of the dog's chest over the heart. Press down and release.

5. Repeat twelve to fifteen times, followed by a breath to the nose.

6. Check for pulse. If there is none, repeat process immediately.

If at all possible, have someone seek veterinary help while you perform CPR.

HEART MASSAGE

Heart massage is used when no heartbeat can be heard or felt.

TECHNIQUE FOR SMALL DOGS AND PUPPIES:

1. Be sure the dog's mouth is clear.

2. Lay the dog on his right side.

3. Locate the sternum just below the elbows. Grasp the sternum with your thumb on one side and your fingers on the other. Using your thumb and fingers, compress the chest firmly six times. Wait five seconds. The chest will expand. Repeat.

4. Continue until the heart beats on its own.

TECHNIQUE FOR LARGER DOGS

1. As with smaller dogs, the first step is to make sure there are no obstructions to breathing.

2. Lay the dog on his side on a flat surface.

3. Locate the sternum just below the elbow. Using the heel of your hand, compress it firmly six times. Wait five seconds. The chest will expand. Repeat.

4. Continue until the heart beats on its own.

CONTROL OF BLEEDING

Bleeding can be from an artery or a vein. If bright-red blood comes out in a pumping or spurting fashion, the bleeding is from an artery (arterial). If dark-red blood flows out, the bleeding is from a vein (venous).

PRESSURE DRESSING

Simple bleeding can be stopped by a pressure dressing on the hemorrhaging

While using the chest compression technique, always check for breathing.

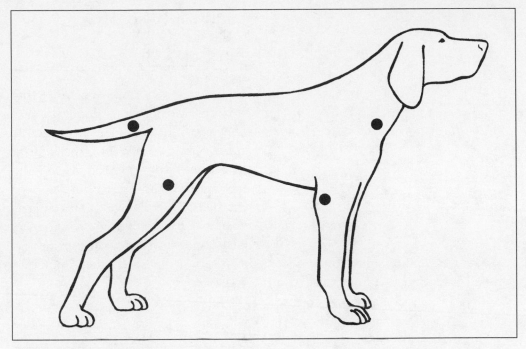

A dog's major pressure points.

area itself. Cover the wound with a sterile piece of fabric or gauze and press directly on it. Hold for eight to ten seconds. See if the bleeding has stopped. If it hasn't but blood is not pouring profusely from the wound, repeat the procedure using another piece of clean material.

PRESSURE POINTS

A second method to stop bleeding is by applying direct pressure to one of four main pressure points as follows:

HEAD AND NECK. Locate the point where the carotid artery coincides with the shoulder. This will control bleeding on that side of the body.

FORELIMB. Apply a pad and bandage or your finger to the brachial artery where it traverses the bone above the inner elbow. The brachial artery crosses over this bone, and direct pressure will stop bleeding in the front leg.

HIND LIMB. Apply pressure to the femoral artery on the upper part of the inner thigh.

TAIL. Apply pressure to the coccygeal artery, which is located beneath the tail. This will control bleeding in the tail area.

TOURNIQUET

If blood is flowing from a severed artery or vein, a tourniquet may be

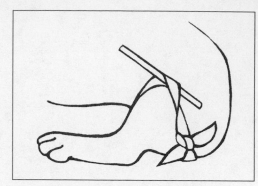

A simple tourniquet may be made out of a piece of cloth and a stick.

necessary. An emergency tourniquet can be made from anything available: a necktie, belt, shoelace, or nylon hose or rope.

If the wound is *arterial* and on a limb or on the tail, the tourniquet should be applied to the leg or tail above the wound—between the wound and the heart. Make the tourniquet by wrapping the material around the limb above the injury. Then insert a stick, pencil, or rolled-up magazine beneath the loop and twist it around until the bleeding stops. Leave the tourniquet on only five minutes so that the area isn't deprived of the normal blood necessary to keep the tissues alive.

If the wound is *venous*, fasten the tourniquet beneath the injured area and turn the tourniquet until blood stops flowing out. Hold in place for one minute at most. Relax the tourniquet slightly. Until the bleeding stops completely, be sure to loosen the tourniquet entirely for two to three minutes after every repetition of the process.

APPROACHING AND HANDLING AN INJURED DOG

If your dog is injured, remember that even the most loving dog may bite reflexively if he is in pain. Be as gentle and soothing as possible, speaking in soft tones. To protect yourself, be very aware of any disturbing or violent behavior triggered by the injury. After you have the dog's confidence, make a noose with a leash or rope and drop it over the head. Then improvise a muzzle.

IMPROVISING A MUZZLE

An emergency muzzle can be made from a gauze bandage, soft rope, necktie, nylon stocking, or anything suitable at hand. Form a loose loop with the material, then place the loop over

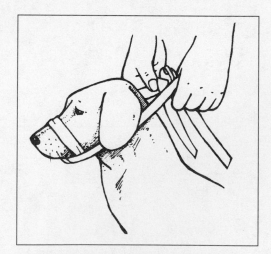

Using a long gauze bandage to muzzle an injured dog.

the snout. Try to place the loop about three quarters of the way up the snout. Tie twice under the jaw. Then take the material from under the chin and bring it straight back, below the ears (the neck's nape). Tie a double knot. This method creates a solid restraint and poses no threat of obstructing your dog's breathing.

TRANSPORTING AN INJURED DOG

Only move an injured dog as much as is absolutely necessary. Improvise a stretcher using a board or other sturdy flat object. If the dog is small, a firm piece of cardboard or even a cookie sheet may be used. You can also improvise a

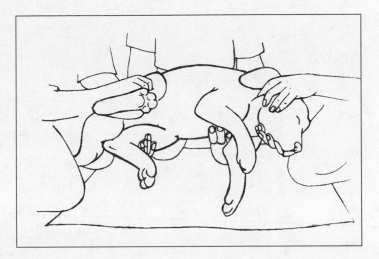

To transport an injured dog, gently place him on a blanket.

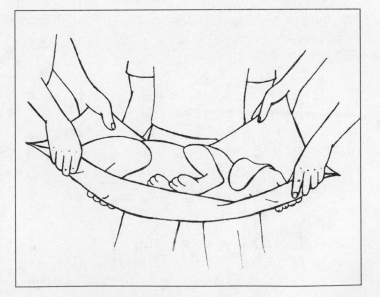

By pulling the corners, you will transform the blanket into a simple stretcher, which will support the dog's spine.

stretcher by spreading a coat or blanket along the ground and under the spine.

1. Gently place the dog on the blanket.

2. Holding the blanket corners, carry it as you would a stretcher. If there is no one to help you, make a sling using your coat or a blanket and drag the dog in it.

COMMON EMERGENCIES

The following section contains all the information you need to deal with common canine emergencies. Not only will we tell you how to treat the emergency situations, but we'll also discuss what their causes may be, which symptoms to watch for, and where possible, even how to prevent the emergency from happening in the first place.

ABDOMINAL PAIN

Severe abdominal pain can be life-threatening. Get immediate veterinary help if your dog shows any symptoms of it.

CAUSES: Acute abdominal pain may be due to urinary stones, internal injury, rupture of the bladder, bloat (see Bloat, p. 246), poisoning (see Poisoning, p. 264), peritonitis, or intestinal obstruction (see Intestinal Obstruction, p. 259).

SYMPTOMS: A sudden onset of abdominal pain accompanied by vomiting, extreme restlessness, whining, crying, and labored breathing. The abdomen is extremely painful to the touch. In later stages, the dog will go into shock (see Shock, p. 261).

FIRST AID: There is no first aid. Get immediate veterinary help.

ALLERGIC REACTIONS (see ALLERGIES, p. 140)

AMPUTATION (NONSURGICAL)

Accidents involving vehicles or heavy machinery can lead to the loss of a limb.

FIRST AID: Because amputation triggers serious bleeding, your initial response must be to fashion a tourniquet (see Control of Bleeding, p. 240), and to seek immediate veterinary care. En route to the veterinarian, treat for shock (see Shock, p. 261). If at all possible, ask someone to warn the veterinarian of your imminent arrival so that the appropriate treatment can begin immediately. Remember, many dogs have lived long and happy lives without all four limbs—the crucial factor is having the wound taken care of before your dog suffers severe loss of blood.

ASPHYXIATION

If your dog is excessively sleepy during automobile trips, check your exhaust system for leaks. Carbon monoxide is an odorless, colorless, tasteless, and very deadly gas. Even in small doses, inhaling it can be fatal to dogs. It causes a condition called asphyxiation, whereby the lungs and blood fail to receive enough oxygen.

CAUSES: In addition to carbon monoxide poisoning, asphyxiation can be caused by inhalation of smoke or gasoline, by drowning (see Drowning, p. 251), by foreign bodies in the airway, and by injuries to the chest.

SYMPTOMS: Labored, strained breathing, extreme agitation, fatigue progressing to coma, dilated pupils, blue tongue and mucous membranes.

FIRST AID: Get your dog into fresh air immediately. Give him oxygen if available. If necessary, treat for chest wound (Chest Wounds, p. 248) or choking (Choking, p. 248). If the dog's breathing is shallow or absent, begin giving artificial respiration.

AUTOMOBILE ACCIDENTS

The automobile is probably the leading canine killer in this country, and it is certainly the leading cause of injury. Even if your dog is not seriously injured, a car accident is still one of the most upsetting things that can happen—to your dog and to you. Familiarizing yourself with the following procedures before an accident happens can help minimize the panic on both sides:

FIRST AID

1. Speaking in a soothing tone, approach the dog.

2. If it is your dog who has been hit, stay with him and send someone else for help. Otherwise your dog could try to run off or struggle.

3. Use a belt or a long piece of fabric to create a makeshift leash. Make a big, secure loop at the end of the material and gently put the dog's head through it.

4. Improvise a muzzle (see Approaching and Handling an Injured Dog, p. 242).

5. Evaluate the dog. Is he breathing? Does he have a heartbeat? What are the extent of his injuries? Is he in shock? If the dog is not breathing, proceed with artificial respiration (see Artificial Respiration, p. 238). If the dog does not have a heartbeat or pulse, administer heart massage (see Heart Massage, p. 240). If he is unconscious, check to be sure the airway is open; clear secretions from the mouth and pull out the tongue. Keep the dog's head lower than his body.

6. Stop bleeding (see Control of Bleeding, p. 240).

7. Immobilize injured limb by carefully tying many layers of newspaper or cloth around it. Use a stick or other rigid object if possible (see Fractures, p. 253).

8. If there are spinal, head, or other internal injuries, improvise a stretcher (see Transporting an Injured Dog, p. 243).

9. Cover the dog with a blanket, coat, or sweaters. This serves two purposes. First, if the dog is suffering from a concussion, he may become confused and try to bite, so use a blanket or coat to protect yourself. Second, if he has lost any blood, his body temperature will drop quickly and he may suffer shock or death.

10. Transport the dog as quickly as possible to the veterinarian.

BLOAT

Bloat is a life-threatening condition that can occur in any dog, but larger breeds are more susceptible. The stomach swells with gas and then suddenly twists, trapping the gas inside. The cause of bloat is unknown, but swallowing air when gobbling down food and vigorous exercise soon after feeding are thought to contribute to it.

SYMPTOMS: In the initial stages, the stomach is taut as a drum. The dog is unable to settle down and is in severe pain, especially if you push on the dog's stomach wall. He breathes rapidly and salivates excessively. He attempts to vomit and defecate, but cannot. This is followed by a sudden and rapid swelling of the abdomen. If the dog is not rushed to the veterinarian, he can collapse and die.

FIRST AID: Rush the dog to the nearest veterinary clinic.

PREVENTION: Discourage the fast intake of food by feeding larger, deep-chested dogs several small meals rather than one large meal a day, and encourage the dog to rest for at least one hour after eating.

BURNS

A kitchen is a dog's pleasure palace. Dogs like to be on hand in case a tasty morsel drops. Unfortunately, they often get burned when they stand next to the stove. Outdoors, a dog may run under a parked car and be burned by dripping corrosives. Puppies suffer electric burns when they make a chew toy out of a plugged-in cord. With so many opportunities for a dog to suffer burns, it is important that you know how to treat such an injury ahead of time, enabling you to act fast. The severity of a burn is measured in degrees. Simple redness indicates a first-degree burn. Swelling plus redness indicates a more serious second-degree burn. A third-degree burn will cause the hair to fall out and the skin may be either charred black or pearly white.

THERMAL BURNS

FIRST AID: If the burn is small, apply ice cubes or bicarbonate of soda solution, then a layer of petroleum jelly to coat the burn and keep it clean. A loose layer of sterile gauze will help protect the area from rubbing and irritation.

Be aware that a dog's skin does not blister when it burns as ours does. Also, a thick coat or long hair could hide a severe burn for several days, until the burn becomes evident by the greenish encrustation of the skin. Usually, this will flake off, revealing a light reddish underlayer. Gently wash this area with soap and lukewarm water and cover it with sterile gauze.

For a more extensive or third degree burn, treat the dog first, if necessary, for shock (see Shock, p. 261). Improvise a muzzle (see Approaching and Handling an Injured Dog, p. 242). Then cover all burned areas with Vaseline and bandages to prevent further fluid loss, which can lead to severe problems. Get the injured dog to a veterinarian as quickly as possible.

CHEMICAL BURNS

CAUSES: Chemical burns are caused by corrosives and caustics found in household cleaners, paints, and various garden and automotive products. The wound will emit moisture and may ooze. The treatment depends on what kind of chemical caused the burn.

FIRST AID: If the burning chemical was an acid (often found in drain cleaners, paint, and automotive products) wash the wound with a rinse made up of one teaspoon of baking soda in one quart of water. Try to keep the dog from licking the wound.

If the burning chemical was an alkali (often found in garden products), wash the area with soap and water. Again, try to keep the dog from licking the wound.

SEVERITY OF BURNS

TYPE	APPEARANCE	POSSIBLE CAUSES
First-Degree	Simple redness under fur	Quick contact with a hot pan or heater, light sunburn
Second-Degree	Deep redness, swelling, blisters	Splash of boiling liquid, deep sunburn
Third-Degree	Skin destroyed, appears white or charred. More than 15 percent of the body surface is burned.	Fire, electrical burn

If the burn is extensive, treat for shock, improvise a muzzle, and cover the burn with Vaseline and bandages just as you would a severe scalding burn. Quickly get the dog to a veterinarian.

ELECTRIC BURNS

Electric-burn injuries are usually found in the mouth because they are most often caused by chewing on cords. The body usually heals by itself. However, if your dog drools excessively or has difficulty breathing, there could be damage to lung tissues. Seek veterinary help (see Electric Shock, p. 251).

CHEST WOUNDS

Chest wounds are often the product of a fall or accident. They pose several serious threats. A dog suffering from a chest wound may lose a significant amount of blood. More dangerous is air entering the chest cavity that surrounds the lungs, a condition that may cause the lungs to collapse.

FIRST AID: If the wound is merely superficial, bandage lightly with moistened gauze (see Chest or Abdomen Wound, p. 86).

If, however, you believe the wound has penetrated the chest cavity, as evidenced by the presence of air bubbles in the blood and labored breathing, take the following steps:

1. Have someone call the veterinarian to warn of your imminent arrival.

2. Create an airtight seal by placing a moistened gauze pad or plastic bag over the wound and firmly holding it in place with your hand. This will help prevent air from escaping. Use more layers of material if necessary.

3. If the wound has been caused by an object like a stick, do not remove it. Bandage around it so as not to aggravate the injury.

4. Check for symptoms of shock and treat if necessary (see Shock, p. 261).

5. Transport dog to immediate veterinary care, placing the animal with his injured side flush against the car seat.

CHOKING

Some dogs love to raid the garbage and unearth bones. Others cannot resist trying to swallow a biscuit in one gulp. The result can be a real emergency—choking.

SYMPTOMS: Rubbing the mouth or throat with a paw or along the ground, excessive drooling, gagging, rasping, attempts to vomit.

FIRST AID: First, remove any object or material that may be blocking your dog's airway. Hold the tongue with some cloth while you use your free hand to carefully remove the object. You may need to perform the Heimlich maneuver, which works on pets as well as humans.

COMA
(see UNCONSCIOUSNESS, p. 263)

THE HEIMLICH MANEUVER

1. Lay your dog on his side, on a hard, firm surface.

2. Place both palms behind the last rib and press down four times, pressing slightly upward.

3. If these compressions don't force the object out of the windpipe, try the process again.

4. If breathing hasn't resumed, try artificial respiration (see Artificial Respiration, p. 238). Get veterinary assistance immediately.

CONVULSIONS (FITS AND SEIZURES)

Convulsions are generalized, severe, spasmodic jerkings of the entire body caused by bursts of electrical activity within the brain. Seeing a dog have a seizure can terrify even the calmest of owners, so it helps to remember that the seizure will be over relatively quickly. Most convulsions last two or three minutes.

CAUSES: Convulsions can have many causes. Two of the most common are epilepsy and distemper (see Epilepsy, p. 173, and Distemper, p. 110). Brain tumors, blows to the head, encephalitis (inflammation of the brain), brain malformations, sunstroke, gastroenteritis, hypoglycemia (low levels of blood sugar), or even a high fever can trigger a seizure. Quick-acting poisons such as strychnine will send a dog into a seizure and a prolonged type of convulsion. In their migration through the bloodstream, heartworms and hookworms may end up in the cerebral ves-sels and cause what are called "worm fits" (see Heartworm, p. 168, and Hookworm, p. 182).

SYMPTOMS: A convulsion often starts with the dog becoming unsettled. His mouth may open and close repeatedly. Then, foam starts to accumulate around his mouth, he shakes his head and flickers his eyes. The dog then collapses, throws back his head, drools, and exhibits facial twitching. His pupils dilate and he makes running movements with his legs. He may lose control of his bowels or bladder. When the dog comes out of the convulsive attack, he will be wobbly and confused.

FIRST AID:

1. If somebody is nearby, ask them to telephone the veterinarian.

2. You may want to remain close to the dog to minimize his stress. However, don't try to calm him by petting or stroking and don't attempt to secure the dog's tongue. Coming into physical contact with the dog may only

aggravate and prolong the condition. You may also be bitten by the dog's jaw movements.

3. If there is any possibility that your dog may come in contact with sharp-edged furniture when experiencing a convulsion, throw blankets over the furniture to avoid additional injury.

4. The fit should not last more than a few minutes. When it is over, telephone your veterinarian (if somebody else nearby has not done so already) and allow your dog to recover.

5. Following a seizure, the dog will be disoriented, confused, and unresponsive. He may continue salivating and start pacing back and forth. The dog may recover from this condition quickly or could remain in a recovery state for several hours. Help him through recovery by keeping him in a quiet and dark environment, if possible. Calmly pet him and speak to him quietly to assure him of your presence. Let him have a drink of water and encourage him to relax.

6. If the convulsion lasts more than five minutes, immediate veterinary care is imperative. In between convulsions, lift the dog by the scruff of his neck, supporting his body with your free hand. Place the dog carefully in the car. Continue to keep the dog restrained (see Restraining a Dog, p. 85) while you transport the dog. If somebody else can help you, ask them to drive the car so that you can remain close to the dog. If you are unable to handle the dog, contact your veterinarian for advice.

DOGFIGHTS

Interaction with other dogs is often a healthy aspect of a domestic dog's life. However, if your dog happens to bump into a particularly aggressive dog, a fight may occur that could result in severe injury.

If you witness an attack on your dog, you will surely want to break it up. However, you will need to be very careful in your actions, or you may wind up being injured. Keep your hands away from the dogs' heads, necks, and faces; if you don't, you will have very little reaction time should either try to bite you. Instead, yank and pull from a tail, or knock one dog off balance by grabbing his back leg. A sudden dousing with cold water may shock the dogs out of battle—use this method if at all possible.

FIRST AID: Treat the injury by the type of wound inflicted.

LACERATED WOUNDS

Lacerated wounds zigzag the flesh, tearing the skin. Apply direct pressure to the wound. Clip the hair surrounding the affected area. Flush the wound with warm water or a hydrogen peroxide solution. If the bleeding is heavy, apply direct pressure and take the dog to the veterinarian. Stitches may be necessary.

PUNCTURE WOUNDS

A puncture wound can be more serious than it looks. Punctures are caused by objects, including tacks, sharp twigs, and teeth, that penetrate the skin. Because the object can pierce through several layers of tissue, puncture wounds can easily become infected.

Because of this risk, it is important to flush the puncture with warm water or hydrogen peroxide, and then seek veterinary treatment.

NOTE: Since any animal bite may transmit rabies, be sure to keep up on all vaccinations. (See Chapter Five, Vaccinations.)

DROWNING

A puppy or elderly dog left unattended near a pool, spa, or hot tub is an accident waiting to happen. Even a dog who likes to swim and is good at it can sometimes find himself in trouble in the water.

FIRST AID:

1. Call nearby people for assistance. Any support can only help, especially when the rescue involves a situation that could also be dangerous to you.

2. If your dog is within reaching distance, try to grab him with your hand.

3. If rescuing your dog involves swimming out to him, bring some type of flotation device with you. When you approach him, secure him by grabbing his tail or the scruff of his neck and bringing his front legs over the flotation device. Keep him secure while you swim to shore.

4. Upon reaching safety, begin to empty the water from the dog's lungs. To do this, you must be sure the dog's head is lower than his chest. Lift the dog either by wrapping your arms around his abdomen and under his hind legs or by picking him up behind the ribs, wrapping one arm around the abdomen. If the dog is particularly small, you can hold him upside down from his hind legs. Shake the dog a few times, allowing the excess water to drain. Extract any foreign objects that may have become lodged in the mouth.

5. If consciousness does not return, lay the dog on his side and begin artificial respiration (see Artificial Respiration, p. 238).

6. Check for a pulse. If there is still no heartbeat, begin CPR (see Cardiopulmonary Resuscitation, p. 239). Holding ammonia spirits before the dog's nose may help to revive him.

7. If the dog was rescued from especially cold water, you may also have to treat the dog for frostbite (see Frostbite, p. 256) and hypothermia (see Hypothermia, p. 257).

8. When consciousness returns, wrap the dog in a jacket or warm blanket and take him to a veterinarian.

ELECTRIC SHOCK

Puppies, and even some dogs, love to chew. Providing them with bones and toys satisfies their oral fixations. Sometimes, however, they turn to dangerous pursuits, such as chewing a cord connected to a socket, and the result is electric shock.

HOW TO PREVENT ELECTRIC SHOCK

Since most cases of canine electrocution involve chewing on electrical cords, take steps in your household to prevent this. One bite-proofing method is to cover electrical cords with those spiral plastic covers intended for telephone cords. Another is to tape the cords to the floor with duct tape and then cover the cords with carpet.

SYMPTOMS: Labored breathing; visible burns of lips, tongue, and fur around the mouth; abnormal salivation; unconsciousness.

FIRST AID: If your dog has received a shock and is thrown away from the cord, he could go into cardiac arrest. If so, you should begin CPR immediately (see Cardiopulmonary Resuscitation, p. 239).

The lungs may fill with fluid, but do not elevate the body above the head in an attempt to drain it, because this could cause the condition to worsen. Get immediate veterinary attention.

WARNING: If you catch your dog in the act and he still has the cord in his mouth, *do not touch him*. If you do, you could be electrocuted. Shut off the main source of electricity, pull the plug out of the wall with rubber gloves, or pry the dog away from the cord with a rolling pin or wooden kitchen spoon.

EYE INJURIES

Any injury to the outside covering of your dog's eye, the cornea, or the eyeball should be considered an emergency.

FIRST AID: Handle any eye injury with great care; your dog's eyesight could be at stake. Keep the eye moist by covering it with a wet gauze square or cloth. Secure this wet cloth by wrapping more gauze or a crepe bandage over the wet cloth and around the dog's head, using his ears for anchorage. Be careful not to wrap the wound too tightly, as you could cut off blood supply.

EYE OUT OF ITS SOCKET

An eye out of the socket is a common emergency in dogs with large bulging eyes, such as Boston Terriers,

If an eye is out of its socket, cover it with a damp cloth and seek veterinary attention.

Pugs, Pekingese, and Maltese. But it can occur in any breed, especially after a hard blow to the head.

FIRST AID: Quick action is required to save the dog's eyesight. Cover the eye with a wet cloth to keep it moist and seek immediate veterinary attention.

FITS (see CONVULSIONS, p. 249)

FRACTURES

If your dog is limping badly, the muscles may be damaged but the leg probably is not broken. In most cases, if the leg is broken the dog will put no weight on it all.

In young dogs, bones tend to crack rather than break, causing what is called a greenstick fracture. The bones of elderly dogs are brittle and more likely to break completely.

Complete breaks can be simple or compound. A simple fracture does not break the skin. In a compound fracture the bone is exposed, either through an open wound or because the bone has broken through the skin from the inside.

FIRST AID: The most common fractures seen in dogs are leg fractures caused by accidents. Remember that with any kind of fracture the dog probably is in considerable pain and should be approached with caution (see Approaching and Handling an Injured Dog, p. 242). Once the dog is muzzled, check for signs of shock, which should be treated before the

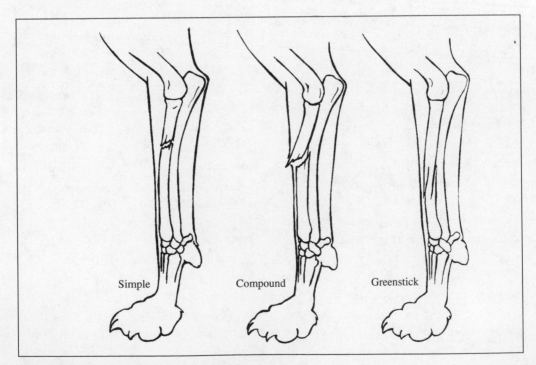

Simple   Compound   Greenstick

Simple, compound, and greenstick fractures.

HOW TO MAKE A SPLINT

1. Gently lay down the dog so you have easy access to his injured part.

2. Wrap the injured part in soft cloth or cotton.

3. Place thin cardboard or newspapers under the injured part. Then, wrap this stiff material around the injury and fasten with adhesive tape.

4. Be certain not to fashion too snug a fit. This could inhibit circulation to the injured area. If you notice any swelling near the splint, redo it, loosening it slightly.

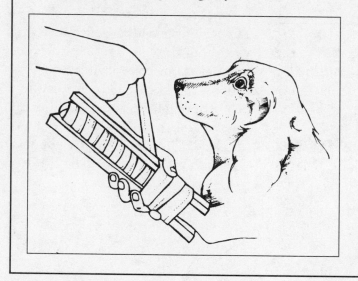

Finish a splint by wrapping the rigid material with adhesive tape.

fracture (see Shock, p. 261). Any fractures should then be immobilized, because excessive movement of broken limbs can cause tearing, further bleeding, or blood clots.

To immobilize the fracture, apply a splint to the bone at the point of fracture. The splint should cross the joint above and below the injury to hold the broken bones in place. Do not attempt to straighten broken bones; this will cause extreme pain.

Remember, a splint is only a temporary measure until professional help is obtained.

LEG FRACTURES

SYMPTOMS: Pain on walking or standing, swelling, obvious deformity in leg (but not always).

FIRST AID: If the injury occurs in the upper leg, there isn't much you'll be able to do on your own, since this is a particularly difficult area to splint. Instead, transport your dog to the veterinarian, preventing as much movement as possible.

If the injury occurs in the lower leg, apply a splint and seek veterinary treatment.

FOOT FRACTURES

SYMPTOMS: Swelling, pain, lacerations on and around foot, or localized in toes.

FIRST AID: Seek veterinary help.

JAW FRACTURES

SYMPTOMS: Jaw droops, drooling.

FIRST AID: Support the area by tying a long strip of cloth under the jaw and around the head, just below the ears. Tie the cloth tightly enough to hold in place, but be sure not to restrict breathing. Seek veterinary assistance.

PELVIC FRACTURES

SYMPTOMS: Severe pain (and probable collapse) upon any attempt to put pressure on hind legs.

FIRST AID: Keep your dog as still as possible until veterinary care is available. A radiograph will reveal whether or not the pelvis has been fractured.

SKULL FRACTURES

SYMPTOMS: Sluggishness, incoordi-nation, loss of consciousness, blood stemming from nose or ears.

FIRST AID: Control bleeding (see Control of Bleeding, p. 240). Treat for shock if necessary (see Shock, p. 261) but do not give any drugs or fluids. Do not bandage the skull. Seek immediate veterinary help.

SPINAL FRACTURES

SYMPTOMS: Following an accident or trauma to the back, paralysis in rear legs; possible paralysis in front legs; lack of response to touch or pinching of foot.

FIRST AID: Do your best to restrict all movement so as to prevent injury to the spinal cord. Gently slide the dog on to a board or stretcher. If the dog doesn't show resistance, tie him in place, but *do not* force the issue. Small dogs can be placed in a carrier. Take the dog to the veterinarian immediately.

TAIL FRACTURES

SYMPTOMS: Paralysis of the tail from the point of fracture downward.

FIRST AID: If the suspected fracture is at the tail's base, do not do anything other than seek veterinary care. If another part of the tail has been broken, immobilize with adhesive tape (see Paw, Limb, or Tail Wound, p. 86) and seek veterinary care. Your dog's doctor will ensure that the nerves in the tail remain functional.

FROSTBITE

Many people think that a dog's fur coat will protect him from frostbite. This is partly true, but remember that your dog, just like you, is still vulnerable to frostbite on his extremities: toes, ears, scrotum (in male dogs), and tail tip.

SYMPTOMS: As the blood supply diminishes, the affected area of the dog's skin will become pale. It will resemble a burn and become red, swollen, scaly, and painful and itchy to the dog when circulation returns. The dog may shed hair and dead skin.

FIRST AID: Affected parts should be thawed out slowly by tying towels soaked in water, at about the temperature of a baby bottle, over the area for fifteen or twenty minutes. Avoid squeezing or rubbing the area, as this may aggravate the injury.

If your dog is experiencing pain when you touch the area or if the area remains red and swollen, the tissue may be severely damaged. Immediately consult your veterinarian, who will prescribe antibiotics to get rid of the infection and, in some cases, pain relievers. Failure to attend to infection may result in gangrene, where the affected skin scabs and darkens. This rarely results in amputation or life-threatening infection if it is immediately treated.

GANGRENE (see FROSTBITE, above)

HEATSTROKE

When your dog pants rapidly on a hot day, he is trying to cool off. Dogs do perspire through their pores, but their main heat regulator is rapid breathing—exchanging warm air for cool air. The problem is, there just isn't much cool air around on a sweltering day, and your dog cannot tolerate heat as well as you can. This is why he is susceptible to heatstroke.

CAUSES: Leaving a dog in a poorly ventilated parked car, especially on a hot day, is very likely to result in heatstroke. Carriers and other enclosed travel aids must be large enough for a dog and allow air to circulate properly, or else they too can create the conditions necessary for heatstroke. Bulldogs, pugs, and other breeds with short snouts are prone to heatstroke. Obese dogs as well as dogs with respiratory problems are also vulnerable.

SYMPTOMS: Rapid breathing through the mouth, increased heart/pulse rate, reddened gums, vomiting, moisture accumulating on feet, a dull staring expression, thickened saliva. Body temperature may eventually reach 110 degrees Fahrenheit.

FIRST AID: Heatstroke requires immediate action. In mild cases, move the dog to cooler surroundings and give him a drink of cold water. If he has a high temperature or is unsteady on his feet, give him a cold-water bath or shower. Apply ice packs to his head, chest, and thighs. Get the dog to the veterinarian as quickly as possible.

HYPOTHERMIA (LOW BODY TEMPERATURE)

Frostbite and hypothermia often go hand in hand. Exposure to cold water or weather can send a dog's body temperature plummeting to below ninety-nine degrees Fahrenheit, a dangerous condition. Toy breeds and short-haired dogs are the most susceptible. The dog can die if his temperature drops as low as seventy-five degrees.

SYMPTOMS: Uncontrollable shivering, low body temperature, fatigue.

FIRST AID: Wrap the dog in a blanket, your jacket, or whatever else is available, and take him indoors to a warm room. Dry a wet dog off with a towel or a blow dryer emitting warm (but not hot!) air. Gradually raise his body temperature to 100 degrees (see How to Take Your Dog's Temperature, p. 82) by placing hot water bottles or packs filled with body-temperature water on him or by allowing him to nestle in a carefully monitored electric blanket or pad set on a low temperature. If your dog's temperature does not return to 100 degrees or he is unconscious, immediately get him to the veterinarian. Your veterinarian will treat him for shock and make sure that the heart and kidney are functioning normally.

INSECT STINGS

BEES, WASPS, AND YELLOW JACKETS

Bee stings are as common a summertime occurrence for dogs as they are for humans. Some dogs see bees as toys, catching them in midair.

This common summer hazard can turn into a real emergency if your dog is extremely sensitive to bee stings (as some humans are), if he is bitten numerous times, or if he is stung in the mouth.

SYMPTOMS: If he was bitten on the face, the dog will continuously stroke his face with his paw or nuzzle it in the grass. The bitten area will swell and a stinger may be visible. If the dog is extremely sensitive to bee stings, he will show severe signs: swellings under the bitten skin and all over the body, vomiting, and diarrhea.

FIRST AID: If the bee stinger is visible, try to remove it with blunt-edged tweezers. Treat the swollen area with a paste of baking soda mixed with water, or with cold compresses. The swelling should disappear within two days. If the dog goes into shock, treat him first (see Shock, p. 261), then get immediate veterinary attention.

SPIDERS

Spiders aren't apt to bite dogs, as a dog's coat and skin are mostly impenetrable to the spider's fangs.

INTERNAL BLEEDING

External bleeding may indicate that there is internal bleeding as well—a life-theatening emergency. You should familiarize yourself with the following symptoms and sources of internal bleeding and what they may suggest, as well as the accompanying first-aid techniques.

BODY PART	CAUSES/SYMPTOMS	TREATMENT
The Eye	Can result from trauma to the head or eyeball.	See Eye Injuries, p. 252.
The Ear	Often seen after fights or car accidents. The bleeding may be from the earflap or from inside the ear.	Gently insert absorbent cotton through the ear opening into the ear canal—just enough to fill the ear. Consult with your veterinarian. If left untreated, such bleeding could develop into a serious middle-ear infection.
The Nose	Possible causes include a sharp blow, tumor, decayed tooth socket, foreign bodies in the nose, high blood pressure.	Sponge the nostrils dry with absorbent cotton. If you can see a foreign body, you may be able to remove it yourself with a pair of tweezers. Do not randomly poke around in your dog's nose, as the mucous membranes lining the nostrils can be easily damaged. If the cause of the nosebleed is not immediately evident, keep your dog as quiet as possible. Apply cold compresses to the bridge of the nose but do not pack the nostrils; this could cause your dog to sneeze and increase the bleeding. Most nosebleeds eventually subside on their own. This does not mean you should not be concerned. A nosebleed can be symptomatic of a disorder, and its cause should be determined by a veterinarian.

SYMPTOMS: If a dog is bitten on the leg, he will hold the leg up and shake it feverishly because of the spreading pain. The bite of a brown recluse spider, black widow, or tarantula is toxic. There is pain; later the dog can develop chills, fever, and labored breathing. He can also go into shock.

BODY PART	CAUSES/SYMPTOMS	TREATMENT
The Mouth	May indicate a broken tooth, a broken jaw, a bitten tongue, or a cut gum. **Note:** Profuse bleeding usually stems from a bitten tongue, which is a serious injury. The tongue is moist and constantly in motion, which makes it difficult for a clot to form. A deep cut in the tongue can actually cause a dog to bleed to death.	If your dog has bitten his tongue—and if he will allow you to do so—hold the tongue in a cotton pad to reduce the bleeding while you take him to the veterinarian.
The Lungs	Indicated by vomiting of frothy blood. The froth is air mixed with blood.	Immediate veterinary attention is required.
The Lower Intestinal Tract	If a dog is bleeding bright-red blood from the rectum, he may be hemorrhaging from the lower intestinal tract.	Immediate veterinary attention is required.
The Stomach	If a dog is vomiting dark-red blood, he may be bleeding from the stomach. The blood is mixed with gastric juices, causing the darker-than-normal color.	Immediate veterinary attention is required.
The Upper Intestinal Tract	If a dog is bleeding dark brown or black blood, the hemmorhaging is coming from the upper intestinal tract. The blood is darker than normal because it is mixed with digestive juices.	Immediate veterinary attention is required.
The Urinary Tract	Blood in the urine can indicate bladder or kidney stones. In female dogs, it can indicate tumors or cysts in the urethra or an infection of the uterus.	Immediate veterinary attention is required.

FIRST AID: Treat for shock if necessary (see Shock, p. 261), apply cold compresses to the bite area, and seek immediate veterinary attention.

INTESTINAL OBSTRUCTION

Even if your dog manages to swallow that large bone, stick, stone, or dog toy, the object may still become stuck in his small intestine. The object may make it through the thick-walled esophagus but will inevitably become caught in the less pliable small intestine and cause a serious emergency.

The closer the blockage is to the stomach, the more acute the emergency. If an object punctures the intestinal wall, peritonitis, the seepage of intestinal material into the abdominal cavity, will ensue.

Younger dogs are susceptible to intussusception: Frequent diarrhea causes the small intestine to turn in on itself, much like a sleeve turned inside out. Part of the bowel is trapped, causing bowel blockage. Circulation to the affected area often stops, causing the tissue to die. This condition requires surgery.

SYMPTOMS: Acute vomiting, dehydration, lethargy, listlessness, constipation. In later stages the abdomen stiffens and becomes very tender. The dog will go into shock.

FIRST AID: There is no first aid. Get immediate veterinary help.

PARALYSIS

A paralyzed dog is a heart-wrenching sight. Not only is the poor dog unable to move, but sometimes he cannot even swallow.

CAUSES: Accidents, cerebral hemorrhage, a slipped or herniated disc (see Herniated Disc, p. 173), milk fever (see Milk Fever, p. 215), and the bite of certain ticks (see Ticks, p. 150).

SYMPTOMS: Symptoms vary, depending on the cause.

Tick paralysis begins with a loss of strength in the hind legs. It eventually renders the dog incapable of standing.

Radial paralysis is usually seen after automobile accidents and is the result of damage to the radial nerve of the front leg. It is most obvious when the dog drags the injured leg. When paralysis is partial, the dog may be able to stand, but he stumbles when he takes a step.

A severely damaged nerve may result in permanent paralysis. In many cases, the nerve is only bruised and functioning will slowly return. This process can take a few days or as long as six weeks.

Paralysis from a slipped or herniated disc comes on gradually, starting with slight incoordination in the rear legs. The dog does not want to move and often arches his back.

Paralysis from milk fever begins with subtle changes in the way a dog walks. Soon, the dog has difficulty keeping his balance, and experiences stiffness in his legs.

FIRST AID: Move the dog carefully (see Transporting an Injured Dog, p. 243) and get him to the veterinarian immediately.

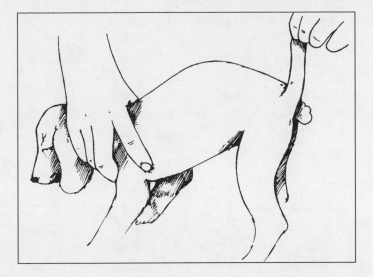

Rectal prolapse must be treated immediately to prevent gangrene.

RECTAL PROLAPSE

In a rectal prolapse, which can be a serious emergency condition, the rectum pops out like an inside-out sock. Rectal prolapse is fairly common in puppies and occurs occasionally in older dogs as a result of severe untreated diarrhea, which breaks down the tissue that holds the rectum in place, causing the prolapse.

Rectal prolapse also can be caused by straining when a dog is constipated, or by rectal tumors.

SYMPTOMS: If your dog has a rectal prolapse, you will see a lump ranging from the size of a red marble to that of a frankfurter protruding from the dog's rectum.

FIRST AID: Get the dog to the veterinary hospital immediately. Delay could result in gangrene and major surgery to remove a section of the rec-

tum. Keep the lump moist with cotton soaked in warm water until you reach the hospital.

SEIZURES (see CONVULSIONS, p. 249)

SHOCK

Shock is a physiological response to severe injury, blood loss, trauma, certain toxins, severe fright, or illness.

When a dog goes into shock, his circulatory system slows down and is no longer able to supply the tissues of the body and brain with enough oxygen to keep him alive. Death can result from shock and not from the injury that caused it.

SYMPTOMS: Check by looking at the dog's gums. Pale and grayish gums indicate shock.

Press your finger into the gum of a dog in shock and the skin will turn white. Normally the gums will regain their pinkish color within a second or two. If shock is present, it will take longer.

Other symptoms include weak and rapid heartbeat, low body temperature, a bluish cast to the skin, rapid and shallow breathing.

FIRST AID: Check for breathing and maintain an open airway. Artificial respiration may be necessary (see Artificial Respiration, p. 238). Control bleeding if present (see Control of Bleeding, p. 240). Rush the dog to veterinary care.

If immediate veterinary care is not available, make a solution of one teaspoon salt, a half-teaspoon baking soda, and one quart lukewarm water. This will replace lost elements crucial to proper functioning. Pour the liquid slowly into the side of the mouth. *Only give liquids if the dog is conscious and is not having seizures or convulsions.*

Once the veterinarian determines the cause of shock, treatment can begin. Your dog will probably require a transfusion, especially if blood loss has triggered the shock.

SNAKEBITE

If your dog comes home from a stroll in the country with a large swollen mass around his face or on his front leg, snakebite may be the cause.

SYMPTOMS: The bite of a poisonous snake leaves two fang marks. The bite of a harmless snake leaves toothmarks

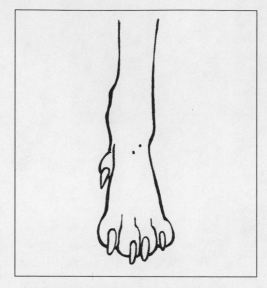

A poisonous snake leaves two fang marks, while a nonpoisonous snake leaves toothmarks in a horseshoe arrangement.

in the shape of a horseshoe, but no fang marks.

Other symptoms include: pain, weakness, swelling, dark discharge at wound site, excessive salivation, vomiting, shock, convulsions.

FIRST AID: Snake bites are extremely painful, so the first step is to muzzle the dog. Then apply a flat tourniquet between the bite and the heart. Tie a handkerchief, piece of cloth, bandage, or gauze about one inch above the wound. This should not be as tight as a tourniquet used to control bleeding, but tight enough to keep the poisonous blood from reaching the heart.

Treatment will be easier for the veterinarian if you can identify the type of snake that bit the dog, but it isn't crucial, so don't risk getting attacked yourself.

Keep the dog quiet, because excitement or exercise increases the rate of the venom's absorption. Lift and carry the dog, if possible. Take him immediately to the veterinarian for treatment with antivenoms (substances that counteract snake venom).

SPINAL CORD INJURIES (see PARALYSIS, p. 260)

STROKE

A stroke is the sudden rupture or blockage of a blood vessel in the brain.

SYMPTOMS: Sudden collapse, impaired movement or breathing, walking in circles, droopy eyelids, partial paralysis, eye flicking.

FIRST AID: If you see these signs, consult your veterinarian immediately.

UNCONSCIOUSNESS (COMA)

Unconsciousness, commonly called a coma, usually develops in stages. At first the dog may seem lost or unusually sad. Then he may appear drunk, uncoordinated, and, finally, he will collapse and lose consciousness.

CAUSES: A coma can be caused by a heart attack: because of circulatory failure, the dog will faint. There will be light, rapid breathing, barely detectable pulse, and loss of color in gums.

Hypoglycemia (low blood sugar) can also cause a coma. Toy breeds, puppies, and hunting dogs are particularly susceptible to this condition.

Other causes of unconsciousness include carbon monoxide poisoning; poisoning by barbiturates, arsenic, or cyanide; brain injuries; cerebral hemorrhage; fits and convulsions; and shock.

FIRST AID: An unconscious dog can inhale his own saliva or vomit, so the first step is to pull out the tongue and clear the airway with your fingers.

Then, gently lift the dog by the hind legs and set him on a table with his head hanging over the side. Wrap the dog in a blanket.

Pass some smelling salts under his nose. *Never give him anything by mouth* until he regains consciousness.

Begin artificial respiration if necessary (see Artificial Respiration, p. 238).

Once the dog fully revives, you can pour small amounts of whiskey or brandy *slowly* into the side of his mouth. Call your veterinarian.

WOUNDS (see DOGFIGHTS, p. 250)

POISON CONTROL

It's amazing to consider how indiscriminate a dog's palate seems to be. If often seems as if dogs will eat anything that fits into their mouths. Clearly, the threat of toxicity doesn't faze them.

Poisons are everywhere in a domestic dog's world. Medications, plants, household cleansers, and cosmetics surround a dog in the house, while pesticides, automotive products, sidewalk salt, rotted garbage, and fertilizers might be a temptation to him outdoors.

One of the trickiest aspects of treating poisoning effectively is the fact that you probably won't see your dog swallowing the toxic substance. Instead, you probably will not even suspect that something is wrong until the poison begins to interact with your dog's system. It is frequently difficult to determine what type of poison has been ingested—the symptoms don't provide instant answers. Also, the symptoms that do occur can indicate conditions other than poisoning.

However, there is a set of basic techniques you can follow to treat most poisoning cases. Above all, *always seek veterinary help as soon as possible*. If you cannot get to your veterinarian, call the National Animal Poison Control Center at 1-900-680-0000 ($20.00 for five minutes) for assistance.

GENERAL SYMPTOMS OF POISONING

The most obvious sign that your dog has ingested a toxic substance is an open medication bottle or a vessel containing a poison situated near the dog or his quarters. Also, look around his mouth and snout for any foreign substances.

Other key symptoms include vomiting, burns in the mouth, diarrhea, bleeding, staggering, tremors, seizures, and unconsciousness.

GENERAL PROCEDURES

In general, treatment involves three steps:

STEP 1:   If you are certain your dog has been poisoned, and if the dog is conscious, make the dog vomit, *unless* the dog has ingested a corrosive. *If the dog has ingested an acid, alkali, or petroleum product, do not induce vomiting.* The idea is to get the dog to vomit the suspected poison before it is absorbed into the bloodstream. Act quickly. Seconds may save your dog's life.

STEP 2:   The second step in treatment is to delay absorption of the poison in the dog's intestinal tract. Mix two to three tablespoons of activated charcoal (available at most drugstores) with one cup of warm water. Spill

TO INDUCE VOMITING
(AFTER INGESTION OF NONCORROSIVES ONLY)

Do not induce vomiting if your dog is unconscious, or having seizures.

Sores or burns inside the mouth, as well as oral swelling, indicate the presence of an acid or corrosive. In this case, *do not* induce vomiting. Instead, if your dog is conscious and not having convulsions, administer olive oil. (Feed your large dog up to one pint; feed a smaller dog four to six ounces.)

If you know your dog has not ingested a corrosive and vomiting is recommended, use one of the following:

HYDROGEN PEROXIDE.   Pour a 3 percent hydrogen peroxide solution mixed with equal parts of water into the side of the dog's mouth.

SALT.   Throw the crystals as far back in the dog's throat as you can, or dissolve in one cup warm water. If dissolved, pour the liquid slowly into the side of the dog's mouth.

DRY MUSTARD.   Dissolve in one cup of cold water. Pour into the side of the dog's mouth.

Use these substances in the following amounts:

3% HYDROGEN PEROXIDE	SALT	DRY MUSTARD
I teaspoon of both hydrogen peroxide and water per 10 lbs body weight every ten minutes—three times total	I teaspoon mixed in I cup water	I tablespoon mixed in I cup water

slowly into the dog's mouth. If charcoal isn't available, use undiluted milk, egg whites, or vegetable oil.

STEP 3:   The third step is to speed the poison's elimination. About thirty minutes after Step 2, administer milk of magnesia—one teaspoonful per five pounds of body weight. If milk of magnesia is not available, administer a warm-water enema, which is available in all drugstores.

WARNING: If your dog begins to show signs of nervous system involvement such as incoordination or seizures, he is in serious trouble. Get him to a veterinarian as quickly as possible. Try to take a sample of his vomit or, ideally, of the poison itself.

If the dog is hyperexcited or is having convulsions, protect him from hurting himself (see Convulsions, p. 249).

FIRST AID FOR SPECIFIC POISONS

In the following guide, substances toxic to dogs are divided into these categories:

Automotive Products
Food
Gardening Products
Household Cleaners
Insecticides
Medicines
Pesticides
Plants
Remodeling Products
Miscellaneous

If you know the identity of the poison ingested by your dog, take the steps outlined in the specific sections below.

AUTOMOTIVE PRODUCTS

BATTERY ACID

SYMPTOMS: Abdominal pain, oral ulcers, bloody vomit, shock.

FIRST AID: Treat for shock if necessary (see Shock, p. 261). *Do not* induce vomiting. Instead, administer sodium bicarbonate (5 percent solution) or milk of magnesia. At the very least, strongly encourage your dog to drink water. Seek immediate veterinary care.

ANTIFREEZE

Antifreeze poisoning is not uncommon because the chemical has a sweet taste that is attractive to dogs.

SYMPTOMS: The amount of antifreeze consumed determines the effects. If a great deal has been consumed, poisoning results in vomiting or staggering. If a lesser amount has been consumed, the dog will show signs of kidney damage (see Kidney Disease, p. 191).

FIRST AID: Induce vomiting and give Kaopectate to coat the stomach and intestines. Rush the dog to the veterinarian.

MOTOR OIL

FIRST AID: *Do not* induce vomiting. Rush the dog to the veterinarian.

FOOD

Food poisoning is common in dogs who are allowed to poke through garbage. Harmful bacteria in discarded meat can do great harm to your dog's system, especially if the food is contaminated with salmonella or clostridium. Salmonella is especially dangerous to younger dogs—puppies stricken with this bacteria can die within hours.

SYMPTOMS: Signs of poisoning begin with vomiting and abdominal pain, followed sometimes by diarrhea (often bloody). If the poisoning is complicated by a bacterial infection, shock may develop.

Poisoning by clostridium bacteria is characterized by partial to complete paralysis, since these bacteria give off a toxin that affects the nervous system.

FIRST AID: Induce vomiting and follow the procedures outlined above (see p. 264) to delay absorption and speed elimination. Call the veterinarian immediately.

GARDENING PRODUCTS

FERTILIZERS

SYMPTOMS: Difficulty breathing, blue tongue and mucus membranes, congested lungs.

FIRST AID: Administer mineral oil. Call for immediate veterinary assistance.

WEED KILLERS

Most weed killers are toxic only if ingested in large amounts. Some can be absorbed through the skin.

PREVENTING POISONING

Minimizing your dog's exposure to toxic agents is an important responsibility for any dog owner. Every room in the house, including the garage, spells potential trouble for your pet. Here are some commonsense measures you can take to help prevent accidental poisoning:

1. Keep medications out of reach, preferably in a locked cabinet.
2. Never store poisons in old food or drink containers. Your dog may think he has found food or water.
3. Check on the quality of any ceramic food or water dishes you use to make certain they do not leak lead into your pet's food.
4. Whenever possible, use nontoxic fertilizers and weed killers. If this is not possible, keep your dog off treated lawns until they have dried.
5. Keep poisonous plants out of your dog's reach.
6. If you use insecticides indoors, keep your dog out of the room until it has aired out and the poison has dried.
7. Keep pesticides out of your dog's reach.
8. Keep garbage cans tightly covered.

FIRST AID: Induce vomiting. Call the veterinarian.

HOUSEHOLD CLEANERS

CLEANSERS, TOILET BOWL CLEANERS, DRAIN CLEANERS

FIRST AID: *Do not* induce vomiting. These substances are corrosive and will cause further damage if the dog vomits them up. Pour diluted vinegar or several tablespoons of lemon juice *slowly* into the side of the dog's mouth. Call for immediate veterinary assistance.

FURNITURE POLISH

FIRST AID: *Do not* induce vomiting. Call for immediate veterinary assistance.

LAUNDRY DETERGENTS

SYMPTOMS: Vomiting, excessive salivation, diarrhea.

FIRST AID: *Do not* induce vomiting. Call for veterinary help.

PINE-OIL CLEANER

FIRST AID: Call for immediate veterinary assistance.

INSECTICIDES

INSECT SPRAY, ROACH TRAPS, FLYPAPER, FLEA COLLARS

SYMPTOMS: Facial twitching, collapse, seizures, coma.

FIRST AID: Insecticides can be absorbed through the skin as well as ingested. If your dog gets the insecticide on his skin, give him a bath in warm soapy water to wash the residue from his coat. If you are certain your dog has ingested an insecticide, induce vomiting. In both instances, call your veterinarian immediately.

PYROPHOSPHATES

Pyrophosphates are compounds used in insecticides such as Malathion. They're also found in agricultural products as well as in flea and tick dips. Pyrophosphate poisoning in dogs often results from dipping too long in flea and tick dips.

SYMPTOMS: Salivation, pinpoint pupils, abdominal cramps, vomiting, diarrhea, twitching, and convulsions.

FIRST AID: Wash the dog off immediately, tuck him in some warm blankets, and rush him to the veterinarian.

PREVENTION: When preparing and using a flea or tick dip, follow the package directions carefully.

MEDICINES

ANTIHISTAMINES, TRANQUILIZERS, BARBITURATES, AMPHETAMINES, HEART PILLS, VITAMINS

There is a huge veterinary pharmacopia for animals. Sometimes these pet medications are overused or abused, or your dog may find an open bottle of your pills or other medication that is to his liking. Veterinarians are frequently summoned to aid a dog who has swallowed pills intended for his owner. Because dogs are unusually sensitive to drugs or medications, any of these substances can create a medical emergency.

SYMPTOMS: May include vomiting, pain, lack of coordination, convulsions, coma.

FIRST AID: Induce vomiting if the animal is conscious. Otherwise, your dog may choke on his own vomit. Give one teaspoon of milk of magnesia per five pounds of body weight. Call the veterinarian immediately.

ASPIRIN

Aspirin can be very toxic to dogs if large enough quantities are eaten.

SYMPTOMS: Lack of appetite, nervousness, vomiting (possibly bloody), seizures.

FIRST AID: Induce vomiting (see To Induce Vomiting box, p. 265) if many aspirin have been eaten. Call your veterinarian.

PESTICIDES

ARSENIC

Arsenic is found in rat, mouse, and ant poisons. It is also found in snail and slug bait.

SYMPTOMS: Arsenic can kill a dog quickly, especially if he has ingested a large quantity. A small amount may evidence itself in gastric upset, vomiting, diarrhea, lack of coordination, garlic-smelling breath, and unconsciousness.

FIRST AID: Induce vomiting if the dog is alert (see To Induce Vomiting box, p. 265). Get immediate veterinary attention. The veterinarian will administer an antidote.

STRYCHNINE

Strychnine is commonly found in pesticides as well as rodent poisons.

SYMPTOMS: Anxiety, restlessness, tremors, and twitching. Convulsions occur suddenly, then increase in frequency until they seem to be set off by even the most insignificant trigger— i.e., someone coughing.

FIRST AID: If your dog shows signs of poisoning but does not have convulsions, induce vomiting (see To Induce Vomiting box, p. 265). If convulsions have begun, cover your dog with a coat or blanket and transport him to the nearest veterinarian.

WARFARIN

This rat poison is supposedly nontoxic to dogs, yet warfarin poisoning is often seen by veterinarians. It serves its function by inhibiting blood circulation, or clotting. Poisoning can be caused by repeated doses over a period of time or by a single dose.

PLANTS POISONOUS TO DOGS

There are many potentially poisonous plants and shrubs—more than 700 types of plants in the Western Hemisphere alone. Identification of all these species is not possible here, but a selected list of common plants that can be toxic follows:

TOXIC HOUSEPLANTS

SYMPTOMS: Some dogs who eat these plants will exhibit no symptoms; others may drool, vomit, have diarrhea, swelling on side and around the mouth, or difficulty in breathing.

Amaryllis
Asparagus fern
Azalea
Bird of paradise
Castor bean (can be fatal)
Cherry (Jerusalem and ordinary)
Creeping Charlie
Crown of thorns
Dieffenbachia (can be fatal)
Easter lily (nontoxic in humans
    but often fatal in dogs)
Elderberry
Elephant ears
Glocal ivy
Heart ivy

Ivy
Japanese yew
Lily of the valley (can be fatal)
Mistletoe (can be fatal)
Needlepoint ivy
Ornamental yew
Philodendron (can be fatal)
Poinsettia (leaves can be fatal)
Pot chrysanthemum
Rhubarb
Ripple ivy
Spider chrysanthemum
Sprangeri fern
Umbrella plant

FIRST AID: Induce vomiting, unless your dog is unconscious or having convulsions. Get immediate veterinary assistance.

SYMPTOMS: Labored breathing, bloody stool, bloody vomit, rapid, faint pulse, staggering, coma.

FIRST AID: Treat the dog very gently to prevent internal bleeding. Keep him warm while you transport him to the veterinarian.

TOXIC OUTDOOR PLANTS

SYMPTOMS: Unless otherwise noted, most of these plants cause vomiting, abdominal pain, cramps, and diarrhea.

American yew
Angel's trumpet
Apricot, almond
Arrowgrass (can be fatal)
Azalea
Bird of paradise
Bittersweet (the berries can be fatal)
Black locust
Buttercup
Cherry tree (foliage and bark can cause cyanide poisoning)
China berry (causes convulsions)
Coriara (causes convulsions)
Daffodil
Delphinium
Elderberry (can cause cyanide poisoning)
English holly
English yew
Foxglove
Hemlock (can be fatal)
Jasmine

Jimsonweed (can be fatal)
Larkspur
Lily of the valley
Locoweed (can be fatal)
Lupine
Mescal bean
Mistletoe
Mock orange
Moonweed (causes convulsions)
Mushrooms and toadstools (can be fatal)
Peach tree (leaves and bark can cause cyanide poisoning)
Pokeweed
Privit
Rhododendron
Rhubarb (can cause convulsions and death)
Skunk cabbage
Soapberry
Spinach
Tomato vine
Wisteria

FIRST AID: Unless your dog is having convulsions, induce vomiting. Follow the procedures outlined at the beginning of this section to delay absorption and speed elimination. Get prompt veterinary assistance.

PLANTS

Many plants that adorn your house or garden can be toxic to dogs, who frequently munch on greenery.

If your dog likes to make a snack out of a plant, consider moving all houseplants out of his reach, and watch him carefully when he plays near your garden.

Dogs are prone to eating grass, especially when they suffer from digestive upset. Scientists believe that ancient dogs turned to grass to induce vomiting: They regurgitated digested food in order to feed their litter. Moderate grass-eating is fine from time to time, as long as you are sure the grass has not been chemically treated.

SYMPTOMS: The symptoms of plant poisoning are as varied as the plants that produce them. Most cause vomiting, abdominal pain, and cramps. Others cause tremors and heart, respiratory, and kidney problems.

FIRST AID: Induce vomiting unless the dog is having convulsions (see Convulsions, p. 249). Follow the three steps listed (see p. 264) to delay absorption and speed elimination. Call the veterinarian immediately.

REMODELING PRODUCTS

PAINTBRUSH CLEANER, PAINT THINNER, TURPENTINE

SYMPTOMS: Vomiting, difficulty in breathing, tremors, convulsions.

FIRST AID: On the skin: Flood with water and wash with mild detergent.
If ingested: *do not* induce vomiting. Call immediately for veterinary assistance.

PUTTY

FIRST AID: Call immediately for veterinary assistance.

PLASTER

FIRST AID: *Do not* induce vomiting. Call immediately for veterinary assistance.

OIL-BASED PAINT

FIRST AID: On the skin: Clean with turpentine, then flood with water and wash with mild detergent.
If ingested: Call for immediate veterinary assistance.

LEAD POISONING

Lead poisoning usually occurs in young dogs who chew and ingest old painted objects, old linoleum, plaster, or putty. Chronic, slow buildup of poisons can occur.

SYMPTOMS: Abdominal pain, vomiting, appetite loss, nervousness, whimpering, sensitivity to light, staggering, paralysis.

FIRST AID: A dog will die of lead poisoning unless treated. Induce vomiting (see To Induce Vomiting box, p. 265) if substances containing lead have been eaten within the previous half hour. Call for veterinary assistance.

MISCELLANEOUS POISONS

BALLPOINT PENS

FIRST AID: Induce vomiting (see To Induce Vomiting box, p. 265). Call the veterinarian.

GOLF BALLS

Some golf balls' liquid centers contain a substance that can be explosive as well as potentially toxic. A second hazard is intestinal obstruction (see Intestinal Obstruction, p. 259).

FIRST AID: Call for veterinary assistance.

GLUES AND PASTES

SYMPTOMS: Oral discomfort, excessive salivation, smacking of mouth.

FIRST AID: Strongly encourage the dog to drink milk or water. Call for veterinary assistance.

KITCHEN MATCHES

The head of a match contains potassium chlorate. If ingested, this substance can trigger abdominal discomfort and possibly vomiting.

FIRST AID: Induce vomiting (see To Induce Vomiting box, p. 265). Call the veterinarian if symptoms persist.

NAIL POLISH

FIRST AID: *Do not* induce vomiting. Call for immediate veterinary help.

PENCILS, CRAYONS

FIRST AID: Induce vomiting (see To Induce Vomiting box, p. 265). Call the veterinarian.

SHOE POLISH

FIRST AID: Induce vomiting (see To Induce Vomiting box, p. 265). Call the veterinarian.

SHAMPOO

FIRST AID: Induce vomiting (see To Induce Vomiting box, p. 265). Call the veterinarian.

SIDEWALK SALT

SYMPTOMS: Vomiting and diarrhea. Sore, swollen feet.

FIRST AID: Give the dog plenty of water. If symptoms persist, call the veterinarian.

SKIN CREAMS CONTAINING HEXACHLOROPHENE

Skin creams containing hexachlorophene, such as Phisohex, can cause brain damage in very young puppies.

SYMPTOMS: Lethargy and listlessness.

FIRST AID: Call the veterinarian immediately.

RECORDING YOUR DOG'S HISTORY

NAME _____

SEX _____

DATE OF BIRTH _____

DATE OF ADOPTION _____

PLACE OF ADOPTION _____

BREED _____

PARENTS' NAMES AND BREEDS _____

_____

Appearance _____

COAT COLOR _____

EYE COLOR _____

PHYSICAL DISTINCTIONS _____

NORMAL WEIGHT _____

TASTES

BELOVED FOODS _____

DESPISED FOODS _____

FAVORITE TOYS AND GAMES _____

FEARS _____

VACCINATIONS

	TYPE	*FIRST VACCINATION*	*BOOSTER*
CANINE DISTEMPER			
RABIES			
DHLPP			
OTHERS			

MEDICAL

NAME OF VETERINARIAN _____

ADDRESS _____

PHONE NUMBER(S) _____

DATE OF ANNUAL CHECKUP _____

OTHER VISITS _____

SPECIAL CONDITIONS _____

FOOD ALLERGIES _____

ALLERGIES/SENSITIVITIES TO MEDICATIONS _____

INJURIES _____

RESOURCES

Adoption Information:
Defenders of Animal Rights, Inc.
P.O. Box 4786
Baltimore, Md. 21211

Allergy Information:
The Associated Humane Societies, Inc.
124 Evergreen Ave.
Newark, N.J. 07114

Animal Ambulances:
The Associated Humane Societies, Inc.
124 Evergreen Ave.
Newark, N.J. 07114

Animal-Assisted Therapy Programs:

Canine Companions for Independence
P.O. Box 446
Santa Rosa, Ca. 95402

San Francisco SPCA
2500 16th St.
San Francisco, Ca. 94103

The Humane Society of New York
306 E. 59th St.
New York, N.Y. 10022

The Chicago Anti-Cruelty Society
157 W. Grand Ave.
Chicago, Il. 60610

Anti-Cruelty Societies:
The American Society for the Prevention
of Cruelty to Animals
442 E. 92nd St.
New York, N.Y. 10028

Associations:
American Animal Hospital Association
P.O. Box 150899
Denver, Co. 80215

American Kennel Club
51 Madison Ave.
New York, N.Y. 10010

Attorneys:
Animal Legal Defense Fund
333 Market St.
San Francisco, Ca. 94105

Animal Behaviorists:
Animal Behavior Therapy Clinic
Animal Medical Center of New York
510 E. 62nd St.
New York, N.Y. 10021

Breed Clubs:
The American Dog and Cat Breeders
Association and Referral Service
33222 N. Fairfield Rd.
Round Lake, Il. 60073

Cemeteries:
Bide-A-Wee Pet Memorial Parks
Wantagh & Beltagh Avenues
Wantagh, N.Y. 11793

Los Angeles SPCA
Pet Memorial Park
5068 North Old Scandia Lane
Calabasas, Ca. 91802

Crematoria:
Marble Hill Crematory for Pet Animals, Inc.
418 W. 219th St.
New York, N.Y. 10034

Death of a Pet:
Free brochure from
The American Animal Hospital Association
P.O. Box 150899
Denver, Co. 80215-0899

American Veterinary Medical Association
930 N. Meacham Rd.
Schaumburg, Il. 60196

Euthanasia:
Free brochure from the
American Veterinary Medical Association
930 N. Meacham Rd.
Schaumburg, Il. 60196

Physically Challenged, Helping Dogs for the:
Guide Dogs for the Blind
P.O. Box 1200
San Rafael, Ca. 94915

International Hearing Dog, Inc.
5901 E. 89th Avenue
Henderson, Co. 80640

Support Dogs for the Handicapped
P.O. Box 28457
Columbus, Oh. 43228

Health Information:
The American Animal Hospital Association
P.O. Box 150899
Denver, Co. 80215-0899

Animal Health and Nutrition Council
P.O. Box 184
Pennsauken, N.J. 08110

Hospitals:
The American Animal Hospital Association
P.O. Box 150899
Denver, Co. 80215-0899

Animal Medical Center
510 E. 62nd St.
New York, N.Y. 10021

Angell Memorial Animal Hospital
180 Longwood Ave.
Boston, Ma. 02115

Grand Avenue Pet Hospital
1602 N. Grand Ave.
Santa Ana, Ca. 92702

Hotlines:
American Animal Hospital Association
(800) 252-2242
(303) 986-2800

Animal Rescue League
(617) 426-9170

Nationwide Health Line
(212) 895-5175

Toxicology Hotline
(217) 333-3611

Tree House Animal Foundation
(312) 784-5480

Housing Discrimination:
Humane Society of the United States
2100 L St., N.W.
Washington, D.C. 20037

Immunization:
Free brochure from
American Veterinary Medical Association
930 N. Meacham Rd.
Schaumburg, Il. 60196

Legislative Groups:
United Action for Animals
205 E. 42nd St.
New York, N.Y. 10011

Society for Animal Protective Legislation
P.O. Box 3719
Georgetown Station
Washington, D.C. 20007

Publications:
Animals Magazine
350 South Huntington Ave.
Boston, Ma. 02130

Spaying and Neutering Clinics, Low-cost:
Nationwide listing provided by
Friends of Animals
1 Pine St.
Neptune, N.J. 07753

Veterinarian, Selecting:
American Animal Hospital Association
P.O. Box 105899
Denver, Co. 80215-0899

INDEX

Page numbers in *italics* refer to illustrations.